Cinephilia

Cinephilia

Movies, Love and Memory

Edited by Marijke de Valck and Malte Hagener

Amsterdam University Press

Cover design: Kok Korpershoek, Amsterdam
Lay-out: JAPES, Amsterdam

ISBN 90 5356 768 2 (paperback)
ISBN 90 5356 769 0 (hardcover)
NUR 674

Contents

III. Techniques of Cinephilia: Bootlegging and Sampling

Acknowledgements

The idea for this anthology originated with a number of discussions and conferences that took place from 2002 to 2004 in between New York, Amsterdam and London that created so much activity that we decided to put together an anthology. This volume would have been impossible without Elena Gorfinkel and Charles Leary, who initiated the Cinephilia conference series and organized the first conference in New York in February 2002. A meeting in Amsterdam in June 2003 was followed a year later by a conference in London, organized by Jenna Ng and David Forgacs. We have to pay tribute to everybody who participated in making this extended series of exchanges possible. We also thank Thomas Elsaesser and the University of Amsterdam, in particular the Department of Media Studies, for supporting us with the second conference in 2003 in Amsterdam as with this publication.

Marijke de Valck / Malte Hagener
Amsterdam, June 2005

Introduction

Down with Cinephilia? Long Live Cinephilia? And Other Videosyncratic Pleasures

Marijke de Valck and Malte Hagener

Cinephilia in the New Media Age

From a historical perspective, the term cinephilia is Janus-faced. On the one hand, it alludes to the universal phenomenon that the film experience evokes particular sensations of intense pleasure resulting in a strongly felt connection with the cinema, often described as a relation of love. Cinephiles worldwide continue to be captured and enraptured by the magic of moving images. They cherish personal moments of discovery and joy, develop affectionate rituals, and celebrate their love in specialized communities. On the other hand, the term covers practices and discourses in which the term cinephilia is appropriated for dogmatic agendas. The most successful of these practices has beyond question been the *"politique des auteurs."* Colin MacCabe points out that the *"politique des auteurs"* was not only concerned with establishing the primacy of the film-maker-director, but also aimed at the creation of a new "perfect" audience. When watching Hollywoodfilms, the young French film critics Truffaut, Godard, Rohmer, and companions discovered they had passionate preferences for certain filmmakers, mostly popular Hollywood directors, which they consequently set out to legitimize in their writings in *Cahiers du Cinéma.* It is this discourse that MacCabe credits with the construction of an "omniscient *cinéphile*" archetype that became central to the (elitist) mode of film reception known as cinephilia.[1]

Initiated in the 1950s, cinephilia came to full bloom in the 1960s thanks to the success of the Nouvelle Vague in France and abroad, but also the lively debates in the film magazines *Positif, Cahiers du Cinéma* and the discussions by the cinephiles congregating around the Cinema MacMahon and other Parisian movie houses. It is here at this possible point of origin (there are other moments one could single out as foundational[2]) that cinephilia presents its double nature: it dotes on the most popular genre film(maker)s of the most popular national film industry, yet it does so in a highly idiosyncratic, elitist, and often counterintuitive fashion. Cinephilia in its French attire of the 1960s is simultaneously democratic since it takes a popular cultural form very seriously while also being snobbishly aristocratic about it because it replaces traditional hierarchies (in which film was found at the lower end of the continuum) with new, similarly dogmatic taste preferences. In its classic form, cinephilia distinguishes between *"auteurs"* and *"metteurs-en-scène"* on the side of production, and, on the side of reception, between those who can recognize certain distinctions – namely the cinephiles – and those who cannot.

Like Colin MacCabe, Paul Willemen positions cinephilia in the French cultural context. To the unchallenged credits for the "politique des auteurs" he adds influence of the 1920s debates on *photogénie*: "[W]e first of all have to realise that it [cinephilia] is a French term, located in a particular rationalisation or attempted explanation of a relationship to cinema that is embedded in French cultural discourses. The privileged moment of that history seems to me to be the notion of *photogénie*. *Photogénie* was the first major attempt to theorise a relationship to the screen."[3] Because these French discourses went hand in hand with a flourishing and internationally acclaimed film culture, the practice of Parisian cinephiles from the 1950s to the 1970s could acquire the status of a classic case that is often abstracted in essentialist fashion from its historical specificity and mistaken as being synonymous with the phenomenon as such. Despite counter-voices, such as Annette Michelson who reminds us that cinephilia has not one "proper" form but many for different historical periods,[4] the appeal of the Parisian archetype continues to be very powerful and recurrently informs contemporary debates.

When Susan Sontag proclaimed the death of cinema in 1996 she in effect declared the incompatibility of the classic cinephile archetype with the contemporary state of the cinema.[5] In her influential article "The Decay of Cinema" she juxtaposes the heyday of cinephilia – the time when "the full-time cinephile [was] always hoping to find a seat as close as possible to the big screen, ideally the third row center" – with the present in which it is hard to find "at least among the young, that distinctive cinephilic love of movies." A love for movies is not enough for Sontag, but a "certain taste" and continuous investments in "cinema's glorious past" are necessary as well. Thus even in her seemingly neutral choice of words Sontag is crystal clear about the superiority of the cinephile movement that can be traced back to Truffaut's manifesto on "a certain tendency of the French cinema."[6] She holds on to the memory of classical cinephilia characterized by the persistence of devoted cinephiles to track down and watch rare movies projected in off-beat and often run-down exhibition venues in a segregated atmosphere of elevated pleasure. The discrepancy of the contemporary form of cinephilia with this nostalgic image results not in a revision of her conception of cinephilia but in a declaration of its death.

Our contention is that, since the 1980s, cinephilia has transformed itself. Nowadays it is practiced by a new generation of equally devoted cinephiles

1805
who display and develop new modes of engagement with the over-abundance of cinematic material widely available through advanced technology. A large part of the public debate that followed Sontag's obituary to cinephilia in fact concentrated on the impact of new technologies. The online journal *Senses of Cinema* dedicated a dossier to this discussion entitled "Permanent Ghosts: Cinephilia in the Age of the Internet and Video" in 1999. One of the main oppositions that is played out in the debate is "going out" versus "staying in." Value judgements differ with regard to the question which specific examples qualify as cinephile practice. The younger generation tends to defend the technology of their home video and internet education as a democratizing tool that not only allows a global, non-metropolitan public access to cinema culture, but also gives them control over their beloved films.[7] The critics of video and bootleg copies, on the other hand, lament the possibilities to fast-forward, freeze-frame, and zap through the sacred cinematic texts and stipulate the superior technology and immersed experience of the theatre.[8]

The recognition that the opposition between "going out" and "staying in" could be irrelevant for the contemporary cinephile condition is clearly put forward by Jonathan Rosenbaum and Adrian Martin in their jointly edited anthology *Movie Mutations*, a recent and important edition that clearly puts the topic of cinephilia on the agenda. The publication grew out of five years of correspondence and collaborations between film critics and filmmakers of which the first round of letters was published in the French magazine *Trafic* in 1997. The project was started as "an exploration of what cinephiles (and in some cases, filmmakers) around the planet have in common and what they can generate, activate and explore by linking up together in various ways."[9] Thus, the subtitle "The Changing Face of World Cinephilia" could have been replaced by "The Changing Interface of World Cinephilia," for what Rosenbaum and Martin observe and encourage is a new transnational *mode of interaction* between cinephiles. These interactions are not only inspired by the new home technologies of video, internet and DVD, but also take place at global forums like international film festivals and conferences. The book succeeds in convincingly describing the new global cinephilia moving beyond distinctions between "staying in" and "going out," but disappoints as a stronghold in terms of normative taste hierarchy. *Movie Mutations* presents a lineup of the usual suspects of contemporary world cinema (art/avant-garde) favorites – Abbas Kiarostami, Tsai Ming-liang, Wong Kar-Wai, Jacques Rivette, John Cassavetes et al. Like Sontag, Rosenbaum and Martin are not primarily interested in describing the universal phenomenon of cinematic pleasures in its rich variety of relations to the screen, but pursue the specific agenda of positioning "certain tendencies" in the globalized movie world as the new norm for cinephilia. As is evident from the fact that their favorite hunting ground remains the film festival, *Movie Mutations'* authors still put their stake on the projected celluloid image on a cinema screen, whereas we prefer to see cinephilia as an umbrella term for a number of different affective engagements with the moving image. We are therefore also highly critical of terms such as "videophilia"[10] or "telephilia"[11] as they only replace one kind of medium specificity with another (also implying a certain taste hierarchy). Instead we prefer to complement our revised concept of cinephilia with the notion of "videosyncrasy" because we see today's cinephiles as moving easily between different technologies, platforms, and subject positions in a highly idiosyncratic fashion that nevertheless remains connective and flexible enough to allow for the intersubjective exchange of affect, objects and memories.

Martin and Rosenbaum's anthology is not the only sign that points to a comeback of cinephilia as a concept. France, the homeland of cinephile orthodoxy, has recently seen two contributions to the field that go a long way towards historicizing a practice that has been hugely influential in shaping cinema culture: A collection of articles from the pages of cinephilia's central organ, *Cahiers du Cinéma*, delineates the activities of a previous generation[12] while Antoine de Baecque's expansive history and theory of cinephilia comprehensively covers the classical period, but historically stops in the late 1960s and theoretically with the introduction of new technology.[13] Both books are important additions to a historical understanding of cinephilia, but they do not address the transformation that we want to focus on. This collection takes a different turn from the established film theoretical agenda by considering contemporary cinephilia in its own right and investigating the issues arising from various non-academic practices that constitute new methods of loving film. This book, ultimately, aims to conceptualize a period break and in doing so introduce Cinephilia 2 as a marker for future research. New technological developments replay this basic dialectical relationship of cinephilia on several levels while also adding new layers to the concept. Rethinking cinephilia along several lines – a common denominator of the papers collected in this anthology – is a fruitful endeavor and opens up new theoretical and historical perspectives.

The Film-Historical Imaginary

In theoretical discussions, there is a discernible tendency to investigate cinephilia as an act of memory. Many of the reflections on cinephilia as a critical concept emphasize its interpenetration with the past. Paul Willemen explains the necrophilia overtones in the cinephile moment with the observation that cinephilia "relat[es].. something that is dead, past, but alive in memory."[14] Thomas

Elsaesser also describes cinephilia as "the love that never dies," the love that binds the present to the past in memory.[15] Willemen and Elsaesser differ in their attitude towards the role of new technologies in the cinephile's maintenance of memory, as Drehli Robnik points out in his contribution. Where Willemen sees cinephilia as being threatened with extinction by electronic images, Elsaesser describes new technologies as the contemporary way of remembering. This book provides case studies and articles that support the latter perspective. The technological changes are intimately connected with a transformed sense of memory, the past and history. Moreover, in the contemporary context, cinephilia's interconnected flirtation with the past is rearticulated in a second important way. Not only in the entangled web including technological changes, economic platforms and social structures, but also in the contemporary films themselves where a different relation to the past is visible. Arguably the most eye-catching characteristic of contemporary cinephilia is its cultural-aesthetic fusions of time and space, its radically different way of employing the historical signifier. On the temporal level, past, present, and future are fused into a media time that is increasingly disconnected from the traditional historical time. Cinephilia in the new media age thus not only celebrates discoveries and classic masterpieces, but also engages in popular reworkings of what we propose, following Elena Gorfinkel's contribution, to call "the film-historical imaginary."

The tendency of contemporary films – mainstream, art and avant-garde, Western and others – to use history as a limitless warehouse that can be plundered for tropes, objects, expressions, styles, and images from former works has often been noticed. This historicist (rather than historical) practice has been given many names: "allusionism,"[16] "nostalgia and pastiche"[17] or "recycling."[18] A good example is DOWN WITH LOVE (USA: Peyton Reed, 2003) in which the reworking of (film) history takes place solely within the feedback loops of the media machine. The film opens with a spatial displacement so glaringly obvious not even the nerdish IMDB-category goofs lists it[19]: While descending the stairs outside New York's Grand Central Station, Barbara Novak (Renée Zellweger) finds herself opposite the UN-headquarters which is in fact six blocks to the east. And a reverse angle reveals the Empire State Building as just a few steps down Park Avenue (when in fact it is some eight blocks south and on Fifth Avenue). The creative geography of the first brief sequence turns New York into a city firmly anchored in the realm of the (media) imaginary: the Pan Am building, UN Plaza, the Empire State Building and Grand Central Station within the space of one block, enough markers for even the slowest spectator to recognize the Big Apple. Moreover, as is so often the case in cinema, the ultimate time-space-machine, space is also substituted for time (or, for that matter, vice versa) because this opening economically indicates how the rest of the film will treat time as historical as well as media-historical which may – as some contributions in this volume indicate – very well be the same thing for us as spectators in the early 21st century. This shift from space to time takes place for the first time when the taxi that Barbara is about to enter releases a handful of activists with posters stating "Down with the bomb," which is also a pun on the film title in the shift from the personal to the political. Because the opening commentary has just informed us that the time is "now, 1962," it is hard to imagine an anti-atomic bomb demonstration which definitely marks a general category of 1960s-ness. The film throughout makes use of such anachronisms and *anatopisms*, as you might call them. Even the most casual visitor to New York knows that the UN building is not opposite Grand Central Station, while even somebody who has never been to New York might actually realize this. For instance, a cinephile with a modestly intact film historical background might know this, for example, from Alfred Hitchcock's NORTH BY NORTHWEST (USA: 1959), a film that prominently features both places in its narrative. In a similar movement, the historical reference to anti-war protesters in 1962 is equally giving itself away as "wrong" as much as the spatial displacement does. Yet, on another level, this displacement is less a "mistake," and more a condensation of clichés for which the film contains numerous examples: in the party sequence, the San Francisco drug culture beatnik scene is as stereotyped as the Madison Avenue advertising and black tie crowd while the various views from the penthouses and apartments reference an imaginary New York much more than they represent any actual architectural reality that is (or was) visible from a specific window in the city: from Barbara's large panorama apartment window we can see the Empire State Building, the Chrysler Building, and the Statue of Liberty all at a similar distance and a similar height, which is of course a topographic impossibility.

Yet our point is not the idea that DOWN WITH LOVE has spatially or temporally "incorrect" references or to wink at the knowing spectator who recognizes the inconsistencies, allowing one to feel superior to the film and to the other spectators. The film already operates in a mode where history (and spatial relations) outside the media machine simply do not exist, where such displacements and condensations consciously alert the audience for all the anachronistic and *anatopistic* references that will follow like the constant references to the space age, from push-up bras to garterless socks, from the astronaut Zip Martin to the rocket to the moon, before the space age had really taken off. These references index our idea of "1962" more than any historical reality, which might be old news to deconstructionists or new historicists, but the fact that a mainstream movie takes the audience for a ride on this pretense is surely highlighting a fundamental shift in Hollywood's approach to history. Indeed, one could argue that this mode of historical referencing is borrowed from the European art cinema of the 1970s where this strategy was used in a variety of ways. In analyzing Rainer Werner Fassbinder's DIE EHE DER MARIA BRAUN (Germany:

1978, THE MARRIAGE OF MARIA BRAUN), Thomas Elsaesser has aptly described the film-historical imaginary:

> ... [T]he past is seen across the traces which it has left in the present, fixed in the representations of that past, across the styles, the gestures, the images that evoke this past in and for the present. [The film] functions as a trigger of memories, but at one remove: not so much recalling a reality, as setting up a chain of associations, stories remembered from one's parents, pictures seen in the family album, in short, the standard version of the 1950s as present in the culture at large of the 1970s... thus explicitly repudiating the relevance of authenticity or documentary truth. On the contrary, it was the artefacts turned memorabilia, and the visual records turned coffeetable books, which made them valid as clichés and icons of the postwar period, and thus as the ironically reinstated guarantors of this history.[20]

The care and accuracy that in Hollywood is normally devoted to recreating an authentic image of a period is now devoted to producing media images saturated with memories of pastness evocative enough to give a mass audience a sense of a historical era. History has been congealed into history as presented in the media while the media, in turn, is inseparably intertwined with history.

As if to underscore this point, TV is referenced throughout DOWN WITH LOVE as a marker of history: The promotion of the book on the (historically real) *Ed Sullivan Show* with Judy Garland singing the title song (in a clever montage in the frame of an old Garland clip of the real Garland with a Garland impersonator visible out-of-focus in the background) propels the (fictional) book to the top of the bestseller list. In a montage sequence we see male lead Catcher Block (Ewan McGregor) and Novak (Zellweger) strolling through New York by night with clubs announcing Woody Allen and Bill Cosby who although they had their starts at this time, were surely not yet marquee attractions. Any conceivable attraction from the early 1960s recognizable to an early 21st-century audience is presented in this montage. When Novak's book hits the top of the bestseller list in the *New York Chronicle*, she tops a certain John Fitzgerald Kennedy (with his book *Profiles in Courage*) whose cardboard cut-out figure is, in one memorable shot, being taken out of a display window and replaced by Novak's. In this scene, the film *literalizes* how "real" history is no more than a cardboard cutout that can easily be replaced by any kind of ready-made filmic fiction that employs certain signifiers of pastness in a mixture of fact and fiction.

Stylistically, the film is also making clever use of dated tropes of filmmaking: back projections are used for conversations in cars, very much in the vein of 1960s technology which certainly cannot compete with the standards of realism as established in digital productions like GLADIATOR (USA: Ridley Scott, 2000) or TROY (USA: Wolfgang Petersen, 2004), nor can the painted backdrops used as the skyline as seen from various apartment windows.[21] If this is a period piece adorned with costumes and props lovingly exhibited as "from another time," the film certainly does not adhere to Hollywood's rules of verisimilitude in which you have to see hundreds of extras in period costume, dozens of cars, and large stretches of streets making you marvel at the sheer scale and extravagance. Instead, the film is right in your face with its artificiality and constructedness, which is in fact its essence. The film is shamelessly shot in the studio and on the Universal backlots with a handful of extras who return in every scene as the director proudly states in the commentary on the DVD, thereby imitating early 1960s films in which Doris Day's and Rock Hudson's New York was entirely (and obviously) constructed in the studio. Even more obvious is the spelling-it-out in detail of Zellweger's final monologue which gives the story another twist which is all played straight to the camera in one take and completely "out of role." Again, the film uses techniques of foregrounding artificiality, marking its distance from classical standards even though the three-act structure, the formation of the couple and many other features clearly adhere to standards of classicality.

Our earlier reference to Hitchcock was not entirely gratuitous. On the surface, DOWN WITH LOVE reworks the plot of the Day-Hudson-vehicle LOVER COME BACK (USA: Delbert Mann, 1961)[22] with some elements such as the split-screen telephone conversations borrowed from PILLOW TALK (USA: Michael Gordon, 1959) and other elements originating with similar romantic comedies of the same period such as WILL SUCCESS SPOIL ROCK HUNTER? (USA: Frank Tashlin, 1957), THAT TOUCH OF MINK (USA: Delbert Mann, 1961) or SEND ME NO FLOWERS (USA: Norman Jewison, 1964). There is, however, another film referred to here, the highly unlikely VERTIGO (USA: Alfred Hitchcock, 1958). Both films feature independent women who represent a riddle to the main character who in turn tries to trick the women into falling for his scheme. Yet, as it turns out, both Barbara/Nancy and Madeleine/Judy are in fact brunettes dyed blonde who are not the person they present themselves to be and are operating on plans that are larger and more sinister than those of their male protagonists. This connection is underscored and spelled out in a scene where Catcher Block deliberately confuses (the fictional) Barbara Novak with (the historically real) Kim Novak, one of Hitchcock's mysterious blondes.

Ultimately though, the film makes an essentialist argument about film-historical time that is packaged as one of Hollywood's memorable battles of the sexes (from 1930s screwball comedies to Hitchcock's cool blondes, from the Day-Hudson vehicles to BRIDGET JONES' DIARY [UK/France: Sharon Maguire, 2001], also starring Zellweger and alluded to by way of a chocolate reference). In DOWN WITH LOVE, the final battle is waged via a duel between two rival magazines, "*Know* – for men who are in the know" and "*Now* – for women who are in the now" strictly delimitating and policing gender differences. The film has, as mentioned earlier, announced itself to be happening "now" which is exactly what it does in at least two senses: The film takes place before our very eyes, so that the time is now while the film's present (its now-ness) is referenced in the diegesis as 1962 and is remembered through the period's media. The little slip from "know" to "now" and back again (including "no" which nobody in this film takes for an answer) points out what is at stake: this basic pairing refers to the knowledge of the spectator who knows that now and "now" are different, yet intertwined, levels. In an anachronistic move, the film announces that it "knows" already "now" (in 1962) what only we know now, namely that what we remember as 1962 in fact is a media construction that depends on popular cinephile knowledge. The anthology that lies before you argues that this type of play with the film-historical imaginary is what sets the contemporary mode of cinephilia apart from previous generations.

The Anthology

The film scholars in this anthology set out to explore the new period of cinephilia in all its diversity. Their essays demonstrate that, beyond the individualist immersion characteristic of the cinephile practice popular from the 1950s to the 1970s, a new diversified brand of cinephilia – simultaneously an individual practice, a collective identity formation, and a critical method – is emerging. The reconstruction of a period break is essential in starting to write an alternative history of (contemporary) cinephilia. Existing publications are dominated by approaches indebted to "classical cinephilia" which still to some extent dominates academia and criticism and has shaped film studies from its inception. The contributions to this anthology, on the contrary, take seriously the watershed marked by the introduction of video, computers, and new media technologies. The collection of essays approaches the phenomenon of cinephilia with a fresh interest that includes the new non-institutional forms of cinephile expression.

The essays in the first part of this anthology approach the phenomenon of cinephilia from a number of theoretical perspectives in order to gauge its usefulness for today's film culture. In his contribution to this volume, Thomas Elsaesser sketches theoretical, spatial, temporal, and personal trajectories across the two kinds of cinephilia in relation to memory, history, and time. Sutanya Singkhra examines the different temporalities at work in THE DREAMERS (Italy/France/UK/USA: Bernardo Bertolucci, 2003), a film about cinephilia by a cinephile of the first generation, which addresses the climax of classical cinephilia from the vantage point of today's retrospection. Drehli Robnik argues that blockbusters, the bread-and-butter of Hollywood in the post-classical period, have developed a film-historical imaginary and describes how they address a public that is radically different from either European art film audiences or those of mainstream productions from the 1960s. Jenna Ng discusses the new transcultural dimension of cinephilia between homage, allusion, and quotation: love – as in cine-philia – offers a solution to the complex problems of transcultural communication for which Tarantino's appropriation of East Asian culture in KILL BILL: VOL. 1/2 (USA: 2003/4) provides the test case.

Part two of this anthology engages with the changes in distribution and exhibition, both in terms of marketing and of a transformed kind of spectatorship. Contrary to the widespread belief that cinephilia in the post-classical era is first and foremost characterized by the shift from a collective audience in a public movie theatre to a privatized and individualized spectator alone at home in front of a TV set, we believe that the contemporary situation offers a whole range of reception possibilities which cannot be subsumed adequately under the heading "individualization." As in classic cinephilia, this practice is dialectically poised between the public and the private, the individual and the collective. The introduction of video, DVD, and CD-Rom, the overabundance of digital production and lately also projection, and the spread of the internet on a consumer market in the last two decades have led to hybrid texts and spectator positions offering various angles of interests for different segments of the audience. New technologies have enabled a new and more active kind of reception in which cinephiles encounter and discuss films in new settings which are increasingly gaining significance such as film festivals, late-night television, home entertainment centers, and internet groups. The essays in part two deal with some of the implications brought about by these new settings. Marijke de Valck examines crucial sites for the construction of contemporary cinephilia: film festivals which have proliferated since the early 1980s. She investigates how contemporary cinephilia can be conceptualized in relation to the International Film Festival Rotterdam. Melis Behlil examines film discussion groups on the internet with a special emphasis put on the *New York Times* website, which has managed to collect a dedicated cinephile community from every corner of the globe and every walk of life.

The intersection of cinephilia, memory, and technological developments is addressed by some of the other contributions to this anthology. The market, the archive, and the filmic text as unstable objects are all mutually dependent upon each other in the contemporary media industry. Charles Leary examines the obstacles confronted while remastering older Hong Kong films for DVD reissues and its economic as well as cultural implications. The notion of speed is crucial here, for while it indexes Hong Kong's status as one of the engines of global capitalism, it is also precisely this speed which proves problematic in the digital editions of these older Hong Kong films. Vinzenz Hediger conceptualizes the transformation from traditional to new media cinephilia across the shift of the film industry from a cinema to a copyright industry. He demonstrates how the "original" is a fetishized construction negotiated in the space between film restorers, marketing departments, and critical-academic discourse. The position of cinema studies is also considered by Wanda Strauven, who discusses how an early Godard film, an object of traditional cinephile devotion, can be fitted into the new framework (in this specific case, a late-night TV broadcast) as it is read across recent academic rediscoveries in early cinema.

Part three of this book is devoted to a discussion of how filmmaking has changed and what a new and emerging cinephile film looks like. Elena Gorfinkel presents a recent and emblematic example for the shift of emphasis in evoking a past time: Todd Haynes' repackaging of Douglas Sirk's Universal melodrama, FAR FROM HEAVEN (USA: 2002). Haynes reworks a media period which in the process is opened up towards a contemporary version of an emblematically intensified past. A similar strategy can be seen in many other contemporary films; Gorfinkel examines here BOOGIE NIGHTS (USA: P.T. Anderson, 1997) and THE ROYAL TENENBAUMS (USA: Wes Anderson, 2001). The cultural-aesthetic fusions of (media) time and space not only display the cinephile engagement of filmmakers, but also point to the broadening of cine-literate audiences through the spread and popularity of festivals, multiplexes, discussion forums on the internet, and DVDs. The tendency for contemporary cinephilia therefore is to move beyond the small and elitist communities of the 1950s–70s and initiate new non-institutional practices (e.g., bootlegging) as well as new institutions (internet platforms, specialized audience festivals on horror, science fiction or fantasy). Lucas Hilderbrand concentrates on Jon Routson's bootleg recordings of theatrical films. While this conceptual appropriation immediately raises the (currently hotly debated) copyright issue, Hilderbrand approaches the issue via the aesthetic and cinephile implications of these recordings and argues that the bootlegs are essentially not reproductions of film, but of the viewing experience. Jan Simons deals with Lars von Trier, one of the most celebrated contemporary filmmakers who not only successfully revived the format of the "new wave," but subsequently also franchised it before abandoning the *Dogma*-dogma in favor of new technological and narrational models. Federico Windhausen discusses the work of experimental filmmaker Morgan Fisher who has redeemed antiquated film formats that have been abandoned by the film industry. Fisher's homage to the filmic insert ( ) (USA: 2003), an underrated sign in the chain of cinematic signification, moves beyond montage as self-expression by adapting models from different artistic and cultural practices. Gerwin van der Pol links A ZED AND TWO NAUGHTS (UK/Netherlands: Peter Greenaway, 1985) to DE WITTE WAAN (Netherlands: Adriaan van Ditvoorst, 1984) in an in-depth account of a cinephile at work, playing the cinephile game of finding similarities and connections between the two films.

Together, these scholars point to an understanding of contemporary cinephilia as a practice that has branched out and embraces and uses technological developments while transforming the lessons of the first generation of cinephilia. Contemporary cinephilia, like its classic predecessor, relates the present to the past, but memory is no longer exclusively cherished in private thought, face-to-face discussions and writings in books and magazines. It is cultivated by consumers, producers, and academics on multiple media channels: audiences flock to festivals, rent videos in specialty stores and buy, download, or swap films on the internet; corporations *repurpose* (old) films as (instant) classics for the booming DVD market; and film scholars help to frame unclassified archival material that is presented at film festivals, in film museums, and at archives. Today's cinephilia is unabashedly consumerist (in the rapidly growing DVD market) and radically anti-capitalist (in its barely legal P2P transactions of films on the internet), often for the same people at different times. Because of its varied use of different technologies, communication channels, and exhibition formats, the contemporary way of remembering is far more accessible than the practice ever was in the 1960s when it was basically limited to a handful of Western metropolises.

The contemporary cinephile is as much a hunter-gatherer as a merchant-trader, of material goods as well as of personal and collective memories, of reproducible data streams and of unique objects; a as much duped consumer as a media-savvy producer, a marketeer's dream-come-true, but also the fiercest enemy of the copyright controlling lawyers involved in the many copyright court cases. Today's film lover embraces and uses new technology while also nostalgically remembering and caring for outdated media formats. It is this simultaneity of different technological formats and platforms, subject positions, and affective encounters that characterizes the current practice referred to as "cinephilia." The transformative power and rejuvenating energy that the love of cinema has demonstrated in its unexpected comeback over the last couple of years shows beyond doubt the enduring relevance of cinephilia for an understanding of the cinema between the stylistics of the cinema text and the practices of film viewing.

Notes

 MacCabe, Colin. *The Eloquence of the Vulgar*, London: British Film Institute, 1999, p. 152.

2. See Thomas Elsaesser's contribution in this volume for genealogical topographies of cinephilia in Paris and London in which spectators ritualistically congregate in their respective temples of worship.

3. Willemen, Paul. *Looks and Frictions: Essays in Cultural Studies and Film Theory,* Bloomington and Indianapolis: Indiana University Press, 1994, p.231.

4. Michelson, Annette. "Gnosis and Iconoclasm. A Case Study of Cinephilia." *October* 83 (Winter 1998): p. 3.

5. Sontag, Susan. "The Decay of Cinema." *New York Times,* 25 February 1996, late final edition: section 6, p. 60.

6. Truffaut, François. "A Certain Tendency of the French Cinema." Nichols, Bill (ed.) *Movies and Methods. An Anthology,* Vol. I. Berkeley, University of California Press, 1976, pp. 224-237. Original French version published in *Cahiers du Cinéma* No.31, 1954: pp. 15-28.

7. See "Essay 2" by Theo Panayides in the "Permanent Ghost: Cinephilia in the Age of Internet and Video" series, <http://www.sensesofcinema.com/contents/00/4/cine2.html>.

8. See "Essay 1" by Steve Erickson in the "Permanent Ghost: Cinephilia in the Age of Internet and Video" series, <http://www.sensesofcinema.com/contents/00/4/cine1.html>. Although Erickson leaves no room to question the superiority of the cinematic medium, he also acknowledges the advantages of the new technologies and argues for a dialogue with the videophiles who share a serious interest in films with the old-school cinephiles.

9. Jonathan Rosenbaum in the preface to Rosenbaum, Jonathan, Adrian Martin (eds.). *Movie Mutations: The Changing Face of World Cinephilia,* London: British Film Institute, 2003, p. vi.

10. See Tashiro, Charles Shiro. "Videophilia. What Happens When You Wait for It on Video." *Film Quarterly,* 45/1 (1991), pp. 7-17. See also Klinger, Barbara. "The Contemporary Cinephile. Film Collecting in the Post-Video Era." Stokes, Melvyn, Richard Maltby (eds.). *Hollywood Spectatorship: Changing Perceptions of Cinema Audiences,* London: BFI, 2001, pp. 132-151.

11. See the dossier edited by Brian Price on "Cinephilia versus Telephilia" in *Framework,* 45/2 (Fall 2004), pp. 36-80.

12. See Baecque, Antoine de (ed.). *Critique et cinéphilie,* Paris: Cahiers du cinéma, 2001. (Petite anthologie des Cahiers du cinéma).

13. Baecque, Antoine de. *La cinéphilie: Invention d'un regard, histoire d'une culture, 1944–1968,* Paris: Fayard, 2003.

14. Willemen, Paul. *Looks and Frictions.* p. 227.

15. Elsaesser, Thomas. "Specularity and Engulfment: Francis Ford Coppola and BRAM STOKER´S DRACULA." Neale, Steve, Murray Smith (eds.). *Contemporary Hollywood Cinema,* London and New York: Routledge, p. 206.

16. Carroll, Noel. "The Future of Allusion: Hollywood in the Seventies (and Beyond)." *October* 20 (Spring 1982).

17. Jameson, Fredric. *Postmodernism or the Cultural Logic of Late Capitalism,* Durham, NC and London: Duke University Press, 1991.

18. Dika, Vera. *Recycled Culture in Contemporary Art and Film,* Cambridge: Cambridge University Press, 2003.

19. Nevertheless, they do painstakingly list "anachronisms": how New York license plates looked in 1962, when the Pan Am building, prominent in the opening shot, was finished, etc.

20. Elsaesser, Thomas. *Fassbinder's Germany: History – Identity – Subject*. Amsterdam: Amsterdam University Press 1996, p. 105.

21. Indeed, in the commentary track to the DVD-version of the film, the director Peyton Reed adds cinephile knowledge for the cognoscenti: He details from which film each back projection is borrowed as this technique of reusing old (and digitally enhanced) back projections was simultaneously cheaper, but also "more real" in the film's reference to the early 1960s. Thus, for a film that is set in 1962 he uses another film from this period.

22. The many astronaut references in Down with Love can be seen as indexing the (invented) story of Jerry Webster's cousin (Rock Hudson) who is circling the Earth on a top-secret NASA mission in Lover Come Back while the song underlying the end titles, sung and performed by Zellweger and MacGregor, states "I'll be your Rock if you'll be my Doris." There are many other references to the Pillow Talk cycle, including of course the Tony Randall cameo. Randall was a fixture as Rock Hudson's inhibited friend in the 1960s cycle.

I

The Ramifications of Cinephilia

Theory and History

Cinephilia or the Uses of Disenchantment

Thomas Elsaesser

The Meaning and Memory of a Word

It is hard to ignore that the word "cinephile" is a French coinage. Used as a noun in English, it designates someone who as easily emanates cachet as pretension, of the sort often associated with style items or fashion habits imported from France. As an adjective, however, "cinéphile" describes a state of mind and an emotion that, one the whole, has been seductive to a happy few while proving beneficial to film culture in general. The term "cinephilia," finally, reverberates with nostalgia and dedication, with longings and discrimination, and it evokes, at least to my generation, more than a passion for going to the movies, and only a little less than an entire attitude toward life. In all its scintillating indeterminacy, then, cinephilia – which migrated into the English language in the 1960s – can by now claim the allegiance of three generations of film-lovers. This fact alone makes it necessary to distinguish between two or even three kinds of cinephilia, succeeding each other, but also overlapping, co-existing, and competing with each other. For instance, cinephilia has been in and out of favor several times, including a spell as a thoroughly pejorative and even dismissive sobriquet in the politicized 1970s.[1]

In the 1960s, it was also a contentious issue, especially during Andrew Sarris's and Pauline Kael's controversy over the auteur theory, when calling one's appreciation of a Hollywood screwball comedy by such names was simply un-American.[2] It was a target of derision, because of its implied cosmopolitan snobbery, and the butt of Woody Allen jokes, as in a famous self-mocking scene outside the New York's Waverly Cinema in ANNIE HALL (USA: 1977).[3] Yet it has also been a badge of loyalty for filmgoers of all ages and tastes, worn with pride and dignity. In 1996, when Susan Sontag regretted the "decay of cinema," it was clear what she actually meant was the decay of cinephilia, that is, the way New Yorkers watched movies, rather than what they watched and what was being made by studios and directors.[4] Her intervention brought to the fore one of cinephilia's original characteristics, namely that it has always been a gesture towards cinema framed by nostalgia and other retroactive temporalities, pleasures tinged with regret even as they register as pleasures. Cinephiles were always ready to give in to the anxiety of possible loss, to mourn the once sensu ous- sensory plenitude of the celluloid image, and to insist on the irrecoverably fleeting nature of a film's experience.

Why then, did cinephilia originate in France? One explanation is that France is one of the few countries outside the United States which actually possesses a continuous film culture, bridging mainstream cinema and art cinema, and thus making the cinema more readily an integral part of everyday life than elsewhere in Europe. France can boast of a film industry that goes back to the beginnings of cinema in 1895, while ever since the 1920s, it has also had an avant-garde cinema, an art-and-essay film club movement, Each generation in France has produced notable film directors of international stature: the Lumière Brothers and Georges Méliès, Maurice Tourneur and Louis Feuillade, Abel Gance and Germaine Dulac, Jean Renoir and René Clair, Jean Cocteau and Julien Duvivier, Sacha Guitry and Robert Bresson, down to Leos Carax and Luc Besson, Cathérine Breillat and Jean-Pierre Jeunet. At the same time, unlike the US, French film culture has always been receptive to the cinema of other nations, including the American cinema, and thus was remarkably free of the kind of chauvinism of which the French have since been so often accused.[5] If there was a constitutive ambivalence around the status of cinema, such as it existed in countries like Germany, then in France this was less about art versus commerce, or high culture versus popular culture, and more about the tension between the "first person singular" inflection of the avant-garde movements (with their sometimes sectarian cultism of metropolitan life) and the "first person plural" national inflection of French cinema, with its love of stars, genres such as *polars* or comedies, and a vaguely working-class populism. In other words, French public culture has always been cinephile – whether in the 1920s or the 1980s, whether it was represented by art historian Elie Faure or author André Malraux, by television presenter Bernard Pivot or the Socialist Minister of Culture Jack Lang – of a kind rarely found among politicians, writers and public figures in other European nations. A respect for, and knowledge of the cinema has in France been so much taken for granted that it scarcely needed a special word, which is perhaps why the particular fervor with which the American cinema was received after 1945 by the frequenters of Henri Langlois' Paris Cinémathèque in the rue d'Ulm and the disciples of André Bazin around *Cahiers du Cinéma* did need a word that connoted that extra dimension of passion, conviction as well as desperate determination which still plays around the term in common parlance.

Cinephilia, strictly speaking, is love of cinema: "a way of watching films, speaking about them and then diffusing this discourse," as Antoine de Baecque, somewhat primly, has defined it.[6] De Baecque judiciously includes the element of shared experience, as well as the need to write about it and to proselytize, alongside the pleasure derived from viewing films on the big screen. The cinephilia I became initiated into around 1963 in London included dandified rituals strictly observed when "going to the movies," either alone or less often, in groups. Cinephilia meant being sensitive to one's surroundings when watching a movie, carefully picking the place where to sit, fully alert to the quasi-sacral feeling of nervous anticipation that could descend upon a public space, however squalid, smelly or slipshod, as the velvet curtain rose and the studio logo with its fanfares filled the space. Stories about the fetal position that Jean Douchet would adopt every night in the second row of the Cinémathèque Palais de Chaillot had already made the rounds before I became a student in Paris in 1967 and saw it with my own eyes, but I also recall a cinema in London, called The Tolmer near Euston Station, in the mid-1960s, where only homeless people and alcoholics who had been evicted from the nearby railway station spent their afternoons and early evenings. Yet, there it was that I first saw Allan Dwan's SLIGHTLY SCARLET (USA: 1955) and Jacques Tourneur's OUT OF THE PAST / BUILD MY GALLOWS HIGH (USA: 1947) – two must-see films on any cinephile's wish list in those days. Similarly mixed but vivid feelings linger in me about the Brixton Classic in South London, where the clientele was so rough that the house lights were kept on during the feature film, and the aisles were patrolled by security guards with German shepherds. But by making a temporary visor and shield out of *The Guardian* newspaper, I watched the Anthony Mann and Budd Boetticher Westerns – BEND OF THE RIVER (USA: Mann, 1951), THE FAR COUNTRY (USA: Mann, 1954), THE TALL T (USA: Boetticher, 1957), RIDE LONESOME (USA: Boetticher, 1959), COMANCHE STATION (USA: Boetticher, 1960) – that I had read about in *Cahiers du Cinéma* and *Movie* Magazine, feeling the moment as more unique and myself more privileged than had I been given tickets to the last night of the Proms at the Royal Albert Hall.

For Jonathan Rosenbaum, growing up as the grandson of a cinema owner from the Deep south, it was "placing movies" according to whom he had seen them with, and "moving places," from Florence, Alabama to Paris to London, that defined his cinephilia,[7] while Adrian Martin, a cinephile from Melbourne, Australia has commented on "the monastic rituals that inform all manifestations of cinephilia: hunting down obscure or long-lost films at suburban children's matinees or on late-night TV."[8] The "late-night TV" marks Martin as a second-generation cinephile, because in the days I was referring to, there was no late-night television in Britain, and the idea of watching movies on television would have been considered sacrilege.

Detours and Deferrals

Cinephilia, then, wherever it is practiced around the globe, is not simply a love
of the cinema. It is always already caught in several kinds of deferral: a detour
in place and space, a shift in register and a delay in time. The initial spatial
displacement was the transatlantic passage of Hollywood films after World
War II to newly liberated France, wh`
ose audiences avidly caught up with the movies the German occupation had
embargoed or banned during the previous years. In the early 1960s, the transatlantic passage went in the opposite direction, when the discourse of auteurism
traveled from Paris to New York, followed by yet another change of direction,
from New York back to Europe in the 1970s, when thanks to Martin Scorsese's
admiration for Michael Powell, Paul Schrader's for Carl Dreyer, Woody Allen's
for Ingmar Bergman and Francis Coppola's for Luchino Visconti these European masters were also "rediscovered" in Europe. Adding the mediating role
played by London as the intellectual meeting point between Paris and New
York, and the metropolis where art school film buffs, art house audiences, uni-
versity-based film magazines and New Left theorists intersected as well, Anglo-
phone cinephilia flourished above all in the triangle just sketched, sustained by
migrating critics, traveling theory and translated magazines: "Europe-Holly-
wood-Europe" at first, but spreading as far as Latin America in the 1970s and
to Australia in the 1980s.[9]

On a smaller, more local scale, this first cinephilia was – as already implied –
topographically site-specific, defined by the movie houses, neighborhoods and
cafés one frequented. If there *were* displacements, they mapped itineraries within a single city, be it Paris, London or New York, in the spirit of the Situationists'
detournement, circumscribed by the mid-week movie sorties (in London) to the
Everyman in Hampstead, the Electric Cinema on Portobello Road, and the NFT
on the South Bank. Similar maps could be drawn for New York, Munich, or
Milan, but nowhere were these sites more ideologically fixed and more fiercely
defended than in Paris, where the original cinephiles of the post-war period
divided up the city's movie theatres the way gangs divided up Chicago during
prohibition: gathering at the MacMahon close to the Arc de Triomphe, at the
Studio des Ursulines in the 5é or at La Pagode, near the Hotel des Invalides,
each cinema hosted a clan or a tribe that was fiercely hostile to the others. If my
own experience in London between 1963 and 1967 was more that of the movie
house *flaneur* than as a member of a gang, the first person inflection of watching
movies by myself eventually gave rise to a desire to write about them, which in
turn required sharing one's likes, dislikes, and convictions with others, in order

to give body to one's love object, by founding a magazine and running it as a collective.[10]

However spontaneous, however shaped by circumstance and contingency, the magnetic pole of the world's cinephilia in the years up to the early 1970s remained Paris, and its marching orders retained something uniquely French. The story of the *Cahiers du Cinéma* critics and their promotion of Hollywood studio employees to the status of artists and "auteurs" is too wellknown to require any recapitulation here, except perhaps to note in passing another typically French trait. If in *La Pensée Sauvage*, Claude Levi-Strauss uses food to think with; and if there is a time-honored tradition in France – from the Marquis de Sade to Pierre Klossowski – to use sex to philosophize with, then it might not be an exaggeration to argue that in the 1950s, the cinephile core of French film critics used Charlton Heston, Fritz Lang, and Alfred Hitchcock, in order to theologize and ontologize with.[11]

One of the reasons the originary moment of cinephilia still occupies us today, however, may well be found in the third kind of deferral I mentioned. After detours of city, language, and location, cinephilia implies several kinds of time delays and shifts of temporal register. Here, too, distinctions are in order. First of all, there is "oedipal time": the kind of temporal succession that joins and separates paternity and generational repetition in difference. To go back to *Cahiers du Cinéma*: the fatherless, but oedipally fearless François Truffaut adopted Andre Bazin *and* Alfred Hitchcock (whom Bazin initially disliked), in order to attack "le cinéma de papa." The Pascalian Eric Rohmer (of MA NUIT CHEZ MAUD [France: 1969]), "chose" that macho pragmatist Howard Hawks *and* the dandy homosexual Friedrich Wilhelm Murnau as his father figures, while Jean-Luc Godard could be said to have initially hedged his bets as well by backing *both* Roberto Rossellini *and* Sam Fuller, *both* Ingmar Bergman *and* Fritz Lang. Yet cinephilia also connects to another, equally deferred tense structure of desire: that of a lover's discourse, as conjugated by Roland Barthes: "I have loved and love no more;" "I love no more, in order to better love what I once loved;" and perhaps even: "I love him who does not love you, in order to become more worthy of your love." This hints at a third temporality, enfolding both oedipal time and the lover's discourse time, namely a triangulated time of strictly mediated desire.

A closer look at the London scene in the 1970s and early 1980s, under the aspect of personal friendships, local particularities and the brief flowering of film magazines thanks to funds from the BFI, would indicate the presence of all these temporalities as well. The oedipal time of "discovering" Douglas Sirk, the dissenting re-assessments of neo-realism, the rivalries over who owned Hitchcock: *Sight & Sound, Screen* or *Movie*. The argument would be that it was a delayed, deferred but also post lapsarian cinephilia that proved part of the driving

force behind what came to be known as Screen theory.[12] The Theory both covered over and preserved the fact that ambivalence about the status of Hollywood as the good/bad object persisted, notwithstanding that the love of cinema
was now called by a different name: voyeurism, fetishism, and scopophilia.[13]
But naming here is shaming; nothing could henceforth hide the painful truth
that by 1975, cinephilia had been dragged out of its closet, the darkened womb-
like auditorium, and revealed itself as a source of disappointment: the magic of
the movies, in the cold light of day, had become a manipulation of regressive
fantasies and the place of the big male escape from sexual difference. And
would these torn halves ever come together again? It is not altogether irrelevant
to this moment in history that Laura Mulvey's call to forego visual pleasure and
dedicate oneself to unpleasure was not heeded; and yet, the feminist project,
which took its cue from her essay, made this ambivalence productive well beyond the cinema.`

The Uses of Disenchantment

These then, would be some of the turns and returns of cinephilia between 1960
and 1980: love tainted by doubt and ambivalence, ambivalence turning into disappointment, and disappointment, which demanded a public demonstration or
extorted confession of "I love no more." Yet, instead of this admission, as has
sometimes happened with professional film critics, leading to a farewell note
addressed to the cinema, abandoned in favor of some other intellectual or critical pursuit, disappointment with Hollywood in the early 1970s only helped re-
new the legitimating enterprise at the heart of auteurism, converting "negative"
or disavowed cinephilia into one of the founding moments of Anglo-American
academic film studies. The question why such negativity proved institutionally
and intellectually so productive is a complex one, but it might just have to do
with the time shifting inherent in the very feeling of cinephilia, which needs the
ever-present possibility of disappointment, in order to exist at all, but which
only becomes culturally productive against the knowledge of such possible
"disenchantment," disgust even, and self-loathing. The question to ask, then –
of the cinephile as well as of the critics of cinephilia – is: What are the uses of
disenchantment? Picking the phrase "the uses of disenchantment" is, of course,
alluding to a book by Bruno Bettelheim, *The Uses of Enchantment*, where he studies the European fairy tale and its function for children and adults as a mode
of storytelling and of sensemaking. What I want to borrow from Bettelheim is
the idea of the cinema as one of the great fairy-tale machines or "mythologies"
that the late 19th century bequeathed to the 20th, and that America, originally

inheriting it from Europe, has in turn (from the 1920s up to the present day) bequeathed to Europe under the name of "Hollywood," from where, once more since the 1980s, it has been passed to the rest of the world.

By turning Bettelheim's title into "dis-enchantment" I have also tried to capture another French phrase, that of "déception," a recurring sentiment voiced by Proust's narrator Marcel whenever a gap opens up between his expectations or anticipations and the reality as he then experienced it. It punctuates *À la recherche du temps perdu* like a leitmotif, and the gap which disenchantment each time signals enables Marcel's mind to become especially associative. It is as if disappointment and disenchantment are in Proust by no means negative feelings, but belong to the prime movers of the memory imagination. Savoring the sensed discrepancy between what is and what is expected, constitutes the semiotic act, so to speak, by making this difference the prerequisite for there to be any insight or feeling at all. Could it be that a similarly enacted gap is part of cinephilia's productive disenchantment? I recall a Hungarian friend in London who was always waiting for the new films by Losey, Preminger or Aldrich "with terrible trepidation." Anticipated disappointment may be more than a self-protective shield. Disenchantment is a form of individuation because it rescues the spectator's sense of self from being engulfed by the totalizing repleteness, the self-sufficiency and always already complete there-ness that especially classic American cinema tries to convey. From this perspective, the often heard complaint that a film is "not as good as [the director's] last one" also makes perfect sense because disappointment redeems memory at the expense of the present.

I therefore see disenchantment as having had a determining role within cinephilia, perhaps even going back to the post-World War II period. It may always have been the verso to cinephilia's recto, in that it lets us see the darker side, or at any rate, another side of the cinephile's sense of displacement and deferral. In the history of film theory, a break is usually posited between the auteurism and cinephilia of the 1950s-1960s, and the structuralist-semiotic turn of the 1960s–1970s. In fact, they are often played off against each other. But if one factors in the temporalities of love and the trepidations of possible disenchantment, then Christian Metz and Roland Barthes are indeed key figures not only in founding (semiologically inspired) film studies, but in defining the bi-polar affective bond we have with our subject, in the sense that their "I love / no longer / and choose the other / in order to learn / once more / to love myself" are the revolving turnstiles of both cinephilia *and* its apparent opposite – semiology and psychosemiotics. Disenchantment and its logic of retrospective revalorization hints at several additional reversals, which may explain why today we are still, or yet again, talking about cinephilia, while the theoretical paradigm I have just been alluding to – psychosemiotics – which was to have overcome cinephilia, the way enlightenment overcame superstition, has lost much of its previously compelling power.

Raymond Bellour, a cinephile (almost) of the first hour, and a founding figure in film studies, is also one of the most lucid commentators on cinephilia. In an essay entitled – how could it be otherwise – "Nostalgies," he confesses:

> There are three things, and three things only, which I have loved in the same way: Greek mythology, the early writings of the Bronte sisters, and the American cinema. These three worlds, so different from each other, have only one thing in common which is of such an immense power: they are, precisely, worlds. By that I mean complete wholes that truly respond at any moment in time to any question which one could ask about the nature, the function and the destiny of that particular universe. This is very clear for Greek mythology. The stories of gods and heroes leave nothing in the dark: neither heaven nor earth, neither genealogy nor sentiments. They impose an order on the idea, finite and infinite, in which a child could recognise its fears and anxieties. [...]
>
> Starting with the invention of the cinema there is an extraordinarily matching between cinema as a machine (apparatus?) and the continent of America. [Because] America recognised straightaway in this apparatus for reproducing reality the instrument that it needed for inventing itself. It immediately believed in the cinema's reality.[14]

"America immediately believed in the cinema's reality": this seems to me one of Bellour's most felicitous insights about cinephilia-as-unrequited love and perhaps even envy, a key to perhaps not only French fascination-in-disenchantment with Hollywood. For it is around this question of belief, of "croyance," of "good faith" and (of course, its philosophically equally interesting opposite "bad faith," when we think of Jean Paul Sartre's legacy) that much of French film theory and some of French film practice, took shape in the 1970s. French cinephile disenchantment, of which the same Cahiers du Cinéma made themselves the official organ from 1969 onwards, also helped formulate the theoretical-critical agenda that remained in force in Britain for a decade and in the USA for almost two. Central to the agenda was the need to prove that Hollywood cinema is a bad object, because it is illusionist. One might well ask naively: What else can the cinema be, if not illusionist? But as a cinephile, the pertinence of the problem strikes one as self-evident, for here, precisely, arises the question of belief. If you are an atheist, faith is not an issue; but woe to the agnostic who has been brought up a believer because he will have to prove that the existence of God is a logical impossibility.

This theological proof that heaven, or cinephilia, does not exist, is what I now tend to think screen theory was partly about. Its radicalism can be most plausibly understood, I suggest, as an insistent circling around one single question, namely how this make-belief, this effect of the real, created by the false which is the American cinema, can be deconstructed, can be shown to be not only an act of ideological manipulation but an ontology whose groundlessness has to be unmasked – or on the contrary, has to be accepted as the price of our modernity. It is one thing to agree that the American cinema is illusionist, and to define what "believing in its reality" means. For instance, what it means is that one takes pleasure in being a witness to magic, to seeing with one's own eyes and ears what the mind knows to be impossible, or to experience the uncanny force of cinema as a parallel universe, peopled by a hundred years of un-dead presences, of ghosts more real than ourselves. But it is something quite other to equate this il-lusion or suspension of disbelief with de-lusion, and to insist that we have to wake up from it and be dis-enchanted away from its spell. That equation was left to *Screen* to insist on, and that is what perhaps was fed to film students far too long for film theory's own good, percolating through university film courses in ever more diluted versions.

But what extraordinary effervescence, what subtle intellectual flavors and bubbling energy the heady brew of screen theory generated in those early years! It testifies to the hidden bliss of disenchantment (which as Bellour makes clear, is profoundly linked to the loss of childhood), which gripped filmmakers as well as film theorists, and did so, paradoxically, at just the moment, around 1975 when, on the face of it, practice and theory, after a close alliance from the years of the Nouvelle Vague to the early work of Scorsese, Paul Schrader or Monte Hellman, began to diverge in quite different directions. It is remarkable to think that the publication of Stephen Heath's and Laura Mulvey's famous articles coincides with JAWS (USA: Steven Spielberg, 1975), THE EXORCIST (USA: William Friedkin, 1974) and STAR WARS (USA: George Lucas, 1975-77) – films that instead of dismantling illusionism, gave it a fourth dimension. Their special-effect hyperrealism made the term "illusionism" more or less obsolete, generating digital ontologies whose philosophical conundrums and cognitive-perceptual puzzles still keep us immersed or bemused. Unfortunately for some of us, the time came when students preferred disbelieving their eyes in the cinemas, to believing their teachers in the classroom.

Cinephilia: Take Two

It is perhaps the very conjuncture or disjuncture between the theoretical tools of film studies and the practical film experiences of students (as students *and* spectators) that necessitates a return to this history – the history of cinephilia, in order to begin to map the possible contours of another cinephilia, today's cinephilia. For as already indicated, while psychosemiotics has lost its intellectual luster, cinephilia seems to be staging a comeback. By an effect of yet another act of temporal displacement, such a moment would rewrite this history, creating not only a divide, but retrospectively obliging one to differentiate more clearly between first-generation cinephilia and second-generation cinephilia. It may even require us to distinguish two kinds of second-generation cinephilia, one that has kept aloof from the university curriculum and kept its faith with auteur cinema, with the celluloid image and the big screen, and another that has found its love of the movies take very different and often enough very unconventional forms, embracing the new technologies, such as DVDs and the internet, finding communities and shared experiences through gender-bending *Star Trek* episodes and other kinds of textual poaching. This fan cult cinephilia locates its pleasures neither in a physical space such as a city and its movie houses, nor in the "theatrical" experience of the quasi-sacral space of audiences gathered in the collective trance of a film performance.

I shall not say too much about the cinephilia that has kept faith with the auteur, a faith rewarded by that special sense of being in the presence of a new talent, and having the privilege to communicate such an encounter with genius to others. Instead of discovering B-picture directors as auteurs within the Hollywood machine, as did the first generation, these cinephiles find their neglected figures among the independents, the avant-garde, and the emerging film nations of world cinema. The natural home of this cinephilia is neither the university nor a city's second-run cinemas, but the film festival and the film museum, whose increasingly international circuits the cinephile critic, programmer, or distributor frequents as *flaneur*, prospector, and explorer. The main reason I can be brief is not only that my narrative is trying to track the interface and hidden links between cinephilia and academic film studies. Some of the pioneers of this second generation cinephilia – the already mentioned Jonathan Rosenbaum and Adrian Martin – have themselves, together with their friends in Vienna, New York, San Francisco, and Paris, mapped the new terrain and documented the contours of their passion in a remarkable, serial publication, a daisy-chain of letters, which shows the new networks in action, while much of the time recalling the geographical and temporal triangulations of desire I have already sketched above.[15]

Less well documented is the post-auteur, post-theory cinephilia that has embraced the new technologies, that flourishes on the internet and finds its *jouissance* in an often undisguised and unapologetic fetishism of the technical prowess of the digital video disc, its sound and its image and the tactile sensations now associated with both. Three features stand out for a casual observer like myself, which I would briefly like to thematize under headings "re-mastering, re-purposing, and re-framing."

Re-mastering in its literal sense alludes, of course, directly to that fetish of the technical specification of digital transfers. But since the idea of re-mastering also implies power relations, suggesting an effort to capture and control something that may have gotten out of hand, this seems to me to apply particularly well to the new forms of cinephilia, as I shall try to suggest below. Yet re-mastery also hints at its dialectical opposite, namely the possibility of failure, the slipping of control from the very grip of someone who wants to exercise it. Lastly, re-mastering also in the sense of seizing the initiative, of re-appropriating the means of someone else's presumed mastery over your emotions, over your libidinal economy, by turning the images around, making them mean something for you and your community or group. What in cultural studies came to be called "oppositional readings" – when countering preferred or hegemonic readings – may now be present in the new cinephilia as a more attenuated, even dialogical engagement with the object and its meaning. Indeed, cinephilia as a re-mastering could be understood as the ultimate "negotiated" reading of the consumer society, insofar as it is within the regime of universalized (or "commodified") pleasure that the meaning proposed by the mainstream culture and the meaning "customized" by the cinephile coincide, confirming not only that, as Foucault averred, the "control society" disciplines through pleasure, but that the internet, through which much of this new cinephilia flows, is – as the phrase has it – a "pull" medium and not a "push" medium.[16]

One of the typical features of a pull medium, supposedly driven by the incremental decisions of its users, is its uncanny ability to re-purpose. This, as we know, is an industryterm for re-packaging the same content in different media, and for attaching different uses or purposes to the single product. It encompasses the director's cut, the bonus package of the DVD with its behind-the-scenes or making-of "documentaries," as well as the more obvious franchising and merchandising practices that precede, surround, and follow a major feature film release. The makers of THE MATRIX (USA: Andy & Larry Wachowski, 1998) or LORD OF THE RINGS (USA: Peter Jackson, 2001-2003) already have the computer game in mind during the filming, they maintain websites with articles about the "philosophy" of their plots and its protagonists, or they comment on the occult significance of objects, character's names and locations. The film comes with its own discourses, which in turn, give rise to more discourses. The critic – cinephile, consumer guide, enforcer of cultural standards, or fan – is already part of the package. Knowledgeable, sophisticated and expert, this ready-made cinephilia is a hard act to follow, and even harder is it to now locate what I have called the semiotic gap that enables either unexpected discovery, the shock of revelation, or the play of anticipation and disappointment, which I argued are part of cinephilia take one, and possibly part of cinephilia *tout court*.

This may, however, be the jaded view of a superannuated cinephile take one, unable to "master" his disenchantment. For there is also *re-framing*, referring to the conceptual frame, the emotional frame, as well as the temporal frame that regulates the DVD or internet forms of cinephilia, as well. More demanding, certainly, than selecting the right row in the cinema of your choice for the perfect view of the screen, these acts of reframing require the ability to hold in place different kinds of simultaneity, different temporalities. What is most striking about the new cinephilia is the mobility and malleability of its objects, the instability of the images put in circulation, their adaptability even in their visual forms and shapes, their mutability of meaning. But re-framing also in the temporal sense, for the new cinephile has to know how to savor (as well as to save her sense of identity from) the anachronisms generated by total availability, by the fact that the whole of film history is henceforth present in the here-and-now. Terms like "cult film" or "classic" are symptomatic of the attempt to find ways of coping with the sudden distance *and* proximity in the face of a constantly re-encountered past. And what does it mean that the loved object is no longer an immaterial experience, an encounter stolen from the tyranny of irreversible time, but can now be touched and handled physically, stored and collected, in the form of a videotape or disk? Does a movie thereby come any closer or become more sensuous or tangible as an experience? In this respect, as indeed in several others, the new cinephilia faces the same dilemmas as did the old one: How to manage the emotions of being up close, of "burning with passion," of how to find the right measure, the right spatial parameters for the pleasures, but also for the rituals of cinephilia, which allow them to be shared, communicated, and put into words and discourse? All these forms of re-framing, however, stand in yet another tension with the dominant aesthetics of the moving image today, always seeking to "un-frame" the image, rather than merely reframing the classical scenic rectangle of stage, window, or painting. By this I mean the preference of contemporary media culture for the extreme close-up, the motion blur, wipe or pan, and for the horizon-less image altogether. Either layered like a palimpsest or immersive like a fish tank, the image today does not seek to engage the focusing gaze. Rather, it tries to suggest a more haptic contact space, a way of touching the image and being touched by it with the eye and ear. Contrast this to the heyday of mise-en-scène, where the art of framing or subtle reframing by the likes of Jean Renoir, Vincente Minnelli, or Nicholas Ray became the touchstone of value for the cinephiles of the first generation.

Cinephilia take one, then, was identified with the means of holding its object in place, with the uniqueness of the moment, as well as with the singularity of sacred space, because it valued the film almost as much for the effort it took to catch it on its first release or its single showing at a retrospective, as for the spiritual revelation, the sheer aesthetic pleasure or somatic engagement it promised at such a screening. On all these counts, cinephilia take two would seem to be a more complex affair involving an even more ambivalent state of mind and body. Against "trepidation in anticipation" (take one), the agitation of cinephilia take two might best be described by the terms "stressed/distressed," having to live in a non-linear, non-directional "too much/all at once" state of permanent tension, not so much about missing the unique moment, but almost its opposite, namely about how to cope with a flow that knows no privileged points of capture at all, and yet seeks that special sense of self-presence that love promises and sometimes provides. Cinephilia take two is therefore painfully aware of the paradox that cinephilia take one may have lived out in practice, but would not ultimately confront. Namely, that attachment to the unique moment and to that special place – in short, to the quest for plenitude, envelopment and enclosure – is already (as psychoanalysis was at pains to point out) the enactment of a search for lost time, and thus the acknowledgement that the singular moment stands under the regime of repetition, of the re-take, of the iterative, the compulsively serial, the fetishistic, the fragmented and the fractal. The paradox is similar to what Nietzsche expressed in *Thus Spake Zarathustra*: *"doch alle Lust will Ewigkeit"* ("all pleasure seeks eternity"), meaning that pleasure has to face up to the fact of mortality, in the endless repetition of the vain attempt to overcome it.

Looking back from cinephilia take two to cinephilia take one, it once more becomes evident just how anxious a love it has always been, not only because we held on to the uniqueness of time and place, in the teeth of cinema's technological change and altered demographies that did away with those very movie houses which were home to the film lover's longings. It was an anxious love, because it was love in deferral and denial. By the 1960s, we already preferred the Hollywood films of the 1940s to the films made in the 1960s, cultivating the myth of a golden age that some cinephiles themselves have since transferred to the 1960s, and it was anxious in that it could access this plenitude only through the reflexiveness of writing, an act of distancing in the hope of getting closer. It was, I now believe, the cinephile's equivalent to the sort of *mise-en-abyme* of spectatorship one finds in the films of early Godard, such as the movie-house scene in LES CARABINIERS (France: 1963, THE RIFLEMEN), where Michel-Ange wants to "enter" the screen, and ends up tearing it down. Writing about movies, too, was trying to seize the cinematic image, just as it escaped one's grasp. Once the screen was torn down, the naked brick wall that remained in Godard's film is as good a metaphor for this disenchantment I am speaking about as any. Yet cinephilia take two no longer has even this physical relation to "going to the movies" which a film as deconstructive, destructive, and iconoclastic as LES CARABINIERS still invokes with such matter-of-factness. Nowadays, we know too much about the movies, their textual mechanisms, their commodity status, their function in the culture industries and the experience economy, but – equally important, if not more so – the movies also know too much about us, the spectators, the users, the consumers. The cinema, in other words, is that "push" medium which disguises itself as a "pull" medium, going out of its way to promote cinephilia itself as its preferred mode of engagement with the spectator: the "plug," in Dominic Pettman's words, now goes both ways.[17]

Cinephilia take one, I suggested, is a discourse braided around love, in all the richly self-contradictory, narcissistic, altruistic, communicative and autistic forms that this emotion or state of mind afflicts us with. Film studies, built on this cinephilia, proceeded to deconstruct it, by taking apart mainly two of its key components: we politicized pleasure, and we psychoanalyzed desire. An important task at the time, maybe, but not a recipe for happiness. Is it possible to once more become innocent and political? Or to reconstruct what, after all, cinephilia take one and take two have in common, while nonetheless marking their differences? The term with which I would attempt to heal the rift is thus neither pleasure nor desire, but memory, even if it is no less contentious than either of the other two. At the forefront of cinephilia, of whatever form, I want to argue, is a crisis of memory: filmic memory in the first instance, but our very idea of memory in the modern sense, as recall mediated by technologies of recording, storage, and retrieval. The impossibility of experience in the present, and the need to always be conscious of several temporalities, which I claimed is fundamental to cinephilia, has become a generalized cultural condition. In our mobility, we are "tour"-ists of life; we use the camcorder with our hands or often merely in our heads, to reassure ourselves that this is "me, now, here." Our experience of the present is always already (media) memory, and this memory represents the recaptured attempt at self-presence: possessing the experience in order to possess the memory, in order to possess the self. It gives the cinephile take two a new role – maybe even a new cultural status – as collector and archivist, not so much of our fleeting cinema experiences as of our no less fleeting self-experiences.

The new cinephilia of the download, the file swap, the sampling, re-editing and re-mounting of story line, characters, and genre gives a new twist to that anxious love of loss and plenitude, if we can permit ourselves to consider it for a moment outside the parameters of copyright and fair use. Technology now allows the cinephile to re-create in and through the textual manipulations, but also through the choice of media and storage formats that sense of the unique, that sense of place, occasion, and moment so essential to all forms of cinephilia, even as it is caught in the compulsion to repeat. This work of preservation and re-presentation – like all work involving memory and the archive – is marked by the fragment and its fetish-invocations. Yet fragment is also understood here in a special sense. Each film is not only a fragment of that totality of moving images which always already exceed our grasp, our knowledge and even our love, but it is also a fragment, in the sense of representing, in whatever form we view or experience it, only one part, one aspect, one aggregate state of the many, potentially unlimited aggregate states by which the images of our filmic heritage now circulate in culture. Out there, *the love that never lies* (cinephilia as the love of the original, of authenticity, of the indexicality of time, where each film performance is a unique event), now competes with *the love that never dies*, where cinephilia feeds on nostalgia and repetition, is revived by fandom and cult classics, and demands the video copy and now the DVD or the download. While such a love fetishises the technological performativity of digitally remastered images and sounds, it also confers a new nobility on what once might have been mere junk. The new cinephilia is turning the unlimited archive of our media memory, including the unloved bits and pieces, the long forgotten films or programs into potentially desirable and much valued clips, extras and bonuses, which proves that cinephilia is not only an anxious love, but can always turn itself into a happy perversion. And as such, these new forms of enchantment will probably also encounter new moments of dis-enchantment, re-establishing the possibility of rupture, such as when the network collapses, the connection is broken, or the server is down. Cinephilia, in other words, has re-incarnated itself, by dis-embodying itself. But what it has also achieved is that it has un-Frenched itself, or rather, it has taken the French (term) into a new ontology of belief, suspension of disbelief, and memory: possibly, probably against the will of the "happy few," but hopefully, once more for the benefit of many.

Notes

1. Paul Willemen's essay on "Cinephilia" accurately echoes this severity of tone and hints at disapproval. See "Through the Glass Darkly: Cinephilia Reconsidered," in Paul Willemen (ed.). *Looks and Frictions: Essays in Cultural Studies and Film Theory*, Bloomington and Indianapolis: Indiana University Press, 1994, pp. 223-257.
2. The Andrew Sarris-Pauline Kael controversy can be studied in Sarris, Andrew. "Notes on the *Auteur* Theory in 1962," *Film Culture*, 27 (1962-63), 1-8; Kael, Pauline. "Circles and Squares," *Film Comment*, 16/3 (Spring 1963), pp. 12-26. For biographical background to Sarris' position, see <http://www.dga.org/news/v25_6/feat_sarris_schickel.php3>.
3. ANNIE HALL (USA: Woody Allen, 1977): "We saw the Fellini film last Tuesday. It was not one of his best. It lacks a cohesive structure. You know, you get the feeling that he's not absolutely sure what it is he wants to say. 'Course, I've always felt he was essentially a – a *technical* filmmaker. Granted, *La Strada* was a great film. Great in its use of negative imagery more than anything else. But that simple, cohesive

core.... Like all that *Juliet of the Spirits* or *Satyricon*, I found it incredibly *indulgent*. You know, he really is. He's one of the most *indulgent* filmmakers. He really is...."

4. Sontag, Susan. "The Decay of Cinema," *The New York Times*, 25 February 1996.

5. Jean-Paul Sartre returned to Paris from his visit to New York in 1947, full of admiration for the movies and the cities, and especially about Orson Welles' CITIZEN KANE (USA: 1941). See *Situations IV: Portraits*, Paris: Gallimard, 1964, pp. 34-56.

6. Baecque, Antoine de. *La cinéphilie: Invention d'un regard, histoire d'une culture, 1944–1968*, Paris: Fayard, 2003.

7. Rosenbaum, Jonathan. *Moving Places: A Life at the Movies*, New York: Harper & Row, 1980, pp. 19-35.

8. Martin, Adrian. "No Flowers for the Cinephile: The Fates of Cultural Populism 1960-1988," Foss, Paul (ed.), *Island in the Stream: Myths of Place in Australian Cinema*, Sydney: Pluto Press, 1988, p. 128.

9. For Latin American cinephilia, apart from Manuel Puig's novel *Kiss of the Spider Woman* (1979), see Perez, Gilberto. *The Material Ghost: Films and Their Medium*, Baltimore: The Johns Hopkins University Press, 2000.

10. The cinephile magazine collectives that I headed as editor were *The Brighton Film Review* (1968-1971) and *Monogram* (1971-1975).

11. "Charlton Heston is an axiom. By himself alone he constitutes a tragedy, and his presence in any film whatsoever suffices to create beauty. The contained violence expressed by the somber phosphorescence of his eyes, his eagle's profile, the haughty arch of his eyebrows, his prominent cheekbones, the bitter and hard curve of his mouth, the fabulous power of his torso; this is what he possesses and what not even the worst director can degrade," Michel Mourlet, quoted in Roud, Richard, "The French Line," *Sight and Sound*, Autumn 1960. On Lang, see Moullet, Luc. *Fritz Lang*, Paris: Seghers, 1963; Eibel, Alfred (ed.). *Fritz Lang*. Paris: Présence du Cinéma, 1964. On Hitchcock see Rohmer, Eric, Claude Chabrol. *Hitchcock*, Paris: Éditions universitaires, 1957; Truffaut, François. *Le cinéma selon Hitchcock*, Paris: Robert Laffont, 1966; Douchet, Jean. *Alfred Hitchcock*, Paris: Éditions de l'Herne, 1967.

12. A good account of Screen Theory can be found in the introductions and texts assembled in Phil Rosen (ed.), *Narrative, Apparatus, Ideology: A Film Theory Reader*, New York: Columbia University Press, 1986.

13. Heath, Stephen. "Narrative Space," *Screen*, 17/3 (1976), pp. 19-75; and Mulvey, Laura. "Visual Pleasure and Narrative Cinema," *Screen*, 16/3 (autumn 1975), pp. 6-18.

14. Bellour, Raymond. "Nostalgies," *Autrement: Europe-Hollywood et Retour*, 79 (1986), pp. 231-232. [*Il y a trois choses, et trois seulement, que j'ai aimées de la meme façon: la mythologie grecque, les ecrits de jeunesse des soeurs Bronte, le cinema americain. Ces trois mondes si dissemblables n'ont qu'une chose en commun, mais qui est d'une force immense: ce sont, precisement, des mondes. C'est-a-dire des ensembles complets, qui repondent vraiment, a tel moment du temps, a toutes les questions que l'on peut se poser sur la nature, la fonction et le destin de l'univers. Cela est tres clair dans la mythologie grecque. Les recits des dieux et des heros ne laissent rien dans l'ombre: ni le ciel ni la terre, ni la genealogie ni les sentiments; ils imposent l'idee d'un ordre, fini et infini, dans lequel un enfant pouvait imaginer ses peurs et ses envies....*
Des l'invention du cinema, il y a une extraordinaire adequation entre la machine-cinema et le continent-Amerique. [Car] l'Amerique reconnait d'emblee, dans cette machine a repro-

duire la realite, l'instrument qui lui est necessaire pour inventer la sienne. Sa force a ete d'y croire instantanement.]

15. Martin, Adrian, Jonathan Rosenbaum (eds.), *Movie Mutations: The Changing Face of World Cinephilia*, London: British Film Institute, 2003.

16. The terms "pull" and "push" come from marketing and constitute two ways of making contact between a consumer and a product or service. In a push medium, the producer actively persuades the customer of the advantages of the product (via advertising, marketing campaigns, or mailings). In a pull medium, the consumer "finds" the product or service by appearing to freely exercise his/her choice, curiosity, or by following an information trail, such as word-of-mouth. The search engines of the internet make the World Wide Web the typical "pull" medium, obliging traditional "push" media to redefine their communication strategies.

17. Dominic Pettman, remark at the Cinephilia II Conference, Amsterdam 2003.

Dreams of Lost Time

A Study of Cinephilia and Time Realism in Bertolucci's
The Dreamers

Sutanya Singkhra

What do people do for love? Just about anything. And we all know how easy it is to fall in love. It is probably because of the mysterious nature of an act of love that makes it somehow irresistible. This is why using a phrase as clichéd as "falling in love with love" is not so inappropriate when we talk about "cinephilia" as a love for cinema. But truly, for us cinephiles, love for the cinema is not just an act of watching movies, but rather of *living* them, re-enacting particular scenes or lines that have changed forever our view of everything in our lives.

Many have tried to define and explain the phenomenon of cinephilia, the "crazy, obsessive" love for 24 frames-per-second of truth on screen.[1] What power does cinema possess, what has it gained, and from where? Its unique mechanism of making a series of still images *appear* in real action/real time is one thing. But the more obvious nature of cinema that we find so mesmerizing is its endless abilities to tell stories within affordable and possible "time frames" for the audience. This transforming power of cinema that perfectly instantiates the mysteries of time – *chronos, kairos, aion*[2] – is exactly the magic of cinema, the power that attracts, entertains and encourages the cinephilia.

Cinema does not only store time's physicality, if it has one (though many have argued that time can in no way be retrieved – Bergson with his theory of time as *durée* comes to mind). For the first time in history it also makes the *flow* of time visible, readable, and compatible with the temporal accessibility of human psyche. None of the previous time-storage media – literature, paintings, sculptures, photographs – possesses this ability, this power to visually regain and represent the "passage" of "lost" time in the way that the human mind manages temporality, if we follow Freud, according to whom the psyche reads time as fragments, opposing itself to the relentlessness of time's flow. For Freud, time itself is a violent force, and the mode of temporal discontinuity is the psyche's own protective configurative.

In our contemporary media context, however, the scheme of time lost and regained in cinema has gone beyond the mere matter of recording and representing time (in both the factual and fictional sense). Today's films, so often the products of cinephiles, have become obsessed with the concept of recapturing lost time, an attempt that may easily be read as a reflection on cinema itself. One can see it as a particular drama of "perfect moments" lost and regained through re-enactments, repetitions; the result of the cinephilia complex, reflecting on it-self in the medium of time.

Bernardo Bertolucci's THE DREAMERS (Italy/France/UK/USA: 2003) seems to be the perfect film to respond to this complex – a cinephilia project par excel-lence. The story is set in Paris against the backdrop of the May '68 student riots. Matthew (Michael Pitt), a young American, meets French twins Théo (Louis Garrel) and Isabelle (Eva Green) at the Cinémathèque Française during a de-monstration against the sacking of its co-founder, Henri Langlois. The three quickly grow close, and once the twins' parents leave town Matthew is invited to live in their bourgeois apartment. There the three friends begin a life of reclu-sive bohemia, dismissing the boiling turmoil in the streets of Paris.

After being shown at the Venice Film Festival in 2003, THE DREAMERS came to us with a "faint whiff of scandal." Not only for its outrageous rating of NC-17 due to its extremely explicit sexual content, but also its controversial political context. THE DREAMERS, based on the novel *The Holy Innocents: A Romance* by Gilbert Adair,[3] who also wrote the script for the film, reminisces, or, more pre-cisely, re-enacts the spirits of the era. Bertolucci refers to the Paris of 1968 as a "very magical and intense period,"[4] an era of "revolution" for young people, including him, as a film lover and filmmaker. THE DREAMERS is, therefore, sim-ply a cinephilia project that Bertolucci uses to revive those glorious moments, a dream to trace back and once again experience that "lost" time.

The critics, those who praise and those who damn the film, all raise the issue of the truthfulness not of the events but of the nostalgia that Bertolucci's film enacts. On the one hand, they argue that "lost time" is successfully retrieved by the film's superb visual style and subtle narrative. But on the other hand, the incidents and scenes depicted – which one could call "cinematic time organi-zers" – are attacked for producing false, artificial, and pretentious reminis-cences.[5] However, if we are to consider this film as a project of and about cine-philia, and not a documentary of historical moments, to explore its nostalgia in *factual* terms would in any case be besides the point. Instead, we should read Bertolucci's THE DREAMERS as a search for the micro-moments and temporal orders that he has developed to sustain and embody these several layers of "lost" time.

Time in THE DREAMERS, then can be considered "cinephilia time," for it is a recapturing of key moments from that first generation of cinephiles (in the 1960s) and everything in relation to it. Along with the archival news footage of the student uprising and a re-enactment of some of the major events, the realism of that lost time is nested, and although it is not truthful to the event's concep-tual sense, it is to its chrono-topical one. What is more, to invoke the impossible, Bertolucci has gone to the extent of transferring this lost time of youth, revolu-tion, and the love of cinema simultaneously from the past (1968 – cinematic time) to the present (filming time 2003 – cinephilia time) and back again, by having the key witnesses of that very event, actors Jean-Pierre Léaud and Jean-Pierre Kalfon, read aloud the same petition they read 35 years earlier.

The isomorphism of cinematic time and cinephilia time in these scenes is evidence of how Bertolucci sees the magic of cinema in retrieving and forming time as a root of the culture of cinephilia. He once wrote: "There are two things I love about the cinema: time and light. The whole *Life of* [Mizoguchi's] *Lady O'Haru* – youth, maturity and old age, in 3,000 metres.... The unity of time in [John] Ford's *Seven Women*: one or two days, as in tragedy. The a-temporal time in the films of Godard."[6] Bertolucci, as a child of the cinema, is mesmerized by cinema's unique ability to weave time and portray it in a nutshell – the cinematic techniques of storytelling as time manipulation. The narrative devices he has chosen to regain lost time in THE DREAMERS can be simply categorized by the three major themes of the period of 1968: politics, love of cinema, and sexuality, the subjects which can be explored through specific spaces in the film respectively: the City, the Cinema, and the Body.

The City and Politics

Kevin Lynch, one of the most important figures in contemporary urban studies, compares the City to an artwork. He writes: "Looking at cities can give a special pleasure, however commonplace the sight may be.... At every instant, there is more than the eye can see, more than the ear can hear, a setting or a view waiting to be explored. Nothing is experienced by itself, but always in relation to its surroundings, the sequences of events leading up to it, the memory of past experiences." The City, therefore is, as Lynch describes it, "a temporal art."[7] Without the passage of time, the city would signify nothing but built space.

In THE DREAMERS, the city of Paris is approached as a piece of temporal art. Bertolucci frames the city with a specific scale of time – the spring of 1968. Within this temporal frame, Paris comes to life, attains its own spirit. What then *is* this spirit of Paris in 1968? In general, people link the generation with sex, drugs, and rock and roll; a group of young people who live in a dream world, idealizing freedom, denying reality. But Bertolucci, who was in Paris at the time,[8] strongly disagrees: "I don't think that [sex, drugs, music] was freedom, to want to be free. I think in that very moment, politics was a big part of that." He says, "Sex was together, in sync with politics, music, cinema. Everything was conjugated together.... It was a great privilege to be able to live in that moment... to be a part of big ambitious dreams: to want to change the world."[9] In other words, Bertolucci believes that this "big ambitious dream" is in fact the true spirit of 1968 Paris, and not as one critic has put it: "In THE DREAMERS, to be a May '68 revolutionary is a lifestyle issue." [10]

This dream is explored in THE DREAMERS along with one of the film's major themes – politics. Throughout the film, even though 80 percent of the story takes place inside the French twins' apartment, Paris is preparing for something. The young people are preparing for a "revolution," which the film re-depicts at the very end. And even though historians consider this student uprising against the government to have been a failure,[11] Bertolucci begs to differ, "people who say '68 was a failure are very unfair, a historical mistake. '68 was a revolution, not in political terms, but a change that was terribly important."[12]

With such a strong emotional connection with the time and place, THE DREA-MERS can therefore be seen as the "light" that Bertolucci is always in search of as a filmmaker: "There is a light in La règle du jeu that announces the beginning of the war; there is a light in Voyage to Italy that announces Antonioni's L'Avventura, and with that, all of modern cinema; and a light in Breathless that announces the 60s."[13] Even though the riot the film portrays in the end resulted in a defeat, the "dream" of the generation, the spirit of the city at the time, is in fact a "light" that, for Bertolucci, announces a true revolution to come. As he points out: "What remains of '68? I think people, the relationships between people are very different after '68. Life before '68 was a number of authoritarian figures. Then they disappeared. And the relationship between men and women, '68 triggered something, the women's liberation movement."[14]

We can see this "light" in THE DREAMERS through how the city of Paris itself is approached. The first shot we see is Paris in the springtime, bathed with sunlight. Matthew, a young American, absorbs the city with wistful eyes. Here it should be pointed out that the political angle of the film is conveyed through the eye of an outsider, an American student in Paris, and of course, an Italian filmmaker who has lived those lost moments. This point also stresses the fact that the realism woven into the film is in fact the "impression" of the time.

Through the eyes of the filmmaker, the impression of the era effects how time is treated in THE DREAMERS as well. Time in Paris – in the city streets – is treated as Bergson's durée. It is a flow that cannot and will not be stopped. In this sense, time in Paris is fact, is reality, that which, as Phillip K. Dick observes, even "when you stop believing in it, doesn't go away."[15]

The Cinema and Love for Cinema

Bertolucci, as a cinephile, or, in the 1960s lingo, a film buff, was intimately affected by the government dismissal of Henri Langlois, a man who gave birth to the Cinémathèque Française, a temple for film critics and filmmakers whose work still plays a significant role in the world of cinema today. The student demonstrations in front of the Cinémathèque at the beginning of the film depicts what Bertolucci regards as the 1960s spirit: "In '68 everything started with the Cinémathèque. ... All the ambitions and the thoughts were very connected with cinema. It was like a projection of illusions that have a cinematic value."[16]

And as a cinephilia project par excellence, THE DREAMERS uses movie-going in order to evoke the period. Bertolucci alludes to several groundbreaking films that help revive the elegance of the time. Thus, he has Matthew, Théo, and Isabelle act out passages from the films they have watched, and then marries the scenes with the shots of the films themselves. These include classics such as QUEEN CHRISTINA (USA: Rouben Mamoulian, 1933) and BLONDE VENUS (USA: Josef von Sternberg, 1932), and Cahiers du cinéma favourites like SHOCK CORRIDOR (USA: Samuel Fuller, 1963) and MOUCHETTE (France: Robert Bresson, 1967). One of the major moments in the film, of course, is the scene where the three main characters deliberately re-enact (and try to beat) the record run through Museé du Louvre by the three protagonists of Godard's BANDE À PART (France: 1964). These clips, nested alongside and inside the lives of the characters, only emphasize once again the concept of "cinema is life, and life cinema," showing that "cinephilia time" is not only the wish to *live* the experience of cinema, but to also *prolong* it beyond cinema, into life.

By the 1960s, the cinema had become more than just "truth" *on* the screen. At one point in the film, Isabelle imitates Jean Seberg from Godard's BREATHLESS (France: 1959), one of the founding moments of the New Wave: "I entered this world on the Champs-Élysées in 1959, and do you know what my very first words were? '*New York Herald Tribune*! *New York Herald Tribune*!'" It is not her parents who gave birth to Isabelle, but New Wave Cinema. And at that moment, the concept works both ways. New Wave Cinema was actually born to young people like Isabelle, Théo, and Matthew. For the first time in history, cinema was being made by young directors such as Louis Malle, François Truffaut, Jean-Luc Godard, and Claude Chabrol, who started as film lovers, became critics, and turned their critical love or loving criticism into movies. This movement we know as the French New Wave or Nouvelle Vague, is in fact another "revolution" THE DREAMERS tries to depict. While there was a "revolution" in the streets of Paris, there was also one in the movie theatres. The arrival of the New Wave changed filmmaking forever. New visual styles, themes, and modes of production were introduced to the world.[17] The novelty and innovations in the form of New Wave films not only brought jump cuts or hand-held camera work; they reflected the spirit of the time in other ways, too – dreaming a dream of sovereignty, in the political sense as well. As Françoise Brion writes in *La nouvelle vague*, "The New Wave was a freedom of expression, a new fashion of acting, and a great reform on the level of make-up…. Suddenly, you saw actors who looked natural, like they had just gotten out of bed."[18] Here the concept of time in relation to the cinema is given another dimension in that it documents the lived time of its protagonists, as a literal "awakening."

The Body and Sexuality

A trademark of Bertolucci's films is explicit sexual content and nudity. Internationally, he became famous with LAST TANGO IN PARIS (Italy/France: Bernardo Bertolucci, 1972), one of the first films to show intercourse on screen in European art cinema. Picking up on this earlier work, also set in Paris, THE DREAMERS contains full frontal nudity and graphic scenes of sexual intercourse. However, in contrast to the sexual content in LAST TANGO IN PARIS, which Bertolucci refers to as "something dark, heavy, and tragic," the eroticism and sexuality in THE DREAMERS is "something very light, very joyous."[19] Given some of the more brooding moments of sexual tension in the film, one may disagree with Bertolucci on this, but one can also put the emphasis in the remark on light as opposed to dark, rather than as opposed to heavy.

The concept of "light," which, as previously indicated, always receives special attention in Bertolucci films, here subtly interplays with the exposure of the youthful bodies. In THE DREAMERS "light" should be seen as intertwined with the spirit of dawn and waking up, that is, with the "big ambitious dream" of freedom. The sexual experimentations the three characters perform thus suggest that very dream, by testing the limits of freedom, enacted in the "light" of each other's constant presence. The issues of sexual relationships from heterosexuality, homosexuality, to incest the film deals with function as a step toward the "revolution" which was taking place outside. As Roger Ebert commented, "within the apartment, sex becomes the proving ground and then the battleground for the revolutionary ideas in the air."[20] The glow and radiance of the era, is reflected in the way Bertolucci depicts the protagonists' naked bodies of the three protagonists under warm but intense lights.

Thus, the portrayal of naked bodies in THE DREAMERS serves not as (censorable) representations of nudity, but as an index of a sovereign space, like the city and the cinema, that preserves lost time, the lost dream of the era. However, with the young bodies constantly being exposed, the concept of time as a chronological flow or kairos (moving towards the single event) is also challenged. Time in the elegant apartment, which is the setting for more than half of the film, seems to stop, or at least be suspended. Matthew, Théo, and Isabelle are the "dreamers" who lock themselves in "the marvelous dream,"[21] enacting their ideals about life, art, music, cinema, and even politics. The concept of dream here brings us back to Freud's theory of the unconscious, the psychical virtual space where dreams reside.[22] We know that Bertolucci has always been an avid reader of Freud, and so the Oedipus complex plays an especially important role in his films – e.g., PRIMA DELLA RIVOLUZIONE (Italy: 1964) or THE SPIDER'S STRATAGEM (Italy: 1970). As Robert Phillip Kolker suggests, all his work deals with some aspect of this conflict: "the problems of sexual relationships, for the struggle of children and parents, of generations."[23] In THE DREAMERS, however, Oedipus is less present, and instead, it is Freud's view of the unconscious, and in particular, the idea that time does not exist in the unconscious, that Bertolucci draws on.

In THE DREAMERS, the "dream" the three characters are living in the apartment seems to never end. The three hardly leave the place, or when they do they always rush right back. For there, in the "dream," they are safe from the destructive nature of time. The exposure of their bodies emphasizes the concept of *eternal* youth. This concept of timelessness is captured by the photographic and painterly *mise en scène* of the film. Like time in photographs and paintings, time in the apartment, which engulfs the bodies of the three protagonists is stopped. Bertolucci is known for his use of sculptures and paintings as models for the visual construction of his films,[24] and this influence is evident in THE DREAMERS. Bertolucci makes the sculpture of Venus de Milo come to life with Isabelle's body, and recaptures Francis Bacon's famous triptychs with the bodies of the three, resting together in a bathtub with their reflections on the three-way mirrors.

The film's painterly *mise en scène* here also reflects the spirit of the 1960s in terms of the cross-cultural exchanges that have, in much of the 20th century, brought Paris and New York into close proximity with each other, if we think of all the French artists who moved between the two capitals, and the many expatriate Americans who came to make Paris their home. This history, already revived by the French cinephiles' love of the American cinema, is further re-enacted and prolonged in the figure of Matthew, the young American. His role reminds one of the Americans – young idealists, at once naïve and pragmatic – that people the novels of Henry James. As Ebert suggests, the film forces Matthew to confront these strange Europeans, Théo and Isabelle, in the same way Henry James "sacrifices his Yankee innocents on the altar of continental decadence."[25] All three, as children of the 1960s, possess the idealism of the period, only Matthew, as an outsider, approaches the ideals with a slightly stronger sensibility, and a different sense of reality. The French twins, on the other hand, are entirely drowned in their own idealism, to the degree that it turns into narcissism. The physical nature of twins makes them inseparable. In the case of Théo and Isabelle, however, they are emotionally inseparable as well.

They do everything together, including sleeping naked in the same bed and bathing in the same bathtub. Matthew at one point can no longer stand their childish self-immersion: "I wish you could step out of yourselves and just look. … I look at you, and I listen to you and I think... you're never gonna grow.... Not as long as you keep clinging to each other the way that you do."

The controversial conclusion of THE DREAMERS brings us back to the concept of time. Time, like reality, never goes away. While the three kids are exploring each other in the apartment, where time is no more, the explosions and riots in the streets are occurring. As Bertolucci clarifies, "history is calling them."[26] Here the film's factual, chronological time catches up and unites with the fictional, *aionic* time. But at another level, that of our cinephilia-nostalgia time, it is we the spectators who have to weave together the "intervals," the "fragments" of lost time that Bertolucci presents us with. They constitute the film's realism, at both the memory and the narrative level, not their truth as history.

Conclusion

Considered as a film about "time realism" (in contrast to, say action or representational realism) Bertolucci's THE DREAMERS makes it clear that the birth of cinephilia is indeed a momentous historical event, because it ushers in the revolutions of how time is experienced, which we are only now beginning to come to grips with, while showing just how crucial a role the cinema itself has had in all this, along with other, more directly technological or political factors. Instead, it is cinema's scheme of temporal regulation and time articulations that popularized the medium, and has kept it alive for over a century now. However, in this particular case, cinematic time is no longer either a matter of mastering time at the mechanical level or articulating it through narrative. Bertolucci's film knows all about "timeless time" and the "space of flows" of contemporary globalization, but by attending to the micro-levels of body, domestic space, city, cinema – and their interactions on that plane of immanence which are the loops of cinephilia time – THE DREAMERS can convey how timeless time feels, and how the space of flows affects us in our innermost being. Cinephilia in the current media context, as Bertolucci demonstrates, has shifted from *reliving* the moments – illustrated by Matthew, Théo and Isabelle mimicking memorable movie scenes for each other – to *reframing* them. Reframing is our task as spectators, and it means being able to hold together in a single representational space two different temporalities – here the cinematic time of 1968 and the cinephilia time of our collective memory of "May '68" – and of calling this framing, this holding together "love." Such is perhaps Bertolucci's ultimate dream project: to make us love the cinema once more, in the age of television, the internet and all the other ways we can store time and represent history, by making us first love the love of cinema which his own generation called cinephilia.

Notes

1. There is a quote in Jean-Luc Godard's film Le Petit Soldat (France: 1963) that says "photography is truth, and cinema is truth 24 frames a second."
2. *Chronos* is time as duration, passage, flow, flux. *Kairos* is time as event, appointment, juncture, opportunity. *Aion* is time as a very long period, an age, an eternity.
3. Gilbert Adair's *The Holy Innocents: A Romance* is a typically erudite homage to The Strange Ones/Les Enfants Terribles (France: Jean-Pierre Melville, writing credits: Jean Cocteau, 1950). From Anthony Allison, "Last Perversion in Paris." Review of *The Dreamers*. *Las Vegas Mercury*. 4 March 2004. 16 January 2005 <http://www.lasvegasmercury.com/2004/MERC-Mar-04-Thu-2004/23346923.html>.
4. Bernardo Bertolucci, Interview. *National Public Radio News*. 6 February 2004. 10 January 2005 <http://www.npr.org/dmg/dmg.php?prgCode=DAY.
5. "Théo's instant transformation from armchair Maoist and domestic slob to ardent militant is glib, his visit to the Sorbonne a nod to a clichéd iconography rather than an accurate depiction of events, and money and food shortages figure only in the sense that the three are reduced to drinking papa's vintage Bordeaux." Vincendeau, Ginette. "The Dreamers." Review of *The Dreamers. Sight and Sound*. February 2004. 10 January 2005. <http://www.bfi.org.uk/sightandsound/2004_02/thedreamers.php>.
6. Kolker, Robert Phillip. *Bernardo Bertolucci*, London: BFI Books, 1985, p. 5.
7. Lynch, Kevin. *The Image of the City*, Cambridge, Mass.: MIT Press, 1960, p. 1.
8. Even though Bertolucci said in this interview (*Black Film*. 10 January 2005 <http://www.blackfilm.com/20040130/features/bertolucci.shtml>) that he "was there," he only meant it figuratively, for in May of 1968 he was shooting Partner (Italy, 1968) in Rome, Italy. He made this clear in "The Making of *The Dreamer*" (available on the DVD version).
9. Bertolucci Interview. *Cinema Confidential*. 6 February 2004. 10 January 2005 <http://www.cinecon.com/news.php?id=0402061>.
10. Vincendeau, Ginette. "The Dreamers." *Sight & Sound*. February 2004.
11. Absalom, Roger. *France: The May Events 1968*. London: Longman, 1971, p. 82.
12. Bertolucci Interview. *Black Film*.
13. Kolker, Robert Philip, *Bernardo Bertolucci*, p. 5.
14. Bertolucci interview. *Black Film*.
15. "On Subjectivity and Subjectivism." *Waking Life*. Site created and designed by Jimmy Hernandez. 10 January 2005 <http://www.prism.gatech.edu/~gte484v/wakinglife/subjectivity.html>.
16. Bertolucci interview. *Black Film*.

17. Neupert, Richard. "A History of the French New Wave Cinema." 2002. University of Wisconsin Press. <http://www.wisc.edu/wisconsinpress/Presskits/Neupertpresskit.html&anchor510508>.

18. Idem.

19. Bertolucci interview. *Cinema Confidential*. 6 February 2004. 10 January 2005 <http://www.cinecon.com/news.php?id=0402061>.

20. Ebert, Roger. "The Dreamers." Review of *The Dreamers*. RogerEbert.com: Movie Reviews. 13 February 2004. 10 January 2005. <http://rogerebert.suntimes.com/apps/pbcs.dll/article?AID=/20040213/REVIEWS/402130302/1023>.

21. Bonelli, Valerio. First Assistant Editor. Interview. *BBC Four Cinema*. 27 December 2003. 10 January 2004 <http://www.bbc.co.uk/bbcfour/cinema/features/bertolucci-dreamers.shtml>.

22. Domhoff, G.W. "The 'Purpose' of Dreams." *The Quantitative Study of Dreams*. 19 December 2004 <http://psych.ucsc.edu/dreams/Library/purpose.html>.

23. Kolker, Robert Philip, *Bernardo Bertolucci*, p. 1.

24. Idem, p. 64.

25. Ebert, Roger. "The Dreamers."

26. Bertolucci interview. *Cinema Confidential*.

Mass Memories of Movies

Cinephilia as Norm and Narrative in Blockbuster Culture

Drehli Robnik

If we equate cinephilia with liking certain movies, the term loses its meaning; but it also does so if we disconnect it entirely from the common habit of liking movies. In its relation to the value-generating cultural economy which circulates everyday affection by and for the cinema on a mass scale, cinephilia involves extraordinary cases of ordinary practices: a love for extraordinary films; an intense love for ordinary ones, capable of charging them with extraordinary qualities; love for a medium as a whole, which, totalized into a lovable whole, turns from a medium into an art or a memory.

Something similar can be said of cinephilia when considered as a theoretical perspective. Here, cinephilia's extraordinariness suggests problems that it poses to disciplinary orders of discourse. This becomes clear if we look at two conceptual approaches to cinephilia that emerged in the 1990s, both use cinephilia as a guideline for thinking about cinema in a broader sense. In Paul Willemen's approach, cinephilia designates a surplus not contained by film analysis; in Thomas Elsaesser's it points to cinema's anomaly with regard to historiography. Both focus on the memorial dimension of loving the cinema, and I will try to abstract and mobilize some of their arguments to discuss how aspects of cinephilia have become normalized in today's media culture and how we re-encounter allegories of cinephilia in the ways people act out their love for movies which are extraordinary in the most ordinary way. I will try to clarify my argument about contemporary blockbuster culture with respect to a movie with lots of love – quantified in box-office terms – attached to it, namely TITANIC (USA: James Cameron, 1997).

In Paul Willemen's reconsideration of cinephilia, the term designates a loving attention to moments of "revelation" experienced in confrontations with highly coded cinematic representations (Hollywood genre movies); an attention and a practice of demarcation that appear close to, but nevertheless remain distinct from theoretical practices of structural analysis, of deconstruction or reading against the grain. What makes cinephilia "resist and escape existing networks of critical discourse and theoretical frameworks" – what keeps love distinct from discipline, one might say – is the surplus of revelation, the involuntary "excess of 'the seen' beyond 'the shown.'"[1] In passing, Willemen refers to this as "ghosting" and hints at "overtones of necrophilia, of relating to something that is dead, past, but alive in memory."[2] Here, his understanding of cinephilia comes close to a central aspect in Thomas Elsaesser's view.

Elsaesser offers an understanding of cinephilia that is closer to necrophilia. Cinephilia always reaches back beyond the temporal distance that history's (or life's) progression creates to revive memorial bonds that connect lived presence with past experiences.[3] Relating to something alive only in memory means that cinema is "the love that never dies."[4] Elsaesser takes up Pierre Sorlin's argument of the near-impossibility of writing a history of the cinema, of a medium dedicated to restoring the past, most of all its own past, to life as it is captured in images that move and affect us here and now: "Because of its undead nature, the cinema perhaps does not have a history (of periods, styles, modes). It can only have fans, clans and believers, forever gathering to revive a fantasm or a trauma, a memory and an anticipation."[5]

Elsaesser's and Willemen's views of cinephilia meet in their respective emphasis on images that cannot be fully incorporated into linear, causal narratives – into coded narratives of Hollywood genre movies in Willemen's case, into narratives of traditional historiography in Elsaesser's. They differ, however, in respect to cinephilia's relation to a film history that is embedded in media history. To Willemen, cinephilia becomes critically urgent "now that cinema and film theory are threatened with extinction," now that the predominance of electronified images makes cinephilia inappropriate and television "destroys cinema," even makes it impossible "to remember cinema" – a "crime against culture," as he puts it.[6] In Willemen's critical melancholia, what threatens to become lost in the "visual impoverishment" fostered by digitization and what cinephilia, therefore, has to preserve from oblivion is a "density of the [cinematic] image" that is "infused with a sense of history." Cinephilia mourns a loss of history and at the same time acknowledges history's separating power, because to Willemen cinephilia is a discourse that sees cinema "as being completely locked into the 'before' of the electronification of the image."[7]

For Elsaesser, digitization also provides an horizon for thinking cinema, but his perspective is a lot less negative, and his emphasis is not on a frozen "before," but on a liquified "after": "When we speak of the cinema today, we speak of cinema *after* television and *after* the video game, *after* the CD-Rom and the theme park."[8] Therefore, TV is not the impossibility of remembering the cinema, but just our moment and our way of remembering it.

These two versions of "cinecrophilia" each imply their vitalism of the cinema: a vitalism critically played off against cinema's death by television in Willemen; while Elsaesser's folds around the digital and its own death by media history, thus making its radical outside its non-identical inside. To put it differently: Elsaesser's "afterlives" paradigm (in which trauma points towards fantasmatic retroactivity) allows for a post-critical vitalism to which the death of cinema might be just a death mask that the image puts on in the course of its intermedia transformations. To Elsaesser, this metamorphosis is exemplified not least by the blockbuster as today's motor of cinema's popularity.

With its capability of translating cinematic events into a great variety of media and options for consumption, the blockbuster is digital cinema's most accessible horizon for remembering cinema. Blockbuster culture takes films and film histories apart and reconfigures them, constantly producing memories of film experiences, film experiences as memories. According to Elsaesser, the blockbuster acts as a "time machine" which we might see as a translator or modulator between temporal regimes – times of everyday habitual consumption, times of spectacular experience, times of catastrophic history.[9] It generates and regenerates memories, most of all of itself, that are not easy to get rid of, that want to be lovingly kept, revived and re-lived in commodified terms and on a mass scale. Seen from Deleuze's perspective of control societies, this is how blockbuster culture contributes to the audiovisual engineering of social consensus and to making a normalized type of subjectivity what Nietzsche called the "dyspeptic" incapable of forgetting : "[Y]ou never finish anything."[10]

Since the most ordinary blockbusters perform the most miraculous metamorphoses, it is not surprising to find them described in terms of the supernatural or the religious. While Thomas Schatz at points evokes rhetorics of Christianity or Buddhism in his study of the New Hollywood, its "multimedia regenerations" and "reincarnations,"[11] Elsaesser offers the vampire as a proto-dionysian allegory for affective investments in digitized cinema, for the latter's metamorphic powers, for the retroactivity of remakes, re-issues, revivals or revamping old generic modes. The image of the vampire – of undying love, insatiable hunger for memories, circulating in media culture – stands in a peculiar relation to Willemen's conscious use of catholic vocabulary: He sees the cinephile as a "trawler" whose analytic perception casts a net over a film to dig and fish for revelatory moments.[12] To the trawler we might add a well-known metaphor for a close relative of the cinephile: The term "poacher" was coined in 1988 by Henry Jenkins for fan cultures of TV consumption, for their retroactive tactics of reappropriating and rewriting standardized media products.[13] Today, from the vantage point of digitization which provides the hypertextualization of media products within a normalized technological basis, this image allows itself to be taken apart and reconfigured, i.e., to be remembered.

Blockbuster culture remembers the poachers as well as the treasure-hunting trawlers and their extraordinary activities of reading-as-writing. It reconfigures their subject positions into those of ordinary vampires and media parasites. I am not claiming that mass culture has become popularized and self-reflexive to a degree as to make all of us poachers and trawlers in Jenkins' and Willemen's sense. These consumption practices can be understood as potentially resistant within an older power formation; when blockbuster culture remembers them, it abstracts and retains their disregard for narrative closure and their impulse towards keeping images alive, rescuing them from oblivion; what is *not* remembered, what does *not* return, is the critical, oppositional moment in cinephilia and fandom, is the pathos of dangerous transgression associated with it. To translate a distinction introduced by Jenkins into the present: blockbuster culture offers positions not for rebellious, but for "loyalist" identities of poachers[14] – loyalty not to an order transcending economic norms as in Jenkins, but to brands and product lines as preferred hunting grounds. Polemically speaking, those subjectivities glorified as consumer culture's nightmares since De Certeau, i.e., the fans and the cinephiles (insofar as they are fans), are now the marketing strategists' dreams come true: they accept so many offers for appropriation. This formulation clearly implies a fallback to the derogatory discourse on mass-cultural dupes (to which we are so allergic nowadays) – so I should rephrase my view in more abstract terms: cinephilia, as one of the once-marginalized minority pleasures of transforming industrial products into practices that act out logics of memory and retroactivity, is now offered within the scope of hegemonic cultural norms and on a mass scale. The flexible modulation between audiovisual flows, flows of capital and flows of love allows for a plurality of affective investments in and usages of digital cinema.

A good example of this can be found in the recent transformations of a most ordinary manner of appropriating cinema: the home video/laser disc/DVD collection which raises archival memory to the level of "videophilia." In Charles Shiro Tashiro's Benjaminian account, videophilia points to a subjectivity reminiscent of the "absent-minded examiner": the "Proletarian Epicure" who acts as his or her own projectionist and "waits for it on video." In 1991, Tashiro saw this waiting as ambivalent. On the one hand, it is the anticipation of a religious ecstasy which video, unlike cinema, cannot provide; on the other, it involves a technologically based refusal to wait, to wait for moments of revelation or, to put it more modestly, for favorite scenes: "What we once might have endured," writes Tashiro, we now skip by fast-forwarding, because of a "saturation by classical cinema" and its narrative linearity. To Tashiro, the videophile's remote control over the film manifests a critical, proto-deconstructive disruption of the film's auratic spell and at the same time a commodified pleasure in which "[s]avory replaces rapture." In a manner typical of cultural studies discourse circa 1990, Tashiro sees the self-empowerment of the consumer as giving rise to a "revolutionary hope [for] the destruction of classical cinema."[15] In Barbara Klinger's later, Benjaminian essay on the privatization of cinema in videophilia, this self-empowerment is reconsidered in terms of the user as owner and classifier, fetishist accumulator of cultural capital available through director's cuts and eager disseminator of trivia learned from making ofs.[16]

What these videophiles retain from Willemen's cinephiles is a disregard for narrative integrity in favor of a technophile attachment to the apparatus (which also played its role in traditional cinephilia) and in favor of the trawling of images. The isolated, fetishized "key image" that achieves paradigmatic status in digital cinema can be seen as the mass-cultural aggregate of cinephilia's fascinating, revelatory moment. It is useful to recall Timothy Corrigan's demystifying account of the "film culture of cult" (bearing in mind differences as well as affinities between cinephilia and cult practices): "Those traditionally marginalized cult audiences have... expanded across culture and been reborn as the primary audience position...."[17] This centering of margins emphasizes the VCR, its technologization and normalization of performative and appropriative aspects of cult behavior. Video materializes films as landscapes of textual ruins through which viewers travel, extracting favorite images from them by remote control like souvenirs.[18] Corrigan's video materialism might be reconsidered (remembered) from the vantage point of the DVD, with videophilia now manifesting a necrophiliac, nostalgic aspect with regard to analogue video, its corporeality, its characteristic "grain," its infusion with histories of usage, all this to be mourned in the way scratches were fetishized in vinylophilia after the introduction of the CD in the mid-1980s. The isolated favorite image as a textual ruin becomes literalized in epiphanies specific to video: rental videos confront you with traces, ruined images, left behind by someone else's fascination by a moment.[19]

Fishing for fascinating moments not only acts out what the remote control is there for, but also mimics practices of film design and marketing known as "high concept" and studied, for instance, by Justin Wyatt. High concept means the overall adaptation of the film image to requirements of intermedia dispersal and shareability. Images are abstracted and rendered flexible in order to be fed into various cycles of consumption and for functioning as logos for all manner of merchandise and advertising media. The unprecedented degree to which we nowadays encounter blockbuster images in trailers (theatrical, internet, video-based, or TV trailers) involves a high-conceptual redefinition of love for and memories of the cinema. The trailer – presumed to contain a film's most fascinating, in some ways most revelatory moments – is the mass-cultural reification of an anticipated memory of a film. It is the film lovingly remembered in advance, and at the same time a form close to the image's total dissolution in a pure flow of audiovisual information to be randomly modulated. The high-concept DVD is another instance of the all-purpose blockbuster image catering to modes of consumption that are hypertextual, participatory, cultist, poaching, trawling, vampirist, and cinephile. By caressing all the folds and openings of the audiovisual body offered to you via DVD, you appropriate and remember a film event as you have experienced it in its theatrical aggregate; the film will have been the anticipation of its DVD, and, in a cinephile inflection, the anticipation of revelations because there is so much more to see on a DVD than during a theatrical projection (not least because the big screen shows you more than you can see); or, as a reviewer wrote on the theatrical release of ARTIFICIAL INTELLIGENCE (USA: Steven Spielberg, 2001): "It bristles with hidden quotations from Kubrick, which in their abundance will only reveal themselves on the DVD edition to come."

Let me, finally, turn to TITANIC, to the way this film incorporated cinema's problematic relationship to digitization. As an extraordinary instance of the ordinary global success that blockbusters aim at, TITANIC's box-office triumph was not just due to the common fact that many people found they had liked the movie after they had paid to see it, but it also built on and mobilized versions of cinephilia. While its theatrical release manifested a Catholicism capable of uniting young and old target groups, legend has it – or maybe fan trivia has it, or maybe statistics has it – that one driving force behind TITANIC's monumental box-office figures was the enthusiastic repeat attendance by young girls. This phenomenon might point us towards the cinephilia-turned-to-knowledge in Heide Schlüpmann's feminist reconsideration of cinema as a culture of the lived-body "guided by love" and as a mass public sphere emphatically encompassing post-bourgeois subjectivities of women.[20]

An emphasis on the lived-body and a version of cinephilia, albeit much less feminist, was also manifested in the way the public sphere of journalism (not only in Austria and Germany, I assume) made sense of TITANIC as a movie that sparked and catered to film critics' nostalgic essentialism of authentic great cinema. In reviews on German TV, the display of the bustling life of "the people" on the lower decks inspired a comparison of James Cameron to John Ford; and a Viennese newspaper critic raved about Cameron as the "creator of breathing characters," his "courage to still make breaths sensible."[21] In this we encounter a cinephile vitalism to which populist celebrations of vitality and the sensibility of breathing revealed that Old Hollywood was not dead, and had either risen from the cold grave of marketing formulas or was at least still breathing.

Let us for a moment recall the importance of sensible images and their existential closeness to living, breathing, passionate bodies in recent cinephile discourses that remember the vitality of the cinema by relating to its embodiment of new lives. In this context, the shaky hand-held camera image, usually accompanied by lots of breathing sounds, is a bodily symptom of the cinema that is perceived as incarnating a revival. With some of the Dogma films as well as with THE BLAIR WITCH PROJECT (USA: David Myrick & Eduardo Sanchez, 1999) – a no-budget, teen horror blockbuster event turning its high concept against itself – a shaky noisiness in sound and image signals a creative over-coming of the *rigor mortis* of a cinema that appears as too controlled and too artificial to common-sense cinephile ideologies. By diagnosing breathing hand-held camera images, the symptomatologic connection can be extended to the notorious landing sequence in SAVING PRIVATE RYAN (USA: Steven Spielberg, 1998). Here, on the generic ground of the action spectacle, a traumatic memory of history fused with the cinephile remembrance of a popular cinema that was and is truly "moving" on a mass scale.

Which – although TITANIC contains hardly any hand-held camera images – brings us back to Cameron's film. David Simpson situates it alongside SCHIND-LER'S LIST (USA: Steven Spielberg, 1993) and SAVING PRIVATE RYAN with regard to the "effects produced by cinematic trauma by proxy."[22] To borrow a tagline from Spielberg, TITANIC is one of those historico-memorial blockbusters that "inspired the world to remember." All the care it takes with the dignity of re-membrance points not least to a conception of how TITANIC wants itself to be remembered, thereby accumulating cinephile cultural capital. TITANIC was cele-brated in highly ideological terms as a blockbuster with a difference, one that would leave only genuine memories behind, no commodified ones in the form of sequels, theme park rides or merchandise (although there was, of course, lots of stuff to buy in the film's wake). In TITANIC's narrative and audience address, we can see both Willemen's and Elsaesser's versions of cinephilia at work, two versions of remembering cinema from the vantage point of digitization: There is the fear of losing it, losing cinema, losing history, losing the memory of the re-velation, which is, however, narratively translated into a discourse of revival inspired by the ability of digital cinema to remember this very fear. To put it differently, in Elsaesserian terms: The remedy is more of the same; the acting out of the trauma provides for therapy and folds the death-defying memory of cinema into a remembrance of TITANIC, the catastrophic historical event as well as the film.

The film itself poses the problem of how to remember TITANIC and offers solutions. One of them is, as Diane Negra has pointed out, its alignment with mass-cultural discourses of survivalism. This implies not only an ethics of self-reliance, but also the possibility for the director to pose as a survivor of his own near-disastrous project; and one might note that TITANIC marks the beginning of the prominence of "boot-camp" rhetorics in interviews and making-ofs that escort most blockbusters, with actors noting how they had to undergo military training for their roles and are now traumatized by the exhausting shoot. This subject position is also available to audiences, who become survivors of the TI-TANIC experience and turn to therapy in the form of listening to Celine Dion or re-consuming the film. In this vein, Negra reads the question which in the film's diegesis initiates Old Rose's oral historical account of the disaster as a discursive invitation: "Are you ready to go back to TITANIC?"[23]

Simpson is probably not alone in comparing the old survivor's struggling verbalization of the TITANIC "story that has to be told" to media images of the oral histories of concentration camp survivors.[24] By extending this connection, we can draw – without being too frivolous – a link between TITANIC, SCHINDLER'S LIST and THE BLAIR WITCH PROJECT, which represent three conversion narratives aimed at generating a dignified memory appropriate to the suffering of living, breathing people. Three blockbusters, atypical in different ways and in different ways surrounded by intermedia practices of archival memory; three attempts at making use of revelatory, emphatic, memorial, counter-historical powers of cinema in a digitized horizon. So that in the end – to borrow another tagline from Spielberg – "something has survived," at least an image, something to be remembered, to be loved, to be touched and be touched by. Without too much evocation of the traumatophile film-as-boot-camp metaphor, we can see all of these movies constructing narrative allegories of their own production processes: how history's listing of casualties becomes a cinematic "list of life."

In TITANIC's case, what Negra calls a "storytelling contest"[25] is, from a cinephile's point of view, a platonic process of selecting the true image, the one that is the most faithful to the idea of loving memory, by narratively lining up candidates for this title and rejecting false pretenders. The frame story moves from treasure-hunting cynicism that guides us through video images of the underwater wreckage in the film's opening scene to the technophilia of a "forensic" reconstruction of the Titanic's sinking in digital animation. These electronic forms of imaging are being conceived as "too distant" in the course of the narrative and therefore ruled out – in favor of Leonardo Di Caprio's drawings from real life (done by Cameron himself) of which one has survived the disaster. But, of course, the image ultimately capable of embodying memory and deserving of love is not the drawing, but the cinematic image: it has assembled, synthesized, all its rivals and was doubly present from TITANIC's very first shot, a would-be documentary long-shot of the ship departing with a man with a movie camera visible in the foreground. It seems as if the cinematic image could survive and even contain digitization. TITANIC's memorial image on the one hand folds digitization into the splendor of "great cinema" (the invisible special effect of sweeping "camera travelings" above and around the ship); on the other hand, the film is able to remember a Bazinian ontology of the cinematic image. The latter finds its meaning in the context of the narrative fusion of a catastrophic collision with the close encounter of two young, passionate bodies – a sensualism that remembers social and physical mobility in terms of the proto-tactile, moving mobility of the image. Its cinephile discourse culminates in the ontologically testifying imprint that, at the moment of orgasm, Kate Winslet's hand leaves on the dimmed windshield of the car in which two heavily breathing characters make love just before the iceberg hits.

Cinema is the love that never dies, especially when blockbuster culture offers us image treasures saturated with sheer life to be trawled from the bottom of the ocean or from the chapters of our DVDs, and when it makes the survival of history in memory a matter of cinephilia.

Notes

1. Willemen, Paul. "Through the Glass Darkly: Cinephilia Reconsidered." *Looks and Frictions. Essays in Cultural Studies and Film Theory,* London: BFI 1994, pp. 223-257, (pp. 231, 242).
2. Ibid., pp. 239, 227.
3. Elsaesser, Thomas. "Über den Nutzen der Enttäuschung: Filmkritik zwischen Cinephilie und Nekrophilie." Schenk, Irmbert (ed.). *Filmkritik. Bestandsaufnahmen und Perspektiven,* Marburg: Schüren, 1998, pp. 91-114, (pp. 102, 109-113).
4. Elsaesser, Thomas. "Specularity and Engulfment. Francis Ford Coppola and BRAM STOKER´s DRACULA." Neale, Steve and Murray Smith (eds.). *Contemporary Hollywood Cinema,* London and New York: Routledge, 1998, pp. 191-208, (p. 206).
5. Ibid., p. 197.
6. Willemen, "Glass Darkly," op.cit., pp. 225, 243, 254.
7. Ibid., pp. 255, 244.
8. Elsaesser, Thomas. "Digital Cinema: Delivery, Event, Time." Elsaesser, Thomas and Kay Hoffmann (eds.). *Cinema Futures: Cain, Abel or Cable? The Screen Arts in the Digital Age,* Amsterdam: Amsterdam University Press, 1998, pp. 201-222, (p. 204).
9. Elsaesser, Thomas. "The Blockbuster: Everything Connects, But Not Everything Goes." Lewis, Jon (ed.). *The End of Cinema as We Know It: American Film in the Nineties,* New York: New York University Press, 2001, pp. 11-22.
10. Deleuze, Gilles. "Postscript on Control Societies." *Negotiations 1972-1990,* New York, Chichester, and West Sussex: Columbia University Press, 1995, pp. 177-182, here p. 179.
11. Schatz, Thomas. "The New Hollywood." Collins, Jim, Hilary Radner, and Ava Preacher Collins (eds.). *Film Theory Goes to the Movies.* New York, London: Routledge, 1993, pp. 8-36, (pp. 29, 31).
12. Willemen, Paul. "Glass Darkly", op.cit., pp. 237, 240
13. Jenkins III, Henry. "Star Trek Rerun, Reread, Rewritten: Fan Writing as Textual Poaching." Penley, Constance, Elisabeth Lyon, Lynn Spiegel, Janet Bergstrom (eds). *Film, Feminism, and Science Fiction.* Minneapolis and Oxford: University of Minnesota Press, 1991, pp. 171-203.
14. Ibid., pp. 171-203, (pp. 174, 191f).
15. Tashiro, Charles Shiro. "Videophilia: What Happens When You Wait for It on Video." *Film Quarterly,* 45/1 (1991), pp. 7-17, (pp. 13, 11, 15f).

16. Klinger, Barbara. "The Contemporary Cinephile: Film Collecting in the Post-Video Era." Stokes, Melvyn, Richard Maltby (eds.): *Hollywood Spectatorship. Changing Perceptions of Cinema Audiences*, London: British Film Institute, 2001, pp. 132-151.

17. Corrigan, Timothy. *A Cinema Without Walls: Movies and Culture After Vietnam*, New Brunswick, NJ and London: Rutgers University Press, 1991, p. 81.

18. Ibid., pp. 82ff.

19. I recall a late 1990s rental video copy of the erotic thriller WILD THINGS (USA: John MacNaughton, 1998) with the tape all wrinkled by frequent application of the still and review functions during the scene of the "threesome" between Matt Dillon, Denise Richards and Neve Campbell. Of course, I didn't hesitate to add a few wrinkles myself.

20. Schlüpmann, Heide. *Abendroethe der Subjektphilosophie: eine Ästhetik des Kinos*, Basel and Frankfurt am Main: Stroemfeld, 1998.

21. Philipp, Claus. "Rettung durch Untergang." *Der Standard*, 9 January 1998, pp. 34f.

22. Simpson, David. "Tourism and Titanomania." *Critical Inquiry*, 25 (1999), pp. 680-695, (p. 694).

23. Negra, Diane. "TITANIC, Survivalism and the Millennial Myth." Sandler, Kevin S., and Gaylyn Studlar (eds.). *Titanic – Anatomy of a Blockbuster*, New Brunswick, NJ and London: Rutgers University Press, 1999, pp. 220-237, (p. 237).

24. Simpson, "Tourism and Titanomania," op. cit., p. 685.

25. Negra, "TITANIC, Survivalism and the Millennial Myth," op. cit., p. 228.

Love in the Time of Transcultural Fusion

Cinephilia, Homage and KILL BILL

Jenna Ng

I. Introduction

There is an inherent difficulty in defining love. Douglas Hofstadter's ironic definition[1] lies more in demonstrating the impracticalities of general recursion than in a genuine attempt for perspicuity. Love simply seems too mystical a force to be registered compactly by facile explanation; it is lamely compared – love "like a red, red rose,"[2] or love that "resembles the eternal rocks beneath"[3] – or else shrugged off as inexplicable phenomena: "love without reason… No wisdom, no judgement / No caution, no blame…"[4] It is presumably too complicated an emotion to analyse, too multifaceted for deconstruction, too profound for definitive scrutiny.

The love of cinema suffers from a similar ambiguity. Cast more or less in the word "cinephilia,"[5] the concept of "the love of cinema" has taken on a state of amorphousness that stretches from the vehement "we cannot live without Rossellini"[6] 1960s film culture to, borne on the growth of the home video, obsessive film collection and solitary, mole-like viewings in dark bedrooms[7] to, simply, a love of the cinema *sous forme de passion exclusive.*"[8] Paul Willemen's baffled exclamation sums it up: "What is this thing that keeps cropping up in all these different forms and keeps being called cinephilia?"[9]

The complication of defining cinephilia is compounded by an element of dogged historicity that writes cinephilia as a past phenomenon and roots nostalgia as the core of its enterprise. Articulated most resoundingly in Susan Sontag's much-discussed article, "The Decay of Cinema,"[10] Sontag refers to cinephilia as the "special" love that cinema "inspired," "born of a conviction that cinema was an art unlike any other," love which evoked a sense of wonder, whereby "people took movies into themselves" and felt liberated by "the experience of surrender to, of being transported by, what was on the screen." "You fell in love not just with actors but with cinema itself."[11] More significantly, Sontag specifically locates the epitome of cinephilia in a targeted historical period, namely, the early 1950s to late 60s.[12] Noting it as a phenomenon which originated in France before spreading to the rest of Europe, the United States and Canada, Sontag recalls cinephilia as a time characterized by feverish, even ritualized, movie-going[13] and animated film criticism dominated by the editors of *Cahiers du cinéma* and other similar journals and magazines around the world, by the proliferation of cinématheques and enthusiastic film clubs, and by a body of original, serious films whose proclaimed creative value truly represented cinema as the art form of the 20th century.[14]

Inherent in the pursuit of such an affectedly idealized historicity is the inevitable nostalgia, the "they-don't-make-it-like-they-used-to" sentiment. Predictably, Sontag mourns that "the love of cinema has waned": "Cinephilia itself has come under attack, as something quaint, outmoded, snobbish…. Cinephilia has no role in the era of hyperindustrial films."[15] Other naysayers such as Stanley Kauffmann, David Denby, and David Thomson echo her pessimism in varying degrees of abjectness – the good times are gone with the dodo. [16] This lingering preoccupation with the *pastness* that comes with the cessation of a certain historicity prompts the observation by (once again) Willemen: "There is a kind of necrophilia involved."[17] Thus is love in this sense of cinephilia infused with so much else: death, nostalgia, regret, bleakness, longing, hopelessness, reminiscence, and – as I painfully felt in Jean-Luc Godard's ÉLOGE DE L'AMOUR (2001), itself a filmic summation of recent history and culture, most obviously cinema – more than a trace of tragic bitterness.

To that extent, "contemporary cinephilia" is an oxymoron in terms – one cannot have contemporariness in a project located specifically in the past. But the pursuit of cinephilia as an undertaking of specific memory overlooks the sheer *love* that is its core to begin with.[18] And love is myriad, boundless and evincible in a legion of ways: that is the difference between the love of cinema and love of *a* cinema. Nicole Brenez writes of her students "who think only of cinema, awaiting the releases of films by their favourite authors the same way one awaits a fiancée." They read, write and breathe cinema, watch films all day and night and have prescient dreams of them even before their releases.[19] That is love. The film CINEMANIA (USA: Angela Christlieb & Stephen Kijak, 2002) documents four fervent moviegoers who plan elaborate daily schedules, right down to toilet breaks, by which they rush between movie theaters (on public transport!) in order to catch *every single* film screening in New York City. Obsessive as it may sound, that, too, is love. Cinephilia is not just confined to explicit practices either. Willemen, for example, pursues cinephilia in the fetishizing of a moment – "what you perceive to be the privileged, pleasure-giving, fascinating moment of a relationship to what's happening on a screen"[20] – which Christian Keathley develops as "panoramic perception," writing these series of moments as "flashes of another history,"[21] and which Roger Hallas applies to his analysis of found footage in Michael Wallin's DECODINGS (USA: 1988).[22] Adrian Martin locates cinephilia within the larger context of Australian culture amidst questions of, *inter alia*, cultural imperialism and populism.[23] Lalitha Gopalan utilizes cinephilia as a springboard towards a rationalization of the study of popular culture, leading to the framework within which she analyses Indian cinema.[24] In discussing contingency, Mary Ann Doane frames cinephilia – "a love that is attached to the detail, the moment, the trace, the gesture" – within "the moment when the contingent takes on meaning."[25] On a slightly different vector, Annette Michelson identifies and examines "a form of cinephilia," "perverse and highly productive,"[26] in the production, exhibition and reception of works by "American filmmakers of independent persuasion and production."[27] Jonathan Rosenbaum and Adrian Martin compile letters, interviews, and essays on "world cinephilia" and contemporary films which the contributors, scattered across the globe, all love and cherish.[28] At the heart of all these writings lies the love of the moving image in its study and reflection. Cinephilia does not die; it merely takes a different form. Love is ahistorical.

It is in this thread that my essay proceeds – to wrap cinephilia around a practice, a theory, a manifestation of love, rather than the continual witnessing of a ceaseless, helpless spectacle of loss. The focus of my essay is the filmmaker's practice of intertextual referencing, especially strategies which specifically evoke "the love of cinema," such as homages and memorialization. In particular, I argue that a unique thrust of contemporary cinephilia is its fluency of transcultural film literacy, one manifestation of which lies in today's plethora of cross-cultural filmic intertextuality, born from a diversity of film culture experiences afforded primarily by home video, cable networks and most recently the internet and DVD. Further, I demonstrate – using Quentin Tarantino's KILL BILL: VOL. 1/2 (USA: 2003/4) – such a transcultural correspondence in a work of homage whose remarkable strategies of cinematic tributes effortlessly fuse love with diversely cross-cultural references, a delivery of the fluid transcultural expressions with which contemporary cinephilia traverses the globalized, amalgamated world of the 21st century.

II. Transcultural Cinephilia

> *Transcultural: Transcending the limitations or crossing the boundaries of cultures;*
> *applicable to more than one culture; cross-cultural.*[29]

Taking on M.M. Bakhtin's notion of dialogism – "the necessary relation of any utterance to other utterances"[30] – Julia Kristeva first establishes the concept of intertextuality in her oft-cited conclusion of the coincidence within the textual space of the work between the "horizontal axis (subject-addressee)" and the "vertical axis (text-context)": "each word (text) is an intersection of word (texts) where at least one other word (text) can be read."[31] Hence, "the theory of intertextuality proposes that any one text is necessarily read in relationship to others and that a range of textual knowledge is brought up to bear upon it."[32]

Despite its literary origins, the term has resonated within film studies:[33] Stam *et al*, for example, apply Bakhtin's conceptions to cinema *qua* medium as signifying practice;[34] intertextuality has also been invoked in contexts as varied as the films of Kurosawa,[35] New Wave French cinema,[36] film analysis,[37] stardom, auteur theory and the films of Jean Renoir.[38] The strategies used are varied, as Noël Carroll notes under the "umbrella term" of allusion (his preferred term): "*Allusion*...[covers] a mixed lot of practices including quotations, the memorialization of past genres, the reworking of past genres, *homages*, and the recreation of 'classic' scenes, shots, plot motifs, lines of dialogue, themes, gestures, and so forth from film history...."[39]

Ranging from spoof to tribute, the motivations for intertextual reference are likewise as diverse, frequently walking knife edges between tribute and being simply, well, too clever. Consideration as to which side a reference falls elicits earnest discussion: a series of posting exchanges on a film forum, for example, reflected the amplitude of responses from enthusiasm to skepticism to the conviction of their being "technically proficient but pedestrian 'ripoffs.'"[40] Clearly, polemics lie in the way one distinguishes between authentic tribute and the (euphemistically stated) sincerest form of flattery.

Nevertheless, in the context of cinephilia, two strategies may be singled out for their motivations of sheer love and reverence. The first is the *homage*. As Thomas Leitch explains:

> A[n] homage is a remake like Werner Herzog's Nosferatu the Vampire (1982) whose primary purpose is to *pay tribute* to an earlier film rather than usurp its place of honor.... [H]omages situate themselves as secondary texts whose value depends on their relation to the primary texts they gloss... Homages therefore present themselves as *valorizations* of earlier films which are in danger of being ignored or forgotten.[41]

Leitch cites examples such as "the compilation films of Robert Youngson (The Golden Age of Comedy [1958], When Comedy Was King [1959], etc)" as the earliest works "informed" by the "impulse behind homages," as well as more well-known works such as Woody Allen's tributes to Ingmar Bergman (Interiors, USA: 1978; A Midsummer Night's Sex Comedy, USA: 1982) and to Federico Fellini (Stardust Memories, USA: 1980).[42]

The second strategy is identified by Noël Carroll as the practice of *memorialization* – "the loving evocation through imitation and exaggeration of the way genres were." Referring to Star Wars (USA: George Lucas, 1977), Superman I (UK: Richard Donner, 1978), Superman II (UK: Richard Lester, 1979) and Rai-

DERS OF THE LOST ARK (USA: Steven Spielberg, 1981), he remarks on how memorialization is "the filmmaker's reverie on the glorious old days," where

> ...plot implausibilities... and its oxymoronic, homemade surrealist juxtapositions... are not forsaken but *defended as homage duly paid to the very source of charm in the originals*. Despite all the thunder and fury, *Raiders* uses its allusions to produce a sense of wistfulness and yearning.[43]

Thus transpires the cinephilic impulse of intertextual referencing: love shown in tribute and celebration inherent in the practices of homage and memorialization, conveying an uncanny mixture of admiration and affection – the former in implicit acknowledgement of a unique superiority of the original; the latter in the complicity of unspoken recognition deep in an affected and subjective memory.

One reason for the high degree of cine-literacy and film-historical awareness which grounds the practice of filmic intertextuality is the pact of "secret sharer" understanding between filmmaker and film-viewer, which in the 60s and 70s was underpinned by a frenzy of film-viewing from a generation of audiences who, as Carroll puts it, "went movie mad."[44] My first argument is that a similar movie-mania is taking place today, albeit with two vital differences: (i) it operates primarily on unprecedented technological development; and (ii) it is marked by an extraordinary diversity of cross-cultural film experience. Whereas the film connoisseurship referred to by Carroll is confined primarily to films from the Western world[45] watched mostly in the cinema hall, the contemporary viewer, however, is able to access films from all cultures, usually from alternative sources. Thus, I argue that the film experience of viewers today – a crucial driver of contemporary cinephilia – has become fluently transcultural in reception and unprecedentedly global in appetite. Surfing on a wave of movie watching first brought about by the videocassette in the 1980s, the "domestication of film"[46] has been subsequently amplified by cable movie channels, refined in quality (albeit briefly) via laser disc and VCD before coming into fruition in the format of the DVD and, in the near future, the internet via movie streaming.[47] No longer bound by a rigid film schedule of the week's new releases dictated by the (commercial intents of the) cinema hall, access to films – what, when, and how (s)he wishes to watch – is now the consumer's prerogative. Via Amazon.com and eBay, viewers from any part of the world are also able to obtain any film they desire. Postal DVD services like Netflix and Movietrak – a savvy combination of the power of the internet and the supreme convenience of DVD – add further to the ease of access not just to films, but also movie spin-offs, cartoons, and television serials. Modes of film discussion and criticism have also been revolutionized via extraordinary databases like imdb.com and countless other online film review websites, journals and e-zines, where surfers are able to discuss and read up on the obscurest film. Ultimately, film consumption, like the rest of our borderless world, has become adeptly cross-cultural, diverse and global – a paradigm of access *sans* geography. Freed from the pragmatic shackles of territorial distance, the film cultures of the world are now fluid commodities – rentable, downloadable or simply available for purchase.

Following this, my second argument is that, like the film directors of the 1970s and 1980s whose work imbibed so much of the film history of the previous decades, today's films (and by extension, film practices) likewise reflect the medley of cross-cultural influences that come with the radical changes of the cine-scape. While intertextual references thus far, such as those cited above by Leitch and Carroll, have been almost completely transatlantic, the films of the 90s and millennium, on the other hand, reflect to a significantly greater degree[48] a transculturally mutable buffet of East-West cinema influences, made by and comprehensible to only a film generation who had grown up with the surfeit of film cultures gleaned from the luxuries of DVD, cable TV and internet technology. As a sampling, Lalitha Gopalan lists an almost alarming number of Western films in the 1990s that refer to Indian cinema:

> ... In both Srinivas Krishna's Canadian production MASALA (1992) and Gurinder Chadda's [sic] British film BHAJI ON THE BEACH (1994), we find lengthy quotations from Indian cinema: protagonists express desire by resorting to song and dance sequences.... In a more abrupt manner, Rachid Bouchareb's French-Algerian film MY FAMILY'S HONOUR (1997) uses Hindi film songs on the soundtrack and even splices an entire musical number from HUM KISISE KUM NAHIN/WE ARE NUMBER ONE (1977) into its narrative... Terry Zwigoff's GHOST WORLD (2000), narrating traumas of the summer after high school, opens with a song and dance sequence, "Jab jaan pechachan/When we got to know each other" from GUMNAAM (1965), intercutting with the main narrative... Baz Luhrmann confesses to not only having seen Indian popular films, but also being mesmerized enough to deploy several song and dance sequences in his film MOULIN ROUGE (2000). Benny Torathi's Israeli film DESPARADO PIAZZA... splices in a song sequence from SANGAM (1964) to map a different history of migration for ethnic Jews...[49]

Undoubtedly, each of us can think of numerous other examples, such as the unmistakable influences of Hong Kong kung fu films and Japanese *anime* in THE MATRIX (USA: Andy & Larry Wachowski, 1998) and its sequels. Nor are the intertextual/cultural references a one-way East-to-West traverse: Tsai Ming-Liang's WHAT TIME IS IT THERE? (France/Taiwan: 2001), for example, makes numerous references to François Truffaut's LES 400 COUPS (France: 1959, THE 400 BLOWS) in terms of scene recreation (Hsiao Kang's father who, like Antoine on the beach, looks straight at the camera for a few seconds in the middle of *Jardin des Tuileries*); narrative motifs (Hsiao Kang hiding a clock in his jacket before hurrying inside a dark movie theater, compared to Antoine's theft of a milk bottle before darting into an alley to drink it);[50] and ultimately a bodily embodiment in Jean-Pierre Léaud's cameo (who played the teen protagonist of LES 400 COUPS).[51] There is even a direct screening of the film itself, as Hsiao Kang watches two scenes from LES 400 COUPS in his bedroom, a Western-film-within-an-Asian-film reference which itself places the viewer as a simultaneous, doubly ambiguous (in a horizontal sense – watching both WHAT TIME IS IT THERE? and LES 400 COUPS; (as well as in a vertical "Chinese boxes" sense watching a little screen within a big screen) cross-cultural sampler of two (and, judging from Tsai's stature in Taiwanese cinema, significant) polarities in film cultures.

III. A Love Supreme

> *The Bride: And what, pray tell, is the Five-Point-Palm-Exploding-Heart-Technique?*
>
> *Bill: Quite simply, it is the deadliest blow in all of the martial arts. He hits you with his fingertips at five different pressure points on your body. And then, he lets you walk away. But once you've taken five steps, your heart explodes inside your body, and you fall to the floor dead.[52]*

Until this juncture, however, the most prominent example to date of intertextual/cultural referencing has yet to be mentioned. Indeed, it is difficult to find a review of KILL BILL[53] which does *not* refer to the potluck party of Japanese samurai films, SHURAYUKIHIME (Japan: Toshiya Fujita, 1973, LADY SNOWBLOOD) revenge flicks, *anime* aesthetics, Japanese monster classics, Shaw Brothers kung fu productions, Sergio Leone spaghetti westerns, etc. that the film happily hosts. A quick trawl through the trivia section of imdb.com will more than suffice to fill one in on the mixed bag of Quentin Tarantino's borrowings (even some from his own films): the split-screen de Palma sequence of Elle Driver (Daryl Hannah) walking down the hospital whistling Bernard Herrmann's *Twisted Nerve*, the old-style kung fu of Shaw Brothers films, the spaghetti western flashback, the Red Apple cigarettes, the yellow suit of the Bride,[54] to name just a few.

Beyond the diversity of KILL BILL's intertextual references, however, is the sheer love that underpins them. Tarantino is explicit, even emphatic, about his "lifelong obsession with Asian cinema" (including television shows such as KAGE NO GUNDA and KUNG FU) and KILL BILL is a frank homage to them. The deep affection behind the memorialization of the genre (as construed by

Carroll) can be seen in Tarantino's insistence on creating a 70s aesthetics, es-chewing a slicker, smoother style easily afforded by today's technology ("that shit [digital effects] looks good, but it looks like a computer did it"). He specifi-cally replicates the filmmaking practices of the era, most notably "low-tech in-novations" such as the timely puncturing of "Chinese condoms filled with fake blood," "a nod to the recently deceased Chinese director Chang Cheh, who Tarantino says invented the technique for his 1970 film VENGEANCE."[55] KILL BILL is thus such a completely cinephilic work of homage and celebration be-cause it remains utterly true: from the imposition of the Shaw Brothers opening logo (with its almost self-abasing implication that one is, rather, watching "a Shaw Brothers movie") to the washed-out colors and use of the "Shaw Brothers' snap zoom" in the "The Cruel Tutelage of Pai Mei" chapter to the faithful yet quintessentially Tarantinoian quirks regarding fake blood, as he expresses in an interview:

> I'm really particular about the blood, so we're using a mixture depending on the scenes. I say, "I don't want horror movie blood, all right? I want Samurai blood." You can't pour this raspberry pancake syrup on a sword and have it look good. You have to have this special kind of blood that you only see in Samurai movies.[56]

Besides replicating aspects of 70s filmmaking, I argue further that Tarantino employs a unique strategy to pay tribute to the era's Asian films and genres: *he continues their stories as legends to inform the mythological world of* KILL BILL, thus invoking nostalgia not as a petulant lament but as a force to be called up via the echo of mythic power, whereby the stories of the era *became* the cosmic vision of his film. This is achieved in two ways (albeit related): the first is by direct refer-ence to the *character*. For example, the character of Hattori Hanzo (Sonny Chiba), the retired Japanese swordmaker and former master of Bill who subse-quently makes a samurai sword for the Bride as her weapon of revenge, is taken directly from the same-named character (also played by Chiba) in the popular Japanese television series, KAGE NO GUNDA (Shadow Warriors) of which Taran-tino professes to be a fan. The mythic force of "Hanzo steel" in the world of KILL BILL is evident in numerous ways: it is the weapon for which the Bride journeys to Okinawa and insists upon; for which Elle Driver meets Budd (Michael Madsen), later double-crossing him; without which the Bride was lost in her fight against Elle Driver until she spots Budd's own Hattori Hanzo sword; whose edge is gorily testified ("that is truly a Hattori Hanzo sword") by a decapitated (and initially disbelieving) Oren Ishii (Lucy Liu). Thus is homage (with its inherent love and reverence) extended by linking the historical signifi-cance of "Hattori Hanzo" from KAGE NO GUNDA to the mythic force of the "Hattori Hanzo sword" in KILL BILL, a reverence doubly amplified through the employment of Sonny Chiba to play Hanzo, both in terms of Tarantino's own admiration of the actor (he has described Chiba as "the greatest actor to ever work in martial arts films"[57]) as well as the double resonance of Chiba which encompasses both the historical and mythic resonances in one actor and one character.

The second way in which Tarantino links his film to the celebrated bygone era is by direct reference to the *actor*. In much the same way as he draws upon the historical significance of Sonny Chiba playing Hattori Hanzo, Tarantino trades on a similar resonance in casting David Carradine as the title character of Bill. Carradine, as the hero Kwai Cheng Caine, was the star of the TV series KUNG FU, of which Tarantino is also a fan. Unlike the character of Hattori Hanzo, however, Tarantino does not utilize a mythical structure around the character of Bill, for there is no weaving of an earlier story (i.e., of Kwai Cheng Caine) into a thread through the current film. But Tarantino pays a different kind of homage, embodied by Carradine, to the TV series. Here tribute is made not via Carradine as the *character* he played in the series, but as the *actor* that he is who played the character. This is clear from Tarantino's own comment on the subjective significance of Carradine: "What's cool is, for an entire generation, who doesn't know about KUNG FU, who doesn't know about DEATH RACE 2000…, doesn't know about THE LONG RIDERS, he won't be David Carradine, he'll be Bill. *But he'll always be Kwai Cheng Caine to me…*"[58]

A different strategy of tribute is thus pursued here – not, as is the usual case, in relation to an earlier work (as with KAGE NO GUNDA) but its *subjective memory*, a memory which is carried *through* and attached *beyond* the work. Tarantino, of course, does pay homage to KUNG FU vis-à-vis Carradine-*qua*-Kwai Cheng Caine: the flute played by Carradine as Bill, for example, is the same instrument which was used in KUNG FU. However, I argue that the greater significance in his employment of Carradine does not so much involve the *objective* facts of KUNG FU or Kwai Cheng Caine as the *subjective* memories of the television series and in particular Carradine as its star. In light of the signification of Carradine as the *actor* in KUNG FU, by casting him as the eponymous character Tarantino thus pays unique tribute by carrying into his film the power of his memories and their inherent affection over and above their inspiration.

However, I think the most astute act of homage in KILL BILL is Tarantino's canny awareness of the limitations of his tribute, a self-aware sensibility of his qualifications as a fan simply on the basis of his being a Western viewer, a foreigner to the culture. When Beatrix Kiddo arrives to face Pai Mei, the first act of the latter is to castigate the former's foreign-accented attempt to call him "Master" in Mandarin. This frank and completely unexpected slight on the inabilities of a Westerner to grasp the tonal inflexions of Mandarin and its dialects (including Cantonese) is not only a keen observation of an Occidental's difficult attunement to the Chinese culture but also, in a way, a humble admission of his limitations as an admirer – not of his affection, but of his understanding. Through just the first two lines of dialogue between Beatrix and Pai Mei, Tarantino acknowledges the simplest of issues about watching foreign films – that of language. Yet, at the same time, it is an acknowledgement of questions more profound than accents or vocabulary, for "to speak a language is to take on a world, a culture."[59] Indeed, it is an incredibly self-reflexive acknowledgement of a limited love, always to be curbed by translations, prisms of understanding, limitations of assimilation, and cultural barriers.

Yet it is not to be a forlorn conclusion. Wittily, Tarantino manages to make a clever joke out of the issue while at the same time turn ignorance into insight: he creates the "Five-Point-Palm-Exploding-Heart-Technique," the super kung fu move which is, as Bill explains to Beatrix, "quite simply, the deadliest blow in all of the martial arts." It is, of course, the move which the Bride eventually used to, well, kill Bill. Taking advantage of the comicality of translation (particularly of kung fu moves, such as "Hammer of the One Thousand Generous Queens" and "Imperial Thrust of the Short-Tempered Warriors" – believe me, they sound much better in the original), Tarantino plays to the hilt the inadequacy of translation by inventing the similarly hilarious "Five-Point-Palm-Exploding-Heart-Technique." In one sense, Tarantino has paid full tribute to the kung fu films he loves, right up to and including the ridiculous translations.[60] Yet in another sense, he has achieved more than that. George Steiner once wrote that great translations are "not an equivalence, for there can be none, but a vital counterpoise, an echo, faithful yet autonomous, as we find in the dialogue of human love. Where it fails, through immodesty or blurred perception, it traduces. Where it succeeds, it incarnates."[61]

What Tarantino has done via his "Five-Point-Palm-Exploding-Heart-Technique" is to turn the (simultaneously self-aware) limitations of his understanding into an endearing target, to synapse the liminality of linguistic translation by a transferral of affection. Not that the love for the original has been eliminated, for the translation has only been translated – not into another language, but into another object of love. And therein lies the incarnation.

IV. Conclusion

I have endeavoured through the essay to connect filmmaking practice and intertextuality to love, because I am convinced that it is the touchstone of cinephilia, based on the elementary meaning of its root suffix, "philia," meaning "love of or liking for."[62] To that extent, I disagree with Kent Jones's comment: "I think that whether or not we all agree about [Olivier] Assayas or Wong [Kar-Wai] is less important than the fact that our respective responses to them are passionate and informed. *In the end, that's what distinguishes cinephilia from connoisseurship, academicism or buffery.*[63] Besides the obvious syllogistic fallacy (might connoisseurship not be informed? Might buffery not be passionate?), Jones has also omitted the element of love which is the basis of "philia" (although being passionate and/or informed may be, though certainly not the only, evidence of love). Love may, of course, take different forms – as Michelson writes: "…there exists, however, no one such thing as cinephilia, but rather forms and periods of cinephilia"[64] – but ultimately, its existence is unmistakable.

I believe it is the simultaneity of these two aspects – amorphousness yet enduring legitimacy – which relegates scholars to analyzing the *practices* of cinephilia, as opposed to its *concept*. I return to my comments, with which I started this essay, on the myriad aspects of love: its mysticism, its conceptual difficulties, its contiguity to insanity and, yet, its manifest, almost palpable, presence, its patent demonstration in a gaze, a gesture, a word, a practice, an act. How can we theorize love? It is ultimately a phenomenon that is deeply subjective and personal. It cannot be fully contained in objective theory, and that is its glory. We love as we dream – alone.[65]

Notes

1. In writing about general recursion, Douglas Hofstadter illustrates the concept by replacing the main words in the dictionary definition of "love" with, in turn, *their* definitions. His result: "A morally powerful mental state or tendency, having strength of character or will for, or affectionate regard, or loyalty, faithfulness, or deep affection to, a human being or beings, especially as distinguished from a thing or lower animal." The process may be repeated indefinitely. See Hofstadter, Douglas R. *Metamagical Themas: Questing for the Essence of Mind and Pattern*, Harmondsworth: Penguin Books, 1985, pp. 434-5.
2. Burns, Robert. "A Red, Red Rose." Kinsley, James (ed.). *Poems and Songs*, London: Oxford University Press, 1969, p. 582.
3. Brontë, Emily. *Wuthering Heights*, London: Allan Wingate, 1949, p. 94.
4. Lyrics to the musical *Passion* and music by Stephen Sondheim, dir. James Lapine, 2000.
5. The coining of the word is commonly attributed to Ricciotto Canudo. However, it should be noted that Canudo referred to "cinephilia" not as a positive designation or concept but in the context of general skepticism with regards to the endurance of an ever-growing vocabulary of cinema terminology. See Abel, Richard. *French Film Theory and Criticism: A History / Anthology, 1907-1939, vol. I, 1907-1929,* "The Seventh Art," Princeton: Princeton University Press, 1988, p. 297.

6. Dialogue from Prima della rivoluzione (Italy: Bernardo Bertolucci, 1964, Before the Revolution). Cinephilia as a theme also runs through his latest film, The Dreamers (France: Bernardo Bertolucci, 2003).

7. See, in particular, Dinsmore-Tuli, Uma. *The Domestication of Film: Video, Cinephilia and the Collecting and Viewing of Videotapes in the Home*, Ph.D. thesis, 1998, University of London Library depository.

8. "Traverses," *Cahiers du cinéma*, 498 (Jan. 1996), p. 50.

9. Willemen, Paul. "Through the Glass Darkly: Cinephilia Reconsidered." *Looks and Frictions*, London: British Film Institute, 1994, p. 231.

10. Sontag, Susan. "The Decay of Cinema." *The New York Times*, 25 February 1996, subsequently reprinted as "A Century of Cinema" in *Where the Stress Falls*, New York: Farrar, Straus and Giroux, 2001, pp. 117-22.

11. Ibid.

12. She is not the only writer to do so; in his introduction to the 2002 *A New Biographical Dictionary of Film*, David Thomson similarly reminisces about "*the early 1970s*, when it was easy to be in love with cinema" [emphasis added].

13. See also O'Pray, Michael. "Cinephilia." *Art Monthly*, 224 (March 1999), pp. 13-7 for an interesting analysis of the differences between cinema, videos, and gallery installation film viewing.

14. Adrian Martin also analyzes cinephilia in a similar historicity, though with a focus on European (and Australian) fixation on American, specifically Hollywood, cinema. See "No Flowers for the Cinéphile: The Fates of Cultural Populism 1960-1988." Foss, Paul (ed.). *Island in the Stream: Myths of Place in Australian Culture*, Sydney: Pluto Press, 1988, especially pp. 120-21.

15. Sontag, "Decay," op.cit.

16. See Kauffmann, Stanley. "A Lost Love?" *The New Republic*, 9 August 1997 and *Regarding Film: Criticism and Comment*, Baltimore: Johns Hopkins University Press, 2001; Denby, David. "The Moviegoers." *The New Yorker*, 6 April 1998, pp. 94-101; Thomson, David. "Inert, archaic, dead. Just why do we bother with movies anymore? And can MTV save us?" *The Independent*, 4 April 2004 as well as "Long, sketchy, bogus: the movies we get are the ones that we deserve." *The Independent*, 11 April 2004. In his introduction to the 2002 *A New Biographical Dictionary of Film*, Thomson confesses: "I have learned that I like books more than film." See also Erickson, Steve. "Permanent Ghosts: Cinephilia in the Age of the Internet and Video: Essay 1," <http://www.sensesofcinmea.com/contents/004/cine1.html> (visited 9 August 2004); and Schickel, Richard. "Cinema Paradiso (history of America's motion picture industry)." *The Wilson Quarterly*, 22 June 1999. For a similar though relatively more balanced view, see Haskell, Molly. "It Used to Be So Easy. I Remember When…" *The New York Times*, 14 March 2003. For an interesting take (and various projects) on nostalgia, see the curatorial statement by Clare Stewart of the Australian Centre for the Moving Image, "'Remembered By': From Nostalgia to Total Recall," <http://www.acmi.net.au/remembrance/cinema_program/curatorial.html> (visited 9 August 2004).

17. Willemen, "Glass Darkly," op. cit., p. 227.

18. Paul Willemen comes closest to this when he comments: "Cinephilia itself describes simultaneously a particular relationship to cinema (and the question then opens up

of [*sic*] what kind of relationship that might be) *and* it also describes a particular historical period of relating to cinema [emphasis added]." Ibid.

19. Rosenbaum, Jonathan, Adrian Martin (eds.). *Movie Mutations: The Changing Face of World Cinephilia*, London: British Film Institute, 2003, p. 20.

20. Willemen, "Glass Darkly," op. cit., p. 232.

21. Keathley, Christian. "The Cinephiliac Moment." *Framework*, 42 (summer 2000) <http://www.frameworkonline.com/42ck.htm> (visited 9 Aug. 2004).

22. Hallas, Roger. "Celebrating the Moment." *Camera Obscura*, 18/1 (2003), pp. 85-127.

23. Martin, "No Flowers," op. cit., pp. 117-38.

24. Gopalan, Lalitha. *Cinema of Interruptions: Action Genres in Contemporary Indian Cinema*, London: British Film Institute, 2002, esp. pp. 11-16.

25. Doane, Mary Ann. *The Emergence of Cinematic Time: Modernity, Contingency, the Archive*, Cambridge: Harvard University Press, 2002, pp. 226-27.

26. Michelson, Annette. "Gnosis and Iconoclasm: A Case Study of Cinephilia." *October*, 83 (winter 1998), p. 9.

27. Ibid., p. 3.

28. Rosenbaum, Martin, *Movie Mutations*, op. cit.

29. Definition of "transcultural" in *Collins English Dictionary*, Glasgow: Harper Collins, 2000.

30. Stam, Robert, Robert Burgoyne, Sandy Flitterman-Lewis (eds.). *New Vocabularies in Film Semiotics: Structuralism, Poststructuralism and Beyond*, London and New York: Routledge, 1992, p. 203.

31. Kristeva, Julia. *Desire in Language: A Semiotic Approach to Literature and Art*, by Roudiez, Leo S. (ed.). New York: Columbia University Press, 1980, p. 66.

32. Fiske, John. *Television Culture*, London: Methuen, 1987, p. 108.

33. Also of relevance is Gérard Genette's concept of "transtextuality," which consists of: intertextuality, paratextuality, architextuality, metatextuality and hypotextuality. See Genette, Gérard. *Palimpsests*, Lincoln: University of Nebraska Press, 1997.

34. See, in general, Stam *et al.*, *New Vocabularies*, op.cit.

35. See Goodwin, James. *Akira Kurosawa and Intertextual Cinema*, Baltimore: Johns Hopkins University Press, 1994.

36. See Kline, T. Jefferson. *Screening the Text: Intertextuality in New Wave French Cinema*, Baltimore: Johns Hopkins University Press, 1992.

37. See Iampolski, Mikhail. *The Memory of Tiresias: Intertextuality and Film*, Berkeley: University of California Press, 1998.

38. See Reader, Keith A., "Literature/cinema/television: intertextuality in Jean Renoir's Le Testament du docteur Cordelier." Worton, Michael, Judith Still (eds.). *Intertextuality: Theories and Practices*, Manchester and New York: Manchester University Press, 1990, pp. 176-89.

39. Carroll, Noël. "The Future of Allusion: Hollywood in the Seventies (and Beyond)." *October*, 20 (1982), p. 52 (emphasis in original). To this extent, also note the three adaptation strategies (borrowing, intersecting and fidelity of transformation) identified by Andrew, Dudley. "Adaptation." Naremore, James (ed.). *Film Adaptation*, New Brunswick: Rutgers University Press, 2000, pp. 28-37.

40. See the message thread for "De Palma's 'Homage' to Eisenstein," posted in August 1998 on the H-Film Discussion Group on the H-Net Discussion Network, at <http://www.h-net.org/~film/> (visited 2 December 2004).

41. Leitch, Thomas. "The Rhetoric of the Remake." *Literature/Film Quarterly*, 18/3 (1990), p. 144 [emphasis added].

42. Ibid.

43. Carroll, "The Future of Allusion", op. cit., p. 62 [emphasis added].

44. Ibid., p. 54. Significantly, Carroll points out that this "movie mania" includes, beyond thriving film clubs and enthusiastic film viewing, the flourishing of film schools and, most importantly, the introduction of film studies in universities.

45. To that end, it is noted that every single filmmaker or film referred to by Carroll in his essay is either American or European. For example, Carroll describes the vocabulary of the film-historically aware American audience as one "including catch phrases such as '*Langian* paranoia'... – 'x (some new film) has a *Fordian* view of history, a *Hawksian* attitude toward women, an *Eisensteinian* use of montage, and a *Chuck Jones* approach to the body'" [emphasis added]. Ibid., p. 54.

46. Dinsmore-Tuli, "Domestication of Film," op. cit.

47. See Gnatek, Tim. "An Online Supplier for Your Desktop Cineplex." *The New York Times*, 12 August 2004. The French also put it well: "*Aujourd'hui, une autre cinéphilie existe et co'existe avec l'ancienne. Elle passe (presque trop?) facilement de la salle de cinéma au museé, du museé à la télevision, du câble à la cassette vidéo, bientôt de la cassette au vidéodisque.*" See "Traverses," op. cit., p. 50.

48. There are, of course, exceptions, most notably Akira Kurosawa's films such as HAKUCHI (Japan: 1951, THE IDIOT) adapted from Dostoevski's novel, KUMO-NO SUJO (Japan: 1957, THRONE OF BLOOD) and RAN (Japan: 1985) from Shakespeare's *Macbeth* and *King Lear* respectively. Nevertheless, the argument made here is one of degree. To that extent, the films of Kurosawa can be considered *sui generis*, whereas the broader point here is that cross-cultural referentiality is a more common and pervasive phenomenon today.

49. Gopalan, *Cinema of Interruptions*, p. 7. For a more in-depth analysis of the intertextuality of MOULIN ROUGE, see also McFarlane, Brian. "The Movie as Museum." *Meanjin*, 12 January 2001.

50. Koc, Aysegul. "Vive le cinema: a reading of WHAT TIME IS IT THERE?" *CineAction*, 22 June 2003.

51. I am grateful to Malte Hagener for having pointed this out to me.

52. Dialogue from KILL BILL: VOL. 2 (USA: Quentin Tarantino, 2004).

53. As the work was released in two parts, there are technically two films: the first being KILL BILL: VOL. 1 and the second KILL BILL: VOL. 2. However, as both volumes are required to constitute the film in its proper three-act entirety, I have thus chosen to refer to the film as simply KILL BILL, rather than by its volume number.

54. The Bride is a character that can, logically, only be so called *after* the El Paso massacre (i.e., when she was attired in her wedding dress, which gave rise to her character name). By the same logic, she could not have been The Bride *before* the massacre (i.e., when she was not a bride). It is a small point, but for this reason I have decided to use "The Bride" only for Uma Thuman's character post-massacre and "Beatrix Kiddo" pre-massacre.

55. Jakes, Susan. "Blood Sport: Quentin Tarantino's KILL BILL Pays Homage to the Gory, Glory Days of Asian Martial Arts Cinema." *Time International*, 16 September 2002.

56. Ibid.

57. Profile of Sonny Chiba, at <http://killbill.movies.go.com/vol1/castCrew/cast-sc. html> (visited 2 December 2000).

58. Interview with Quentin Tarantino on "The Making of KILL BILL VOL. 2," from the DVD of KILL BILL: VOL. 2 (Region 2, 2004) [emphasis added].

59. Fanon, Frantz. *Black Skin, White Masks*, New York: Grove Press, 1967, p. 38.

60. Tarantino's awareness and exploitation of this issue is patent. In the early script of KILL BILL, one of his specifications is that, in the first meeting between Pai Mei and Beatrix Kiddo, "whenever Mandarin is supposedly spoken, it comes out of their mouths as dubbed English *like in a 70's Shaw Brothers Chop Socky Flick*" [emphasis added]. See the early draft script of KILL BILL, available at <http://www.tarantino. info> (visited 2 December 2004).

61. Steiner, George. *After Babel: Aspects of Language and Translation*, 2nd edition, London and New York: Oxford University Press, 1992, pp. 270-71.

62. *Shorter Oxford English Dictionary*, vol. 2 (N-Z), 5th ed., Oxford University Press, 2002.

63. Rosenbaum, *Movie Mutations*, op.cit., p. 11 [emphasis added].

64. Michelson, "Gnosis", op.cit., p. 3.

65. With apologies to Joseph Conrad.

II

Technologies of Cinephilia

Production and Consumption

Remastering Hong Kong Cinema

Charles Leary

In descriptions of Hong Kong cinema, and Hong Kong itself, one invariably encounters two keywords: "globalization" and "speed," with speed being a factor of globalization, in the rapid production, circulation, and consumption of cultural commodities. The conspicuousness of these terms in studies of the region is partly due of course to the shifting dominion over Hong Kong during its modern history – once a British colony, once Japanese-occupied territory, and now a "Special Administrative Region" for China's "one country, two systems" project – as well as its status as one of the most active financial centers in the world. As a site of a number of distinct streams of immigration (and emigration) throughout the 20th century, the city has long been described as a place of transit, from the West to the East and vice-versa, and its cosmopolitan sensibility has been compared by one critic, for example, with an airport.[1] Hong Kong has even registered itself as a brand name welcoming globalization, with its slogan "Asia's World City."[2] Aside from the transfer of its capital – that is, the move of well-known film personnel to Hollywood – the globalization of Hong Kong cinema is a tale told in its circulation via film festivals, but more emphatically so in video outlets, cable television, and internet sales and discussion – moving, it appears, at a speed for the most efficient circulation.

Speed: Political Economy and Film Form

Consider, for an example of the deployment of "speed" as a keyword in Hong Kong film and cultural criticism, this passage from Esther Yau's introduction to her anthology *At Full Speed: Hong Kong Cinema in a Borderless World*:

> Speed is of prime importance for global access. Cultural productions coming from the major metropolitan centers display an explicit self-consciousness of competitive time, as if they embody the notion that conquest of the vast marketplace can only be possible through fast production and instantaneous dispatches.[3]

Yau is alluding here to the quick production and distribution pace of Hong Kong studio films, that once put out an enormous amount of material, but have now declined in annual output (although mainstream feature films are still made relatively quickly compared to Hollywood productions). Various factors – such as fluctuations in the real estate market, video piracy, and the 1997 Asia financial crisis – led to a decline in production and an increase in Hollywood dominance at the Hong Kong box office beginning in the 1990s.[4] Speed does indeed distinguish Hong Kong cinema's rapid dispersal throughout mainstream and non-mainstream markets. Overseas Chinese communities quickly gain access to and consume Hong Kong films (and television) via video clubs and stores, and the international cult-fan has long relied on video, including poor-quality bootleg copies, to see these films.[5] And in Hong Kong, the Video Compact Disc (VCD), a cheaper digital format with a picture quality inferior to DVD (and more frequently pirated), is a primary means of spectatorship.

Various critical accounts emphasize the phenomenon of quick global access to Hong Kong cinema, but this access must be qualified as indicative of the particular dimension of Hong Kong cinephilia. The reception of Hong Kong cinema is really its reception on video, particularly (but far from exclusively) overseas. New York, for example, recently lost its last remaining Chinatown movie theater, the Music Palace, which was a first-run house for films from Hong Kong. Although the festival circuit has recently enjoyed the popular genre films of Johnnie To, generally speaking, Hong Kong films on the festival circuit are art-auteur productions. In addition, the American distribution of Hong Kong's popular cinema has become a target of frustration and consternation among cinephiles. Miramax, the subject of numerous fan websites – including (with a name presumably inspired by the animal rights group People for the Ethical Treatment of Animals) the *Web Alliance for the Respectful Treatment of Asian Cinema* – has developed a notorious reputation for purchasing the rights to many Hong Kong films and delaying their release for what to some seems an indefinite period of time.[6] For example, after years of anticipation among American fans, the blockbuster SHAOLIN SOCCER (Hong Kong: Stephen Chow, 2001) was finally released in the United States and other Western regions only after being re-edited with added special effects. Miramax also delayed the release of another major box-office success in Asia, INFERNAL AFFAIRS (Hong Kong: Andrew Lau and Alan Mak, 2002), now being remade by Martin Scorsese for Brad Pitt's production company.[7] In fact, the new trend of simply buying remake rights to Hong Kong films seems the most immediate form of circulation. The Hollywood adaptations of the Japanese film RINGU (Japan: Hideo Nakata, 1998) and JU-ON: THE GRUDGE (Japan: Takashi Shimizu, 2000-2003) have thus far proved to be the most successful examples, with a number of what once were Hong Kong horror films now coming to a theater near you soon via Hollywood.[8]

Yau continues, "Riding on the winds of change, the mutations of commercial Hong Kong cinema since 1980 have foretold a new globalization narrative: that of speed, or the emergence of a 'permanent present' that paradoxically erases earlier notions of space and time and invites nostalgia."[9] It is true that films produced as recently as 1980 or later may often be forgotten with the newest release of something comparable, and, with the lack of a legal mandate that many other countries have requiring producers to register a print of the film, many do not make it to the Hong Kong Film Archive. This narrative of globalization predicated on the concept of speed, familiar to the academic work regarding the cultural space of Hong Kong and its cinema, could allow the Hong Kong film past, that is, the perceived "primitive" past of chop-socky kung fu exploitation film of the 1960s and 1970s, to disappear – this past at once stands in for the present and provides the very formal antecedent for the "speed" metaphor with the fast-pace of action cinema. "Speed" often collapses two approaches to Hong Kong film – the political economic reading and film form – into one concurrent sweep, a juxtaposition I return to below in the discussion of the temporal inscription of deteriorated classics in conjunction with their historical context of film industry practice and contemporary re-release. As for Yau's examination of a "permanent present," commensurate with the tenets of postmodernist theory as well as, more specifically, in Yau's persuasive argument, the contemporary Hong Kong genre film's eclipse of parochial "Chineseness" in earlier Hong Kong cinema, it is worth noting that with the emergence of an immediate reference point – that is, the 1997 handover, inviting a before-and-after approach – a frenetic history writing project characterizes much recent activity among government institutions, artists, policymakers, journalists, and academics in Hong Kong.[10]

This search for public memory extends to the realm of film culture, most notably with the establishment of a physical space for the Hong Kong Film Archive in 2001. A visit on any day to the Hong Kong Film Archive quickly dispels the notion that Hong Kong is a postmodern space without a past while also revealing the regrettable gaps in the historical record of Hong Kong film. The irrecoverable loss of a majority of the world's film heritage is a well-known fact, while Hong Kong's film legacy has been hit especially hard, with only a handful of films made prior to World War II surviving. One especially unfortunate example is the possibility that the Japanese army may have melted down many films to extract the silver base during the occupation of Hong Kong from 1941 to 1945.[11] Because of the particularly poor climate conditions for film storage in humid Hong Kong, many artifacts in the Archive have come from closing movie theaters in overseas Chinatowns.

The development of the Hong Kong Film Archive has been peppered with astonishing stories of rescues from the dustbins of history. For example, almost 100 films from the 1950s and 1960s were discovered in a dumpster in an alley in Oakland's Chinatown, previously held in a storage room in the basement of a nearby Chinese restaurant.[12] Many artifacts have also been donated by the family members of filmmakers or collectors, and the Archive has celebrated its relationship with local cinephilia in staging an exhibition of fan magazines and other ephemera accompanied by the stories of the collectors who donated them.[13] Other special exhibits focus not only on film history but the popular culture and everyday life throughout Hong Kong's history, such as projects on fashion and popular literature. The Archive has also functioned as a center of film scholarship in Hong Kong, regularly conducting oral histories, collaborating with local universities on academic conferences and other projects, and releasing a number of richly detailed books on Hong Kong film history. And there seems to be a certain political dimension to the Archive's attention to underappreciated or rare works, providing the unique space to revisit local Cantonese independent productions (prior to the Hong Kong "new wave" of the 1980s) that competed (without much financial success) with major studios, like Shaw Brothers and the Motion Picture and General Investment Company (MP&GI), which produced Mandarin dialect films.

The Hong Kong Film (and Video) Catalogue

The Hong Kong Film Archive is primarily a film-based institution, but in returning to earlier remarks that Hong Kong cinema is often experienced on video, one should also note a few "conservation on video" projects currently underway in Hong Kong. One is led by film producer and critic Roger Garcia, who is duplicating the catalogue of Modern Films onto video, which is comprised of little-known yet significant experimental films from the 1980s.[14] One of the filmmakers represented by Modern Films, Comyn Mo, later became one of the founding directors of the video-art collective videotage, now housed at the Cattle Depot Artists Village.[15] Working with both videotage and the Hong Kong Film Archive, the video artist May Fung began the "iGenerations" project to collect various experimental films from the 1960s to 1980s that had fallen out of circulation. Many of these films were also made by those now considered some of Hong Kong cinema's best-known critics, including Law Kar, Sek Kei and former student filmmaker/critic John Woo.[16]

However, film festival retrospective programs, museums, and repertory theaters across the world, and particularly video stores in Asia and the global Chinatowns, are a testament to a major remastering project of what could be called the Golden Age of Hong Kong Cinema – that of the Mandarin cinema of the two major studios in the 1950s and 1960s, MP&GI and the Shaw Brothers.[17] Hong Kong recovered relatively quickly from the decimation of World War II and the Japanese Occupation, transforming itself from a trade entrepôt to a major industrial center in the 1950s. Part of the impetus in this economic shift was an influx of Shanghai industrialists to Hong Kong, who escaped the ravages of war on the mainland and the political turmoil following the Communist Party's assumption of power in 1949.[18] It was during the late 1940s and 1950s when Hong Kong, flush with the migration of many filmmakers and studios from Shanghai, overtook Shanghai as the capital of Chinese-language filmmaking.[19] In concert with a changing public culture in Hong Kong, two studios based in Singapore would cement this shift. MP&GI – later changed to its better-known name, Cathay – was established by the Cambridge-educated Loke Wan Tho, who inherited a family business of mining and hotel industries and proposed to "modernize the everyday culture of Asia" with state-of-the-art theaters across Southeast Asia.[20] Acquiring the financially-troubled Yung-hwa studio in Hong Kong, he moved from distribution and exhibition to a fully vertically integrated enterprise, producing films in the 1950s and 1960s that focused on contemporary melodrama, comedies, and musicals portraying a middle-class Hong Kong (despite rampant poverty) that had yet to emerge, but soon would.[21] The success of Cathay's Mandarin-language films spurred Run Run Shaw, of the Shaw and Sons distribution and theater enterprise also based in Singapore, to move to Hong Kong and personally oversee the establishment of a huge motion picture production studio. Fierce competition among the two studios yielded a variety of lavish, big-budget films not yet seen in the region, and out of the reach for independent Cantonese-dialect low-budget films. Eventually, Shaw Brothers rose to dominate the market, particularly after the untimely death of Loke Wan Tho in 1964 and the popularity of Shaw's new school "wuxia" (martial arts) film genre introduced in the late 1960s.[22]

In 2000, Cathay began digitally remastering over 200 of their films into a "classic library" for television broadcast, albeit advertised as "digitally restored."[23] Gradually over the past few years, a handful of these "classic" films have been released on VCD and DVD by Panorama Entertainment, a video distributor that recently purchased the rights to the library of the Golden Harvest studio (Shaw Brother's rival in the 1970s and the producer of Bruce Lee's Hong Kong films) and which is now also embarking on film production. A number of Cathay films, as well as related objects and ephemera from the studio library, were also recently transferred to the Hong Kong Film Archive with the eclipse of Cathay's lease on their warehouse.[24] However, these Cathay video releases come on the heels of the more heavily marketed release of classics from what was its major competitor, and surely many have seen the quite explicit homage to Hong Kong cinema's past in Quentin Tarantino's recent film KILL BILL: VOL. 1 (USA: 2003), the credit sequence of which opens with the title card that opened every Shaw Brothers production filmed in "Shawscope," Shaws' version of Cinemascope. Juxtaposed with a welcome message trailer from what perhaps was a grindhouse or B-movie theater, the film squarely situates Tarantino's Hong Kong cinephilia in the realm of cult spectatorship – but, as a nostalgia that specifies watching the films in a movie theater and not on video.[25]

Though not, in fact, a Shaw Brothers production, parts of KILL BILL were filmed at Shaw's Movietown, the studio that once provided the location for the sets of many classic martial arts films but is now the site of the biggest commercial film restoration project ever undertaken. For years, the reigning patriarch of the studio, Run Run Shaw, refused to lend out titles for re-release from the vast film library – not even to educational institutions – after ceasing film production in the 1980s to concentrate on film exhibition and distribution and television production with Television Broadcasts Limited (TVB), the station which provided the training ground for many filmmakers associated with the Hong Kong new wave as well as many of today's stars. In 2002, the Shaw Brothers catalogue, totaling over 760 films, was finally sold to a Malaysian media conglomerate, which established Celestial Pictures to restore and distribute the films on video and on cable television. Celestial embarked on a 24-hour-a-day work schedule to digitally remaster and release an incredible quota of ten to twenty titles per month. In addition to releasing the titles on DVD and VCD, Celestial established a Shaw Brothers cable network that currently airs in various Asian countries. They also own distribution rights to a number of current films and also finance new productions. Thus, we are in Hong Kong perhaps witnessing something similar to Lew Wasserman's purchase of the Paramount library, which allowed him to capitalize on redistributing old product while engaging in television and film production. However, Shaw does maintain an interest in Celestial Pictures, and the two companies are cooperating together with another major studio, China Star Entertainment, to build a new multi-billion-dollar studio complex.

Considering as well the aforementioned Fortune Star's purchase of the Golden Harvest library, these few major remastering projects can be described in terms similar to those which Thomas Elsaesser has used to discuss digitization: as "the totem-notion around which a notoriously conservative industry is in the process of reorganizing – and this usually means reinvesting – itself, in order to do much the same as it has always done."[26] In many ways, the "remastering" project of Hong Kong's golden era of Mandarin cinema is providing the capital to allow Hong Kong cinema and television to restructure itself, including, perhaps, a shift away from local dialect cinema (Cantonese) to a rebirth of Mandarin cinema. Indeed, the satellite station TVB, which includes the Shaws as a major stockholder, has purchased the exclusive rights to show Celestial films on its channel, buying its own product back to re-sell.

The Pathology of Re-Presenting the Past

Celestial's project should be met with some skepticism, not least of all because they are not, in fact, restoring these films into archival quality resolutions, but rather "remastering" them onto DVD for standard broadcast resolution. However, some titles were released for a limited commercial run in theaters across Asia (Miramax holds the North American rights) on digital projection, considered by some experts an inevitable replacement for film projection commensurate with the rise of digital technology for production, post-production, and conservation.[27] Both the New York Film Festivals and Cannes showed a print of Celestial's showcase project, the "restored" COME DRINK WITH ME (Hong Kong: King Hu, 1966), starring Cheng Pei-pei, who has done much promotion for Celestial while her career has enjoyed something of a resurgence after playing the villain in CROUCHING TIGER, HIDDEN DRAGON (Taiwan/Hong Kong/USA/China: Ang Lee, 2001). Though the lab has a mandate to remaster three to four films per week, COME DRINK WITH ME received two weeks of attention, digitally remastered in high definition format and then transferred back to film.[28]

With such a large-scale commercial project, automatic restoration software is typically employed, and Celestial enlisted the American firm DaVinci to use its "Revival" system. As is the case with many such projects, professionals are not conducting the actual pass of the film through the digital output. Operators of the equipment are trained on the job, and a worker interviewed for a fan magazine reported, "when I joined, many of the people there had almost no experience in film and video and the manager who was hired later didn't even know what a Digital Beta tape was!"[29] The film is processed through various modules, such as those termed de-Flicker, de-Shake, de-Scratch, de-Blotch and de-Noise. A hidden module, working constantly in the background, is referred to as "motion estimation." This module addresses the occasional fast motion that will be interpreted as dirt and interpolated with new pixels, the residual trace of the moving object deleted, with the missing object then referred to as an "artifact."[30] The Shaw Brothers' martial arts films presented a particular problem in this regard, requiring the composition of a new algorithm to approximate kung fu action. Thoma Thurau of SGI, which provided the hardware for the project, reported: "An actor would be throwing a punch, and the system would think that the unusually fast motion was dirt."[31]

In the discourse of restoration techniques, this kind of motion – that is, motion that the software cannot track and thus reads as damage – has been termed "pathological motion."[32] Types of motion that are recognized as typically causing problems for the "motion estimation" process are movement of cloth, water, and smoke. Besides the fast movement of bodies in kung fu, these are all typical features of the martial arts film's *mise en scène*. COME DRINK WITH ME also includes all of these elements, highlighting the martial arts film's exploration of the various planes within the phenomenal world. COME DRINK WITH ME is something of a transitional work in the genre's history, still using on occasion typical Shanghai martial arts special effects from the 1930s, as with the Drunken Knight character who has the power to push water and the air. To move through air, or to move air itself, leaves a visible trace, like ripples in water.

Yet why does this movement qualify as "pathological," if we consider the word's connotations? With all the emphasis on other-worldly (or, "unusual") movement in the martial arts film, is there something especially pathological about the genre? Charges of pathology in fact do resonate with the history of the martial arts film. Not only has it occupied a marginal existence in the West as a low-culture, trashy, or cult object, but also in Hong Kong (and its origins and circulations in Mainland China and Taiwan), it has at various periods of "nation building" propaganda in the history of modern China been a target – that is, considered as something to get rid of, to be inoculated from. For example, in the censorship of martial arts films (and, particularly, Cantonese dialect films) in the 1930s in advance of the New Life movement in Republican China, or in the "healthy realism" campaign of Taiwan in the 1950s and 1960s, in which the "health" of the nation was endangered by the "feudal superstitions" and perceived immoral sensationalism of the martial arts film, the genre has come under attack for supposedly immanent moral or political failings.[33]

COME DRINK WITH ME, as the inaugural showcase for Shaw's remastering project, presents an interesting case study. I've already alluded to its transitional stylistic elements, and the film did indeed usher in what was promoted as "Shaw's Color *Wuxia* Century."[34] However, Hu, under contract to the Shaws as an assistant director and actor, directed only this one film for the studio before going independent and moving his operations to Taiwan (and later to Korea and unsuccessfully to America). In considering how the attempts to "remaster" the martial arts action film– that is, to try to catch the action that we always miss – COME DRINK WITH ME presents a particular challenge, following David Bordwell's analysis of Hu's aesthetic as one of "the glimpse." He writes:

> How, we might ask, can cinema express the other-worldly grace and strength of these supremely disciplined but still mortal fighters? The solution he found was to stress certain qualities of these feats – their abruptness, their speed, their mystery. And he chose to do so by treating these feats as only partly visible... Hu makes his action faster than the eyes – and even, it seems, the camera – can follow. Often we are allowed only a trace of the warriors' amazing feats. We do not see the action so much as glimpse it.[35]

Hu pioneered some of the quickest editing in Hong Kong cinema at the time, and had a practice of deleting frames between the beginning and end of even the most mundane movements, creating at times a jumpy or blurry effect.[36] Readers familiar with Bordwell's work may recall that in prefacing his texts, he often makes a point of insisting on reproducing frame enlargements to illustrate his arguments, as opposed to production stills, and thus many of Bordwell's books are gloriously illustrated with color plates. Interestingly, in his essay on Hu, the images he uses reveal the difficulty of attempting to capture the image of motion in the static form of the photograph. All of the photos of the action scenes are blurry and largely illegible. This image is, in a sense, the trace he talks about, and this is the image read as pathological, or "dirty," by automatic restoration processes.

The other unique feature of COME DRINK WITH ME (consistent with some of Hu's other works) is its revitalization of the female heroine tradition that can be traced back to the earliest martial arts films made in Shanghai. The martial arts moves performed by the heroine take on a more radical meaning, as has been argued on occasion, as the woman surpasses the patriarchal order, flying through the air across borders and traveling (often by passing for a man) through the male-dominated spaces of the *jiang hu* and roadside inn (a central setting for many of Hu's films).[37] Keeping in mind the rubric of pathological motion (or movement), we can consider its other appearance in the medical films discussed by Lisa Cartwright in her book, *Screening the Body*. She explains that pathological movement was often interpreted as a sign of perversion, like interpretations of sexual perversion, "putting the body to uses that have nothing to do with immanent purpose."[38] The martial arts movement is often theatrical and not realistic, yet as Zhang Zhen finds in the early Shanghai films – and as Bruce Lee (though the most utilitarian martial arts hero) makes clear in a vengeful attack on a Japanese *dojo* in FIST OF FURY (Hong Kong: Wei Lo, 1972), AKA THE CHINESE CONNECTION – the martial arts' transformative power over the body was in part a relief from, and social uplifting response to, China's denigration as the "sick man of Asia" after it lost, among other things, control of Hong Kong after the Opium Wars. As Zhang describes:

> Unfailingly, the heroine is endowed with extraordinary body techniques that mark her as a cyborg-like creature. One such technique is the ability to effortlessly move the body either horizontally or vertically, such as flying in the sky or leaping over a tall wall. In other words, what makes possible the instant bodily transportation from one location to another hinges upon the capability of losing one's gravity in space and overcoming the restraint of time.[39]

Any anxiety concerning this female embodiment of technological and spiritual strength was quickly displaced by Hu's competitor and the most prolific director under contract to Shaws, Zhang Che. Zhang's martial arts films ushered in what he called a cinema of "staunch masculinity," and promoted the rise of male stars in a popular cinema at the time dominated by female stars (in all genres), a practice that extended far past his retirement, particularly with the films of one of his protégés, John Woo.[40] The shift is most clear in Zhang's GOLDEN SWALLOW (Hong Kong: 1968) something of a sequel to COME DRINK WITH ME that marginalizes Cheng Peipei's heroine character and makes her the damsel in distress, despite her character's name giving the film its title. While Celestial entered Cannes with COME DRINK WITH ME, it returned in 2004 to distribute a new independent Chinese film and, recreate the earlier order of gender representation, with a newly "restored" version of one of the titles of Zhang's classic castration-revenge trilogy, THE NEW ONE-ARMED SWORDSMAN (Hong Kong: 1971).[41]

The rubric of pathology has, finally, also been engaged in the discourse of the relationship of speed with Hong Kong's cinema and cultural space. In *Hong Kong: Culture and the Politics of Disappearance*, Ackbar Abbas describes how with the looming deadline of the 1997 handover, Hong Kong began a reappraisal of the significance of its popular culture, one that takes the explosive form of "disappearance." With the anxiety among Hong Kong citizens over the handover exacerbated by the 1989 Tiananmen Square incident, what was once taken for granted threatened to disappear, revealing a "pathology of presence" where the city space is one of misrecognition, not unlike, perhaps the "pathological movement" that restoration software misrecognizes as something else – a misrecognition that is no longer the sense of coincidence and déjà vu experienced on the city street, but that can only happen with the speed of the immediate electronic transmission.[42]

In the various remastering projects discussed above, the films are indeed moving at full speed, now available in, more often than not, quality formats superior to the state in which they were found; yet, numerous Hong Kong cinephiles will note that there is something missing, particularly among the pixels when these video images are blown up for projection in the repertory theater. The balance of the restrictions of preservation versus public access is a fundamental debate for any archiving project, but with Celestial's corporate mandate, here the "healthy" re-packaging and remembering of this seminal period in Hong Kong's film history has opted for mass consumption. Such accessibility of course runs counter to one of the key symptoms of a cinephile's pathology of desire, that is, assuming exclusive ownership, even authorship, over a coveted film. And the cinephile will also remain fixated on a particular moment in a film as the source of meaning; in the martial arts film, we should suspect such a moment would include this pathological movement that give the films their "other-worldly" quality (or, as Paul Willemen describes the process of cinephilia, "a sense of its own 'beyond'") in excess of a classical narrative's representational limits of realist temporality and visual perspective – the very moments that frustrate the remastering machine's attempts at standardization.[43] Run Run Shaw reportedly screened films for himself and his staff on a regular basis (often going to great lengths to find prints of European films). Now with the keys to Shaw's library, the CEO of Celestial Pictures, William Pfeiffer, claims to screen a few films from the shelves every night, surveying their remastering potential.[44] The remastering project has in part been guided by the spectatorship of both DVD enthusiasts and corporate executives, engaging in that perversion one can diagnose as "cinephilia," while at the same time cleaning things up for the video store.

Thanks very much to Edwin Chen, Malte Hagener, Ann Harris, June Hui-Chun Wu, Sergei Kapterev, J.P. Leary, and Marijke de Valck for their helpful suggestions.

Notes

1. Abbas, Ackbar. *Hong Kong: Culture and the Politics of Disappearance*, Minneapolis: University of Minnesota Press, 1997, p. 4.
2. The strategy for Hong Kong's publicity campaign, and registration of "Hong Kong" as a brand name, is explained online in "Brand Hong Kong" at Hong Kong SAR Government Information Centre. <http://www.brandhk.com.hk>.
3. Yau, Esther. "Introduction. Hong Kong Cinema in a Borderless World." Yau, Esther (ed.) *At Full Speed: Hong Kong Cinema in a Borderless World*, Minneapolis: University of Minnesota Press, 2001, p. 3.
4. Teo, Stephen. *Hong Kong Cinema: The Extra Dimensions*, London: BFI, 1997, p. vii.
5. An interesting sketch of video shops in overseas Chinese communities can be found in Wong Hing-yuk, Cindy. "Cities, Cultures and Cassettes. Hong Kong Cinema and Transnational Audiences." *Post Script* 19.1, 1999.
6. Miramax chairman Harvey Weinstein addressed these critics in a guest column for *Daily Variety*, citing scheduling and marketing logistical difficulties. Weinstein, Harvey. "Climbing the Chinese wall." *Daily Variety*, September 1, 2004: p.15.
7. The Scorsese version is tentatively titled THE DEPARTED, and lists as executive producers Roy Lee and Doug Davison, who produced the Hollywood remake of RINGU. Brodesser, Claude and Cathy Dunkley. "Damon Goes Undercover for WB." *Daily Variety*, July 23, 2004: p. 1.
8. For example, Tom Cruise's production company is producing a remake of the Pang Brothers, THE EYE (Hong Kong/UK/Thailand/Singapore: Oxide Pang Chun and Danny Pang, 2002.) An interesting analysis of the recent phenomenon of Hollywood remakes of Asian films can be found in Xu, Gary Gang. "Remaking East Asia, Outsourcing Hollywood." *Senses of Cinema* 34, 2005.

9.   Yau, Esther. "Introduction. Hong Kong Cinema in a Borderless World." p. 7.

10. The films of the Shaw Brothers are particularly emblematic of popular Hong Kong filmmaking evoking an ahistorical Chinese past, and Sek Kei provides an effective summary of this approach in "Shaw Movie Town's 'China Dream' and 'Hong Kong Sentiments.'" Wong Ain-ling (ed.). *The Shaw Screen: A Preliminary Study,* Hong Kong: Hong Kong Film Archive, 2003.

11. Fonoroff, Paul. *Silver Light: A Pictorial History of Hong Kong Cinema, 1920-1970,* Hong Kong: Joint Publishing HK, 1997, p. xi.

12. Lee, Henry K. "Film Experts Find Treasure in Trash Bin: Vintage Martial-Arts Movies Bound for Hong Kong Archive." *San Francisco Chronicle,* May 28, 1999.

13. For example, see Hong Kong Film Archive, *Archive Treasures.*

14. For further information on Modern Films see Möller, Olaf. "A Lost Era of the Avant-Garde Was Forever in Search of the Elusive Nature of Home." *Film Comment* 40.5, 2004: pp. 20, 22.

15. After 1997, a number of artists' collectives sprung up, squatting in unused former factory spaces. Some of these have come and gone, but a few remain devoted to Hong Kong experimental art, such as Para/Site and the Cattle Depot Artists Village.

16. Fung, May (ed.). *i-GENERATIONs: Independent, Experimental and Alternative Creations from the 60s to Now,* Hong Kong: Hong Kong Film Archive, 2001.

17. One recent touring exhibition that screened in various American cities was sponsored by the Hong Kong Economic and Trade Office, consequently including promotional material for the aforementioned Brand Hong Kong, advertising "Asia's World City."

18. For a history of modern Hong Kong, see Tsang, Steve. *A Modern History of Hong Kong,* London: I.B. Tauris, 2004.

19. Law Kar (ed.). *The China Factor in Hong Kong Cinema,* Hong Kong: The Urban Council, 1990; Fu, Poshek. *Between Shanghai and Hong Kong: The Politics of Chinese Cinemas,* Stanford: Stanford University Press, 2003; Zhen, Zhang. "The 'Shanghai Factor' in Hong Kong Cinema. A Tale of Two Cities in Historical Perspectives." *Asian Cinema* 10.1, 1998: pp. 146-159.

20. Fu, Poshek. "Hong Kong and Singapore. A History of the Cathay Cinema." p. 66.

21. Hong Kong Film Archive programmer Law Kar discussed this notion of the Cathay cinema depicting a future of increased living standards at the MP&GI Symposium presented by the Center for Humanities Research at Lingnan University and the Hong Kong Film Archive. An abbreviated account of the conference proceedings can be found in Liu Suet-wan, collated. "Summaries of HKFA Seminars, MP&GI Symposium. Session 5: 'Studio Style.'" Agnes Lam (trans.). *Hong Kong Film Archive Newsletter* 20, 2002.

22. This is an all too brief rudimentary history of the two studios, condensed for space limitations, leaving out the particularly interesting political implications of the importance of the Taiwan market once the Mandarin-language audience of mainland China closed its borders in 1950. For a more complete history of Cathay/MP&GI, see Lim, Kay Tong. *Cathay: 55 Years of Cinema.* Singapore: Landmark Books, 1991; Yu Mo-wan. "The Cathay Organisation and Hong Kong Cinema." Wong Ain-ling (ed.). *The Cathay Story,* Hong Kong Film Archive, 2002; and Cheung, Stephanie Po-yin. "A Southeast Asian Tycoon and His Movie Dream. Loke Wan Tho and MP&GI." Wong Ain-ling (ed.) *The Cathay Story;* on Shaws see Cheung, Stephanie

Po-yin. "The Industrial Evolution of a Fraternal Enterprise. The Shaw Brothers and the Shaw Organisation." Wong Ain-ling (ed.) *The Shaw Screen: A Preliminary Study,* Hong Kong: Hong Kong Film Archive, 2003.

23. Groves, Don. "Cathay Enters Digital Arena." *Variety* 15-21 May 2000: p. 70.

24. So, Karen. "Bringing Starlight Back to Hong Kong – The Return of the Cathay Films." *HKFA Newsletter,* nr. 29. 2004: n.p.

25. In a script provided to overseas distributors of the film for subtitling, an explanatory parenthetical for this title card reads, "Note that this message harks back to the '70s-era Chinese martial arts/revenge movie genre best exemplified by directors Cheh Chang and the Shaw Brothers, to which the director is paying homage."

26. Elsaesser, Thomas, "Digital Cinema: Delivery, Event, Time." Elsaesser, Thomas, Kay Hoffmann (eds.). *Cinema Futures, Cain, Abel or Cable,* Amsterdam: University of Amsterdam Press, 1998, p. 203.

27. "D-cinema and e-cinema, once well established, will remove colour print film stocks from the market, and with them may go almost all other motion picture photochemical supplies and services. It is not clear how long this will take but it seems inevitable. Estimates of 5-15 years have been put forward" from: "FIRST PROJECT WORKPACKAGE 3. Motion Picture Film Digitization for Preservation and Restoration." *State of the Art Reports,* Project First: Film Restoration and Conservation Strategies, 2003.

28. High definition format being 1080/24p. See "SGI® Technology Powers World's First Large-Scale Digital Film Remastering Center." Mountain View, CA: Silicon Graphics, Inc., 2003.

29. "Cleaning Up the Classics." *Hong Kong Digital* 4.200, n.d. <http://www.dighkmovies.com/v4/200/200.html>.

30. A demonstration can be found on a featurette included as an extra feature on the DVD of the latest *Metropolis* (Fritz Lang, 1927) restoration.

31. "SGI® Technology Powers World's First Large-Scale Digital Film Remastering Center." Mountain View, CA: Silicon Graphics, Inc., 2003, p. 3.

32. Kokaram, Anil, et al. "Robust and Automatic Digital Restoration Systems. Coping with Reality." Amsterdam: International Broadcasting Convention, 2002, p. 405. For further studies of "pathological motion," also see Biemond, J., R.L. Lagendijk, and P.M.B. van Roosmalen. "Restoration and Storage of Film and Video Archive Material." Byrnes, J.S. (ed.). *Signal Processing for Multimedia,* IOS Press, 1999; and Biemond, J., A. Rares, and M.J.T. Reinders. "Statistical Analysis of Pathological Motion Areas." *IEEE Seminar on Digital Restoration of Film and Video Archives,* 2001.

33. On the banning of early martial arts films in China, see Zhen, Zhang, "Bodies in the Air. The Magic of Science and the Fate of the Early "'Martial Arts' Film in China." *Postscript* 20.2 & 3, 2001, p. 55-57.

34. Law, Kar. "The Origin and Development of Shaws' Colour *Wuxia* Century." Wong Ain-ling (ed.). *The Shaw Screen: A Preliminary Study.* Hong Kong: Hong Kong Film Archive, 2003.

35. Bordwell, David. "Richness Through Imperfection. King Hu and the Glimpse." Poshek Fu, David Desser (eds.). *The Cinema of Hong Kong: History, Arts, Identity.* Cambridge: Cambridge University Press, 2000, p. 200.

36. Rayns, Tony. "Director: King Hu." *Sight and Sound* 45.1, 1975/1976.

37. For discussion of the gender politics of the martial arts film see Zhang Zhen, "Bodies in the Air."; and Reynaud, Berenice. "The Book, the Goddess and the Hero. Sexual Politics in the Chinese Martial Arts Film." *Senses of Cinema*, no. 26, May-June 2003. <http://www.sensesofcinema.com/contents/03/26/sexual_politics_chinese_martial_arts.html>.

38. Cartwright, Lisa. *Screening the Body: Tracing Medicine's Visual Culture.* Minneapolis: University of Minnesota Press, 1995, p. 53

39. Zhang Zhen. "Bodies in the Air." p. 54.

40. Chang Cheh. *Chang Cheh: A Memoir.* Hong Kong: Hong Kong Film Archive, 2004, p. 79-103.

41. The castration-fear motif of Zhang's *The One-Armed Swordsman* films is addressed most directly in Stanley Kwan's documentary, YANG YIN: GENDER IN CHINESE CINEMA (Hong Kong/UK: 1996), in addition to a more general discussion of his representation of masculinity. Also see Teo, Stephen. *Hong Kong Cinema: The Extra Dimensions.* London: BFI, 1997; and Lam, Michael. "The Mysterious Gayness in Chang Cheh's Unhappy World." Wong Ain-ling (ed.) *The Shaw Screen: A Preliminary Study.*

42. Abbas, Ackbar. *Hong Kong: Culture and the Politics of Disappearance*, p. 8.

43. Willemen, Paul. "Through the Glass Darkly: Cinephilia Reconsidered." *Looks and Frictions: Essays in Cultural Studies and Film Theory.* London: British Film Institute, 1994, p. 230.

44. Hansen, Jeremy. "Reach for the Sky." *Variety*, 20-26 August 2001: p. 22.

Drowning in Popcorn at the International Film Festival Rotterdam?

The Festival as a Multiplex of Cinephilia

Marijke de Valck

> *Rotterdam was the first international film festival I attended, and those first few years remain precious in my mind as a time of nascent cinephilia, opening my eyes to filmmakers that I never would have discovered staying at home even in such a film savvy city as Toronto, who [sic] has its own excellent festival; anyone concerned that Rotterdam has grown unwieldy in recent years should come to Toronto and try to find anything like a familial environment or an unheralded discovery.*[1]
>
> Mark Peranson, editor-in-chief of *Cinema Scope*

On the night of Wednesday, 28 June 1972, seventeen spectators attended the opening screening of the new film festival "Film International Rotterdam." The sight of an all but empty cinema theatre prompted the Councillor of Arts to return without performing the official opening ceremony for the film week that had been described as "super-experimental."[2] This label was the consequence of the outspoken – and controversial – taste preferences of the founder of the festival, Huub Bals, who was also the co-founder of the Féderation Internationale des Festivals Indépendents that included the Quinzaine des Réalisateurs (Cannes) and the Internationales Forum des Jungen Films (Berlin). Though the festival's consistent focus has been on art cinema, experimental works, and southern (Asian) developing film countries, ever since its foundation, the popularity of the festival has increased dramatically. Today, the International Film Festival Rotterdam is the second largest audience film festival in the world, with an attendance of 355,000 during the 2004 festival.[3] This number also positions the IFFR as the largest multiple-day cultural event in the Netherlands. The IFFR pleases its visitors by offering the best films of the festivals of the preceding year before their release in theatres, national and international premiers that haven't (yet) found distribution, a first feature competition program, thematic programs, and highly popular Q&A sessions with filmmakers themselves, after the screenings of their films.

But we must also remain a bit wary of the attendance figure of 355,000 because, as IFFR's Cinemart director Ido Abram un-euphemistically puts it, "the number is a lie."[4] What we should bear in mind when we read this figure is that it does not represent the number of actual *visitors* to the festival. Festivals work hard to present a positive image in the global competitive context, and so attendance figures are an important measure of success that are artificially boosted – in the case of Rotterdam, the published figure also includes *potential* admissions through tickets sold at the festival box office to people visiting exhibitions at associated cultural institutions – to reach the impressive 355,000. This data is used to support the impression of the IFFR as an important national and international event when it applies for funding on which the festival organization is dependent. However, because all film festivals use similar methods to calculate attendance, the lie rules and so these figures retain their usefulness for comparing festivals.

In general, they point to an explosive increase in attendance in Rotterdam since the mid-1990s.[5] The flattering attendance figures aside, the fact is that the IFFR is very popular with a diverse and devoted audience. As Mark Peranson suggests, not everyone has welcomed the growth of the festival with equal enthusiasm. Film critic and *Filmkrant* editor-in-chief Dana Linssen is among the skeptics, putting a satirical photo of the festival icon – the tiger – drowning in a sea of popcorn on the cover of the festival daily paper no. 5. Linssen expresses her concerns directly to festival director Sandra den Hamer, who will soon be the sole captain on the festival ship, as co-director Simon Field finished his Rotterdam career with the 2004 festival. Her "Dear Sandra" editorial appeared at a time when the director was probably considering some significant changes to the festival that bear her personal imprint. Linssen's cry can be read as a subtext to the drowning tiger collage, as she notes: "I am for example very concerned about the size of the festival, both as a journalist and a film lover.... The real highlights from the 'best of the fests' are sure to be released in Dutch cinema theaters. No matter how proud you may be of this festival with all those sweet, crazy cinephiles who take a week off to watch 50 films here, I can imagine that you also agree with me that it would be better for the culture of wayward, pronounced and artistic films in general if these same people would once in a while go to the cinema during the rest of the year as well.... The IFFR should be smaller, more explicit and more accessible."[6]

Linssen is not alone in her concern about the size of the festival. The logistical handling of Rotterdam's 355,000 visitors is a continuous source of concern for the organization and frustration for the audience. A couple of days before the festival kicks off, the reservation line and ticket sales center are opened. Within hours the most popular screenings are sold out. Tickets are hard to get, especially for the evenings and the weekends. This is frustrating for those not experienced enough to know that you have to either arrive early and physically line up at one of the ticket counters in Rotterdam or persistently redialing on your (mobile) phone(s) until you get through to one of the volunteer operators. In this respect, it is telling that the attempts to launch an online reservation system remain unsuccessful because the early peak in traffic again and again have proven to create a bottleneck that effectively crashes the program.

Before the 2004 festival opened, 130,000 tickets were reserved and 55,000 had already been sold. The idea at stake here, however, is not merely the discussion of attendance figures but, more interestingly, the normative evaluation of festival cinephilia. Both Peranson and Linssen belong to the proponents of traditional cinephilia. They appreciate Rotterdam for its "commitment to young filmmakers, to experimental filmmaking and installations – and less of a commitment to sales agents."[7] They want the festival to be programmed at the cutting edge with an eye for discoveries and remain dedicated to informal and inspiring encounters between the elite communities of film professionals. Linssen, however, mourns the overwhelming presence of an audience not as totally devoted to the Tiger Awards Competition Award (which is awarded for a first or second feature film) and thus her image of the tiger drowning in popcorn, the ultimate low culture symbol for cinema consumption. Peranson devaluates popular taste with the statement that he learned "[a]nother lesson from Rotterdam: the films at the bottom of the audience polls are generally the best."[8]

But do the old high culture versus low culture or art versus commerce oppositions really do justice to the rapidly transforming festival world? Can the criteria of 1960s cinephilia survive throughout the 1990s into the millennium without some transformation? In this regard, I plead for an understanding of festival cinephilia as a process of translation within the changing festival environment and consequently argue that contemporary cinephilia appears in many forms at today's International Film Festival Rotterdam.

The Cinephilia Debates

Initially, festival cinephilia seemed to be marginalized in the late 1990s debates, initiated by Susan Sontag and her article "The Decay of Cinema."[9] As we have shown in the introduction, a lot of the discussions around the alleged death of cinephilia concentrated on the impact of new technologies such as video and the internet. In their anthology *Movie Mutations*, Jonathan Rosenbaum and Adrian Martin present a new (inter)face for world cinephilia that includes new transnational communication modes, such as the internet and film festivals. In the introduction, we also argued that their embrace of technological development has not led to a revised conception of cinephilia: "*Movie Mutations* presents a lineup of the usual suspects of contemporary world cinema (art/avant-garde) favorites – Abbas Kiarostami, Tsai Ming-liang, John Cassavetes et al. Like Sontag, Rosen-

baum and Martin are not primarily interested in describing the universal phenomenon of cinematic pleasures in its rich variety of relations to the screen, but
pursue the specific agenda of positioning "certain tendencies" in the globalized
movie world as the new norm for cinephilia."[10] Writing about the film festival
in Rotterdam, Rosenbaum presents his position with full confidence: "So for
me, a particular pleasure of attending the Rotterdam Film Festival year after
year… is the pleasure of seeing the received wisdom of American commerce
repeatedly confounded. To all appearances, there's a hunger for experimental
work that producers, distributors, and most mainstream reviewers are completely unaware of, and which gives me a renewed faith in the capacities of the
spectator."[11]

Rosenbaum expresses his faith in the IFFR spectators as if he were allowing
them to be part of his transnational community of cinephiles provided that they
can prove to be *capable* of appreciating for instance the "multiple narrative mysteries" of I-Chen Ko's Lan Yue / Blue Moon (Taiwan: 1997). Keep in mind that
Rosenbaum – born to a family that manages an independent cinema chain – is
not alluding to differences in tastes but differences in capability levels. Obviously the larger part of the roughly 90,000 visitors behind Rotterdam's attendance figure of 355,000 would not stand the test, because they do not flock to
the experimental works that are shown at the festival and preferred by film
critics, but to the 'best of the fests' and to the more accessible films that are likely
to receive distribution outside the festival. Like Linssen who tried to convince
Sandra den Hamer to disregard the wishes of "all those sweet, crazy cinephiles"
and concentrate the programming on cutting-edge (experimental) work without
changes for distribution, Rosenbaum is advocating his conception of cinephilia.

If cinephilia were a skill to be mastered, the average festival spectator would
very unlikely emulate such "professional cinephiles" as Linssen, Peranson and
Rosenbaum. The question is whether they *should* in order to qualify as cinephilia practitioners. Or to put it more provocatively in the words of low-culture TV
icon Dr. Phil – "How much fun do you think you are to live with?" In other
words: "How much fun is cinephilia if it restrains the public with professional
criteria?" We have to bear in mind that Linssen, Peranson, and Rosenbaum are
not just cinephiles, but also film critics. Their professional involvement in cinema discourse colors and deepens their cinephile practice and vice versa. The
tentative question then bounces back to the real issue at stake in the video and
internet-driven debates on cinephilia. The issue is fear: professional fear over-
ruling the private passions or "fun" of independent cinephiles. Fear that the
multiplication of distribution channels and the accompanying broadening of
access to film culture will result in a decrease in quality. Fear that original cultural contexts will be misunderstood or misquoted. Fear, finally, that the established spaces for the recognition and appreciation of marginalized film tastes

will be appropriated by others. God forbid that they might be popcorn munchers! Festival cinephilia enters the debate here. What I am interested in finding out is whether the growing popularity of film festivals with its larger audiences really increases exclusion and the marginalizing of marginalized tastes, or does it lead to more inclusion, amounting to a multiple concept of cinephilia? For this we first need to consider the developments in the larger cinema environment.

Transformations on the Festival Circuit

The introduction of video had an effect on both the movie industries and the film festivals. In the early 1980s, the Cannes Film Festival and film market became the epicenter of bustling activity, new independents, and commercial frenzy. Towards the end of the decade, however, the market had consolidated and most of the independents had departed. Those who survived, like Miramax, became subsidiaries of multinational media corporations. When the Hollywood Empire struck back and took measures to bound mass audiences to its products across the various outlets in a smart response to the emergence of the multimedia environment, the film festival circuit went through a fundamental transformation as well. The global proliferation of film festivals during the 1980s and 1990s resulted in the creation of a worldwide alternative film circuit in which a few festivals became the major marketplace and media events, while the majority of festivals performed a variety of tasks from discovering new talent to supporting identity groups such as gays and lesbians).[12] As Julian Stringer argues, following Saskia Sassen's work on global cities, these festivals all compete with each other in terms of the global space economy. "As local differences are being erased through globalization, festivals need to be similar to one another, but as novelty is also at a premium, the local and particular also becomes very valuable. Film festivals market both conceptual similarity and cultural difference."[13] The tension between similarity and difference points to the interdependence of the festivals. All of the festivals are embedded in the international festival circuit that features over 1,900 unofficial and 800 official festival events worldwide.[14] The power of the circuit lies in its constitution as a chain of temporary exhibition venues along which films can travel and accumulate value that will enable and/or support theatrical release or simply support the exposure to festival audiences.

"Best of the Fests" programs underline this interdependence. Takeshi Kitano's ZATÔICHI (Japan: 2003), for example, had its Dutch premiere during the 2004 IFFR and was not directly released in theatres as a tribute to the festival that supported the director on its way to gaining international recognition. Kitano, in his turn, paid his respect to the festival by attending the premiere, thus contributing to the extensive media exposure that most likely enhanced box of- fice revenues. The differences between the conditions of exhibition at film festi- vals can, however, be great. The world's leading festival in Cannes caters almost exclusively to a professional audience and complies with strict hierarchical practices and segregating rituals. Without proper accreditation, it becomes al- most impossible to attend the screenings. Thus for non-professionals, unless they believe that waiting in front of the Palais des Festivals with camping chairs and ladders to get a glimpse of Antonio Banderas, qualifies as a cinephilic prac- tice, then Cannes is not their Mecca of Cinephilia. Moreover, Rotterdam has no red carpets and presidential suites waiting to welcome the guests. The festival in Rotterdam is easily accessible for both professional and non-professional ci- nephiles. It is widely applauded for its open atmosphere, lack of pretentious decoration and many public post-screening Q&A sessions with attending film- makers. In contrast to Cannes, Berlin, and Venice, the IFFR is not compromised by a Hollywood presence. Whereas these "A" category festivals rely on different selection criteria, ranging from star power and media attention to critics' crite- ria, the IFFR is a pure art cinema festival, selecting films on their "quality" and choosing themes according to "social or cinematographical urgency."[15]

The global proliferation of the film festival phenomenon from the 1980s on- wards and the consequent tightening of the individual festivals who embed themselves in the international circuit did not, however, leave Rotterdam unaf- fected. We can discern three key transformations: 1) the growth of the audience; 2) the move to the Pathé multiplex in downtown Rotterdam in 1997; and 3) the introduction of the Tiger Award Competition in 1995. Competitions and awards were initially not included, but because of pressure from an expanding festival circuit, the Tiger Award Competition was launched to keep attracting media representatives coming to the festival. Faithful to Bals' legacy, the award is to be given annually to three *ex aequo* winners for the best first or second feature film. The former two transformations, on the other hand, caused a breach with Bals' idiosyncratic ideas on film. He maintained that his task as a festival direc- tor was to find an audience for his films and not to find films for his audience. The expanding number of films and new programs in the festival cannot, how- ever, be considered separately from the growing audience. The move to the Pathé multiplex was a logistical necessity to facilitate more screenings for more spectators or – should I reverse the order – more spectators for more movies. Despite the call for a smaller festival by Linssen and others like her, the growing popularity of the IFFR has become an irreversible fact.

其实这适用于不仅IFFR.

Preliminary Taxonomy of Cinephiles

分类学

ANT:每个人的存在基于不同的社交网络而言会有不同的身份,人是靠这些关系定义而存在的,除此之外没有"存在"(entity)

The IFFR is very popular with both a professional and a non-professional public. This is a statistical fact and an obvious reality when one visits the festival. I suggest following Latour's actor-network theory (ANT) to study festival cinephilia and complement the picture drawn by official attendance figures. Latour's ANT – which is actually more of a methodology than a theory – will allow us to hear the actors speak for themselves, because it considers actors (objects) in their relation to other entities, that is in conjunction to the network. ANT starts not with a meta-theory, but with empirical data to draw descriptions that will lead to conceptual insights.[16] This perspective is important because it acknowledges the influence of changing circumstances in the festival circuit environment as well as the active, shaping influence of actors (such as cinephiles) especially in relation to each other. Thus, for the IFFR, it is necessary to begin with the film lovers who attend the festival in Rotterdam and describe what they do. The result is a preliminary taxonomy of cinephiles in Rotterdam. The six cinephile types below are prototypical descriptions that fit actual festival visitors on a continuum (allowing for combinations of several types).

The Lone List-Maker

The lone list-maker thoroughly prepares his/her festival visit. The program is thoroughly perused and chosen titles are meticulously composed into a tight schedule that barely allows for commuting between cinema theaters or a quick snack between films. The list-maker typically does not take the preferences or itineraries of others into consideration, but follows his/her own taste that may range from festival toppers to experimental work. Exchanges and discussions on films occur during stolen moments with acquaintances or friends. The list-maker makes a great effort to find time for a multi-day visit to the festival to see as many films as possible.

The Highlight Seeker

The highlight seeker also prepares his/her festival visit, but consciously considers and collects the tips of others in order to not miss any festival highlights. Highlight seekers select established names and are susceptible to pre-festival publications and specials that put certain topics and films on the agenda. They are also on the lookout for the hottest hits that are coming via other festivals and find pleasure in having seeing them before they hit the (art house) theaters.

The Specialist (often professional)

The specialist concentrates on a clearly defined interest, such as experimental films, installations, Asian cult films etc. This might be accented by one of the festival's thematic programs. At the IFFR, visitors interested in discoveries follow the Tiger competition; those who want to delve into art and avant-garde film history may use the filmmakers in focus programs that offer canonical filmographies, or perhaps you are interested in looking beyond traditional forms at points where cinema overlaps with, for example, video games and installation art? Then Exploding Cinema is the showcase for you. Special programs can also include a variety of the preconceived festival categories. Professionals in particular, use the video booth facilities of the festival to ingest the desired artwork purposefully and efficiently.

The Leisure Visitor

The leisure visitor is less determined than the previous types in his/her selection of films. The wish to visit the festival as a leisure activity doesn't include the willingness to sacrifice (a lot of) time and energy in pre-selection and reservations. Leisure visitors typically do not adjust their daily routines to the festival, but look for available and appealing screenings in the evenings, the weekends or other free hours. They may also visit the festival without any reservations and see what is available at the last-minute counter. Also popular with these types of visitors are the composed programs; large institutions, such as the Erasmus University, *VPRO* (public television station) and *de Volkskrant* (quality daily newspaper) offer day programs for their employees and subscribers. In general, leisure visitors are inclined to visit the festival with company.

The Social Tourist

The social element of a festival is central to the social tourist. Many people visit the festival as part of a group (friends, colleagues, family, etc.). With a group, the film selection is typically left up to one person, who will try to accommodate the general taste of the group (e.g., not too much violence, because Helen doesn't like it; one exotic film, preferably set in a desert or other remote environment – featuring for example a cute weeping camel – oh, and definitely something French, something with a bit of extramarital sex). Their visit is primarily seen as an outing and time is calculated for lunch, coffee, and dinner, which will most likely be consumed in the city rather than within the festival buildings.

The Volunteer

The volunteer offers his/her services to the festival in exchange for accreditation and an inside experience. The number of films that can be seen by volunteers is not extremely high, because they have to work a minimum amount of hours during the festival. This, however, is compensated with the experience of being part of the festival. Through their work at the festival, volunteers have easy access to news and can see trends developing firsthand. Some jobs (drivers, guest service) allow volunteers to have (brief) contact with filmmakers. This adds a touch of exclusivity to their positions. Moreover, the volunteer community is a tight-knit group of cinema lovers and younger people who get together after hours and generally have a very good time amongst themselves. Access to the closing party is an important part of the volunteer's compensation.

These various actors make it difficult to isolate one core identity mark of festival cinephilia. Is it about the opportunity to immerse oneself in premieres and un-released films, the encounter with filmmakers, the specialized knowledge at hand, the promise of discovering new talent, the atmosphere of expectations, the joint experience of a popular event, or the inside look? Latour teaches us that in the process of describing an actor's actions we have to pay special attention to the movements, the flows, and changes that circulate between them and the environment, the network, i.e., the festival circuit in general and the festival in Rotterdam in particular. This allows us to see the emergence of multiple forms of Rotterdam cinephilia in conjunction with the changing environment.

The Multiplex of Cinephilia

The popularity of the IFFR has enabled the festival organization to rent the Pathé multiplex in downtown Rotterdam for the festival's duration since 1997. The move has the metaphorical value of capturing some of the essential issues at stake in the transformations of the festival. The multiplex specifically links the film festival to the mass audience it attracts and, at the same time, points to the unavoidable professionalization of the IFFR organization that has occurred both in response to the increased global competitive context, as well as the growth and success of the festival itself. The festival schedule resembles the logistics of the multiplex as a commercial enterprise; films are constantly beginning and festival visitors may come to the multiplex without a clear goal of what they are going to see as last-minute decisions are facilitated by the concentration of cinema screens in one mega-theater.

Furthermore, films from the various programs are screened parallel to each other to accommodate the tastes of a diverse audience. The most popular films – or those expected to be – are programmed in the largest cinema theaters (notably Pathe1) and have the preferred timeslots of around 8 and 10:30 p.m. to give as many people as possible the ability to include these in their festival programming. Because the festival is obliged to rent all of the seating from the multinational exhibition corporation, the logistics of predicting and orchestrating supply and demand is not without its financial consequences. Like the commercial management of the multiplex, the festival pre-calculates how many seats a film is likely to fill (at what time) and takes this into consideration when assigning theaters and timeslots to the various films. Due to the short duration of the festival, the commercial dogma of box office revenues in the opening weekend affecting a film's circulation does not apply, in a strict sense, to the festival's films. The schedule and numbers of screenings per film is set and limited beforehand. However, the juggling with attendance figures (not exclusive to the IFFR) points to a progressive institutionalization of the festival system that has to account for its mass popularity and competitiveness with hard figures.

Because the invention of the multiplex is, moreover, tied to the rise of New Hollywood's high-concept marketing strategies, the combination of festival and multiplex indicates the key role that festivals play in strategies to promote what Alisa Perron calls "indie blockbusters – films that, on a smaller scale, replicate the exploitation marketing and box office performance of the major studio high-concept event pictures."[17] Festivals are not only alternative exhibition sites for films that cannot find theatrical distribution, but also events that help build the profile of niche productions before release. At the level of the contemporary global film market festival, exposure, and preferably awards, constitute world/ art cinema's essential baggage for check-in. For many traditional cinephiles, the commercial changes are cause for some disenchantment, a feeling evoked in particular by the festival's architectural setting. Jonathan Rosenbaum, for example, writes: "In some respects, the Pathé suggests an airport or a train station where crowds are periodically appearing and disappearing between scheduled departures; in other respects, it recalls superstores like Virgin or FNAC – or, in the US, bookstores like Borders and Barnes & Noble – that have become the capitalist replacements for state-run arts centers or public libraries. The disturbing aspect of these stores as replacements of this kind is the further breakdown of any distinction between culture and advertising which already characterises urban society in general. But a positive aspect may also exist in terms of community and collective emotion."[18]

The break with classical cinephilia is great indeed. Where traditional cinephilia often conjures up images of people gathering in run-down establishments with character to catch one special screening, the Rotterdam festival takes place in state-of-the art cinemas (the (post)modern multiplex) and features more than 800 screenings in 12 days.[19] The difference between commercial and festival exploitation in the multiplex is that for the former, market-driven efficiency homogenizes the movie audience while allowing little room for individual identities, whereas for the latter, it has led to the practice of broad programming (from the selection of first and second features for the Tiger Award Competition to the acquisition of festival hits), while still succeeding in avoiding the impersonal anonymity by creating a sense of community for the various types of film lovers. Simply walking to your screening in the Pathé will give you the sensation that you belong to the festival in-crowd as one sees all the other festivalgoers rushing to their respective screenings in the main hall. And attending an evening screening in Pathé1 is sure to generate that specific festival magic that crosses all the various tastes via the sheer thrill of sharing the overcrowded room with an eagerly anticipating large audience. Another major generator of festival "fun" that crosses all taste preferences is the experience of exclusivity one feels within the highlighted setting of this event. For some that means having obtained a ticket to Sofia Coppola's LOST IN TRANSLATION (USA/Japan: 2003), which sold out in four hours, for others it means being part of the first screening of the legendary "lost" Cassavetes, the original version of his first feature SHADOWS (USA: 1958).

I argue that the IFFR's broad programming and its catering to a wide range of cinephiles is the result of the transformations within the international film festival circuit. Embedded in the global competitive context of the festival circuit and dependent on the criteria of support from the Ministry of Culture and the municipality of Rotterdam, the festival needs to be able to address a multiplicity of needs. The festival has to obtain films, secure premieres and persuade filmmakers and journalists to attend the festival. It also has to compete (nationally on the cultural agenda) with other events for audiences, media attention and funding. On the festival circuit, the IFFR has found a niche position with its focus on art, avant-garde, and experimental works. Both the festival organization and (part of) the (professional) public are strongly dedicated to maintaining this aspect. In fact, the strength of Rotterdam when compared to the major festivals in Cannes, Berlin and Venice is precisely this co-existence of cutting edge and uncompromising film programs and a receptive general audience.

Using ANT to compose the preliminary list of cinephiles means being concerned with describing what the actors do. When trying to ground the marginalization fear of the more experimental and artistic works in the festival with these descriptions, the conclusion must be that cinephiles' (actors') behavior tell us otherwise. In fact, many cinephiles are quite open to the experts' selections. They also rely on the festival's programs and might even choose pre-selected day-programs, read reviews, and attend the discussions.

Meanwhile, the social tourist, who considers the festival an outing with friends, might discover new genres or filmmakers they had no idea existed before and return with an agenda that takes into account their new interests. The encounters between the various films, experts, and spectators in the stimulating and dynamic environment of the festival is thus the ideal starting point for the development of taste. The professional cinephiles, the film critics, have an important task in this regard. As Wesley Monroe Shrum Jr., writing on the role of critics at the Edinburgh Fringe Festival (theater), argued: "[T]he difference between high and popular art is not fundamentally a difference in the institutions that promulgate their products or in the class background of consumers but a difference in the process of *mediation*. The relation between producers and consumers of art is not constant. It entails different levels of expert involvement. The higher a work is in the cultural hierarchy, the more important is discourse about the object to its status. Taste in high art is mediated by experts, whereas taste in low art is not."[20] It is precisely this presence of lively discourse and expert mediation that continues to characterize festival cinephilia throughout its many transformations. The festival as a multiplex of cinephilia might evoke visions of capitalist appropriation at first, but then reveals itself as a hopeful metaphor for the event that nurtures cinephilia in its multiple forms. The festival in Rotterdam is a joyful celebration of cinema that, through its popular appeal, introduces a larger audience to the cinephile experience and can potentially even persuade them to continue to deepen this engagement. There is no reason to fear loss of recognition and exclusivity as long as the festival organization and critics remain resistant to the impulse to drown in popcorn. In fact, I argue the opposite: popularity may be a strategy of inclusion that benefits from the ramified network that was the result of the post-1980s transformations of the festival circuit. The IFFR has successfully adjusted itself to the globally dominant model of the media event and managed to use the changing interface of world cinephilia to expand its accessibility and address the needs of a variety of cinephiles.

Notes

1. Peranson, Mark. "Nothing sells better than sex." *Filmkrant in Rotterdam*, no. 4, 25 January 2004: p. 5. <http://www.fipresci.org/criticism/archive/archive_2004/rotterdam/rdam_mperanson.htm>.
2. Bertina, Bob. *De Volkskrant*, June 1972. Also see Heijs, Jan, Frans Westra. *Que le Tigre Danse. Huub Bals, een biografie*. Amsterdam: Otto Cramwinckel Uitgever, 1996: p. 97.

3. The 2004 festival was held between January 21 and February 2 and equalled the attendance record of 355,000 spectators established in 2003. The biggest audience festival is the Berlinale.

4. Abram, Ido. "Cannes Film Festival 2004." This evaluation of attendance figures by Ido Abram is for the 2004 film festival in Cannes.

5. In 1983, the attendance figures were 44,680. By 1996, they exceeded 200,000. The exponential increase after 1996 is related to the new location – the Pathé Multiplex on the Schouwburgplein – that was inaugurated for festival purposes in 1997.

6. Linssen, Dana. "Beste Sandra." *Filmkrant in Rotterdam*, no. 10, 31 January-1 February 2004: p.5. My translation is from the Dutch original: "*Ik maak me bijvoorbeeld grote zorgen over de grootte van het festival, als journalist én filmliefhebber…[D]e echte hoogtepunten uit de 'best of the fests' [komen] toch later in de Nederlandse bioscopen. Hoe trots je ook kunt zijn als festivals op die lieve gekke filmofielen die een week vrij nemen om hier 50 films te gaan zien, ik kan me voorstellen dat je het met me eens bent dat het voor de algehele cultuur van eigenwijze, uitgesproken en artistieke film beter is als die mensen de rest van het jaar ook nog eens naar filmtheater of bioscoop gaan…. Het IFFR moet kleiner, opvallender en behapbaarder worden.*"

7. Peranson, Mark. "Nothing sells better than sex."

8. Idem. In 2004 the public gave Tiger Award winner Kang-sheng Lee's (also known as Tsai Ming-liang's actor of choice) acclaimed debut Bu Jian / The Missing (Taiwan: 2003) an average score of 3.41 out of 5, placing the film at 109th place out of 164.

9. Sontag, Susan. "The Decay of Cinema." *New York Times*, 25 February late final edition 1996: section 6, p. 60.

10. De Valck, Marijke & Malte Hagener. "Introduction."

11. Rosenbaum, Jonathan. "Preface." Rosenbaum, Jonathan, Adrian Martin, eds. *Movie Mutations: The Changing Face of World Cinephilia.* London: British Film Institute, 2003: p.53.

12. See, for example, Kim, Soyoung. "'Cine-mania' or Cinephilia. Film Festivals and the Identity Question." *UTS Review*, vol. 4 no. 2 (November 1998): pp.174-187.

13. Stringer, Julian, "Global Cities and the International Film Festival Economy." Shiel, M. and T. Fitzmaurice (eds.), *Cinema and the City: Film and Urban Societies in a Global Context.* Oxford: Blackwell Publishers, 2001: p. 139.

14. Of the 800 official festivals, 250 have emerged over the last five years. International Film Festival Summit. 17 January 2005. <http://www.filmfestivalsummit.com>.

15. Abram, Ido. Cannes Film Festival 2004.

16. See for the four common misinterpretations of ANT: Latour, Bruno. "On Recalling ANT." Law, John, John Hassard (eds.). *Actor Network and After.* Oxford: Blackwell, 1999: pp. 15-25.

17. Perren, Alisa. "Sex, Lies and Marketing: Miramax and the Development of the Quality Indie Blockbuster." *Film Quarterly*, vol. 55 no. 2 (Winter 2001): pp. 30-39, p.30.

18. Rosenbaum, Jonathan. "Sampling in Rotterdam:" p. 54.

19. Of which there are approximately 250 feature films.

20. Shrum, Wesley Monroe Jr. *Fringe and Fortune: The Role of Critics in High and Popular Art.* Princeton: Princeton University Press, 1996: p. 40.

Ravenous Cinephiles

Cinephilia, Internet, and Online Film Communities

Melis Behlil

> **jbottle – 11:59 AM/EST March 21, 2003** (#8564 of 21182)
> "I guess we all hold onto some movie, usually for personal reasons..."
> Yeah, for some reason I really like MIKE'S MURDER, so I can forgive someone's personal faves. For every LLV [LEAVING LAS VEGAS] lover there's somebody out there who obsesses over routinely dismissed film O.C. & STIGGS and even something as distasteful as RAVENOUS.

> **oilcanboyd23 – 12:04 PM ET March 21, 2003** (#8567 of 21182)
> Obsess – "To preoccupy the mind of excessively."
> While O.C. & STIGGS does haunt me, and RAVENOUS is my 11th favorite movie of all time, neither one preoccupies my mind excessively. I only discuss them when I am asked to do so by a fellow poster. To ignore such requests would be rude. I may have a lot of bad traits, one of which is being not long on truthfully or fairly attributing remarks to others, but rudeness is not one of them.[1]

The above is a fairly classic exchange from two of the more seasoned members of the *New York Times* Film Forums.[2] It contains references to some of the most often-mentioned films of these Forums: *oilcanboyd* often expresses his admiration for O.C. & STIGGS (USA: Robert Altman, 1987), and every time RAVENOUS (Czech Republic/UK/Mexico/USA/Slovakia: Antonia Bird, 1999) or anyone related to that film is mentioned, he makes a point of commenting on it, often noting that it is his eleventh favorite film of all time. "Ravenous" in the title of this article refers not only to this film and the little ritual around it, but also to the position the "forumites" (Forum members) have had vis-à-vis the forums, in the way that this online community satisfied a long-standing hunger for discussions with fellow cinephiles.

The New Cinephilia

With the changes technology has brought to contemporary life, cinephiles – for whom movies are a way of life, films and how they are experienced have undergone major changes. The classic cinephile, as the term was adopted in the

1960s, connected the love of cinema to the actual medium of film, and to the movie-going experience. Being a cinephile involved traveling to distant theaters to track down obscure art films and discussing them with fellow cinephiles, either in ciné-clubs or in respectable film journals. In the late 1970s and early 1980s, the boom in home-viewing technologies and the decline in the number of art house theaters changed things. And with the popularization of the internet in the 1990s, the cinephile world became a whole different scene. For some, like Susan Sontag, David Denby, and David Thomson, this marked the death of cinema and cinephilia. For others, it was merely a new beginning.

In "The Decay of Cinema" Susan Sontag lamented the death of cinephilia. She argued that "going to the movies" was a great part of the movie experience, and that the vanished rituals of the theatre could not be revived.[3] The discussions about the possible death of cinephilia have continued and are linked very closely to the differences between movie-going and home-viewing. Born into an pre-existing home-viewing culture, I am among those who think limiting cinephilia to movie-going is a restrictive and provisional way of perceiving the love of cinema. Not only that, but it is also restrictive in the sense that people living outside of a handful of Western metropolises did not have the chance, until recently, to see non-mainstream fare, on or off the screen. Theo Panayides calls our generation (those born in the late 1960s and early 1970s) "the best generation in which to be a film-buff."[4] We can access films that were never so easily available before, and unlike the subsequent generations, the "vast hinterland of film history" is not yet "impossible to encompass." This is the age of "the new cinephilia," which really got going with the home video,[5] and it is not necessarily inferior to the cinephilia of the 1960s.

The new cinephilia is closely related to technology, in the way that it relies on the gadgets that make home theaters possible: first the VCR, then the hi-fi surround sound systems, and lastly the DVD. The new cinephiles may be called videophiles instead,[6] but it is the same love for an art form. Those bemoaning the demise of cinema often argue that movie theaters have all been cut into movieplexes with many tiny theaters, all showing the most recent, unoriginal and uninspired blockbusters. It is at home, however, that a film lover can watch more or less any film he/she desires, sometimes in conditions that are better than those in some stuffy, tiny movieplex theater. Repeated viewings don't cost extra and favorite scenes can be rewound and rewatched at one's own leisure. The availability of films is assured not only through giant merchandisers like Amazon.com, but also through specialized film stores such as Video Search of Miami,[7] which claims to have "more than 12,000 Cult, Exploitation, Foreign, and Bizarre movie titles" on VHS or DVD. In addition, one can (legally or often illegally) download copies of films from peer-to-peer (p2p) systems, or exchange DVDs or tapes with other cinephiles on the internet.

Not surprisingly, the new breed of cinephilia feeds itself intellectually through the technology of the internet. Various sites on the net are not only the source of great (and unfortunately not always correct) information, but they also provide a space for cinephiles to get together and exchange ideas, and fuel their need to discuss the films they have seen, which is a part of the cinephiliac tradition. In an attempt to build an analogy, one can argue that online communities are to home viewing, what ciné clubs were to the movie-going experience. Similarly, there are online journals such as *Scope, Senses of Cinema* or *Film Philosophy* that are no less stimulating than their printed counterparts, which are also often partly or fully available online to readers who would not have a chance to get hold of this material otherwise. Local film critics and gurus of the 1960s' cinephilia have been joined by online film critics such as James Berardinelli and Mike D'Angelo, who are read by thousands around the world. Online film critics are taken more seriously than they used to be just a few years ago, and many published film critics reach larger audiences through their publications' websites.[8]

Just as it is easier to obtain films and access journals, it is also easier to meet fellow cinephiles on the internet. Fellow film buffs may be easy to find in large cities or on university campuses, but cinephiles living in more rural and less culturally diverse areas are frequently on their own when it comes to tastes in film. However, online film critic Bryant Frazer argues that despite the existing forums and discussion sites, "a real sense of community" is missing online.[9] I disagree with him because I believe that these communities are real, although he does have a point when he says that "discussions that ensue tend to the diffuse – soundbite discussions peppered with moments of insight from a few hardy posters who really shouldn't waste their time contributing to a community that gives them so little in return." However, these are still valid online communities that provide people with an unprecedented sense of camaraderie, and in the case that I will be discussing, can evolve into something that goes beyond "soundbite discussions." My case study starts with the *New York Times* Film Forums, and continues with its spin-offs, the Milk Plus Blog and The Third Eye Film Community.

I will use the term "online" and "cyber" instead of "virtual" since these communities are as "real" as any other. The "realness" of these communities is not to be doubted; as Steven Jones contends: "Internet users have strong emotional attachments to their on-line activities."[10] Howard Rheingold, one of the initial theorists and earliest advocates of online communities, spoke of his "family of invisible friends."[11] While validity of online communities as communities proper has been frequently debated, it has become quite clear that there is a need to redefine community, and that the old definitions and concepts are largely obsolete today.[12] What some adversaries of online communities argue, namely that a virtual community can never truly become a community, is not only restrictive but it also makes the mistake of confusing "the pastoralist myth of the community for the reality" according to Barry Wellman and Milena Gulia.[13] For the cinephiles in question here, there often is no possibility of another, "real" community. In her "Introduction to the second issue of Cybersociology Magazine," Robin Hamman attempts to identify "community." Her definition, using George Hillery's analysis, is as follows: "(1) a group of people (2) who share social interaction (3) and some common ties between themselves and the other members of the group (4) and who share an area for at least some of the time."[14] Each of these items is valid for the community I will be discussing here.

Film-related communal cyberspaces are quite varied, ranging from casual chatgroups to academic mailing lists, from devoted fan-site-rings to theory-oriented e-journals. I will use the *New York Times* Film Forums as an example to look at the way in which an online community functions. The interviews that form part of the research for this article were conducted in January 2002 via email. However, since then, there have been a number of changes in the community, and some members have split up to form different film discussion sites. It is only natural for a community to undergo changes, even more so when this community is based in a constantly changing and growing environment like the internet. One very basic reason for my choice is the fact that I have been a member of these Forums from 1998 to 2003 and have had a chance to observe the dynamics of the community over the years. But I also find it interesting that by being associated with the *New York Times*, the Forums carry a certain weight, a connotation of being a part of one of the leading newspapers in the world. This issue comes up quite frequently in discussions in terms of maintaining a certain level of "quality" in the conversations. One member of the Forums recently described Vincent Gallo as "perverted" and "insane" for making THE BROWN BUNNY (USA/Japan/France: 2003), and asked: "Don't the Times editors have more sense than to promote this disgusting point of view?"[15] In addition, the *New York Times* has required registration on its site and since late 2001, the Film Forums have been a moderated space, requiring special registration with the Forum moderator, resulting in a certain level of commitment to even become a posting member. To demonstrate the dynamics of this online community I will relate my own observations on the Forums, as well as some responses from forumites to questions I posed regarding their film-viewing and online habits. Since some members have preferred not be named with their "real" names, I will refer to them by their online handles, or nicknames.

Movies – Opinionated Readers' Opinions

The *New York Times* Forums were founded in 1996, along with the launch of the *New York Times* website.[16] These were designated according to the major sections of the newspaper and at first hosted by experts in each field. The Film Forums were moderated by Melanie Franklin in 2002, when the first version of this paper was presented, and starting in April 2004, by Joan Hanson. They are located in the *New York Times* "Readers-Opinions section", filed under the heading "Arts" and the subheading "Movies," and are divided into several sections, which have been renamed over the years: *Current Film* became *Hollywood and Movie News*, *International Film* became *Indies and World Cinema*, and *Home Viewing* remained the same. Some headings change every few months, including: *Oscars, Genre Series: Horror Films, The Best 1,000 Movies Ever Made* and *Overlooked Films*, as well as *The Blanche Awards*, to which I will return. Although all of these sections were and still are used as general guidelines, some discussions occurred in unrelated sections, and off-topic conversations used to be very common. Moderation is done on three levels: members need to be registered to post; there is an automated moderation that withholds posts containing certain "improper" words, which are then reviewed by the moderator to see if the post is actually offensive or if it is just a misunderstanding.

In 2002, the 138 registered members were from a variety of geographical locations, age groups, and backgrounds. There were forumites from the USA, Canada, the UK, Italy, Turkey, Austria, Germany, and Australia. The ages ranged from late teens and college students to pensioners in their sixties. Male/female ratio was almost equal. These were mostly amateur cinephiles, but also some film professionals, film critics: but interestingly, no formal film students. I should note that all these data are from posters, and not lurkers (readers). Forum members saw films both in movie theaters and at home. The ratio between the two was approximately 1/3 to 2/3, favoring home-viewing for nearly all forumites. A few members had DVD players, but most still owned VCRs. Most of them went online both from work and from home, making the EST early evening hours the busiest times on the Forums. Most Forum members had never been a member of a film club, nor did they frequent any other film-related online communities.

One thing most members have in common is that their love for film is often known and found peculiar by their "real-life" acquaintances. It is their love of cinema that has drawn them to these Forums and keeps them together, even though the tastes and interests of forumites are quite diverse. I think this is also the key point in terms of cinephilia, as Kent Jones argues: "whether or not we all agree about Olivier Assayas or Wong Kar-wai is less important than the fact that our respective responses to them are passionate and informed ones. In the end, that's what distinguishes cinephilia from connoisseurship, academicism, or buffery."[17] One of the strongest cornerstones of this community remains the fact that it brings together people not only with a similar love for cinema, but also people who, until the Forums, had been unable to engage in intense discussions on the object of their love, simply because of their geographical location. For the members of the Forums from outside large cities (who amount to at least half of the posters), cyberspace is the only option to exchange opinions. What used to be a minority taste in their local surroundings is no longer minority in the global context, reached via the internet.

Rituals and Experiences

Hamman's third definition of community, as cited above, is: "common ties between themselves and the other members of the group." This is the most significant of the four items. Stephen Doheny-Farina argues that a community is "not something you can easily join," but that "it must be lived."[18] In the case of this online community, the first common bond is the love of cinema, but to take a community further, one needs common experiences and rituals; even more so in a cinephile community, since cinephilia is often closely associated with certain rituals. "Rituals" in this case refer to an everyday usage of the word, suggesting "habits." For instance, Sontag notes the ideal seat for a cinephile has to be "the third row center."[19] In the *New York Times* Forums, these rituals presented themselves on various levels. Although membership has changed somewhat, many of the rituals discussed here are still observable, in the original Forums or in their spin-offs. Firstly, there are the little daily rituals concerning dialogues. Certain members have unique expressions or phrases, which function as a signature. This is most visible when *coniraya* is online, since he has a definitive style with incomplete sentences and deliberate misspellings: "some click world a fantasy. ya knewl that graben between virtu/ and re/ality."[20] This is accompanied by *oilcanboyd*'s exclamation "opps!" whenever he and *coniraya* are simultaneously online. *Oilcanboyd* is also responsible for another ritual, involving Rave-nous, related in the introduction of this article.

On another level, Forum members discuss their film-viewing rituals. There has been a section titled *Personal Experiences*, where forumites shared their memories related to films: for instance, *tirebiter*'s proposing to his wife-to-be at the Wilmette Theater during a screening of Marcel Carné's Les Enfants du Paradis (France: 1945). Frequently, members describe the exact circumstances in which they watched a particular film, mentioning the movie theater, the weather; or if at home, where they got their film from, what they ate before watching it, and what kind of wine they drank while watching it. There are many threads with lists of favorite use of a song in a film, best possible imagined cast for different movies, and many others, similar to the "Top 5" lists so endearingly made in Stephen Frears' HIGH FIDELITY (UK/USA: 2000), a movie about (among other things) the love of records. Many members frequently announce their "Top 10 films of the year so far," demonstrating a near-obsession with making lists, which culminates in the Blanche Awards, coinciding with the Oscars every year. The awards, although laid-back in terms of eligibility (all films that opened in the forumite's country of residence that year qualify), has a fairly strict voting procedure. It involves a two-tiered voting, where nominees are determined by open voting online, and winners by a second round, done via emails sent directly to the volunteering counter. This tradition continues on the Milk Plus blog, where the awards have been renamed Droogies.

Moderation of the Forums, while sometimes limiting the use of certain words, used to be very relaxed in terms of off-topic postings. Although these did get out of hand at times, off-topic postings also provided Forum members with background information about the other forumites, making the exchanges a lot more personal and friendly, a point frequently made in the emails sent to me by the members. Some forumites have met outside the net and/or correspond regularly. There have been occasions that brought members together, when one member became a father, when one opened a bar in Las Vegas, and when one of the much-loved members of the community lost his wife. But possibly the single most important experience has been 9/11, when discussions were focused on one section, and functioned as a roll call to make sure members in New York and Washington were alright. As *pokerface11* said in her email: "I could help by staying on-line, getting updates, helping people through the shock who actually lived in the city."[21] The *New York Times* Opera Forum in fact lost a member in the attacks, and the funeral was attended by some Forum members.

I mentioned earlier that a large percentage of the members come from outside the large cities, where they have limited access to films and opportunities to discuss cinema. This also helps to build strong ties between forumites, since within this group, they are no longer isolated film buffs, but just one of the crowd. If it is any sign of the "film-buffness" of its members, the level of trivia questions thrown about is extremely high. When asked what they find advantageous about the Forums, nearly all of the members regard forming friendships with like-minded people and sharing opinions as their highest priority. Most are also happy with the level of writing, and believe that writing about a film "forces [one] to think about it, and to clarify [one's] response"[22] and that the Forums have offered them "a place to test some of [their] ideas or things that [they] have learned [at school]."[23]

On the cyber-level, the dynamics of the community show strong parallels with those of any offline film group. There are members who get along well with one another, and those who declare their clear dislikes of certain other forumites. Every now and then, some members leave the community, accusing others (who have left) of being too superficial, as in the words of *jeremybroad*: "the likes of *joshuasilver*, *balmung*, *xerxes* and others, who instinctively feel that erudition can only thrive in a dry atmosphere, that because levity and seriousness are near antonyms they are mutually exclusive."[24] There have been those who leave because they find the Forums no longer satisfying, or because their interests take them elsewhere. But the largest number of defectors can now be found at two different newer communities, a communal weblog (blog) called Milk Plus[25] and a forum called The Third Eye Film Community.[26]

Milk Plus and The Third Eye

Milk Plus was founded on 10 March 2002 by *mcbain* (Albert Goins), who wrote:

> Milk Plus: the Korova Milkbar for the intelligentsia. Starting a group of friendly members from the NYT Movie Forum, and adding on from there, we've assembled a collective of valuable contributors for a message board where films can be discussed at length and with both great debate and sympathetic analysis. Cutting out the moronic trolls that plague the NYT Forum as well as the endless white noise chatter, this format will encourage a more fruitful and efficient way for all of us to communicate across the globe on the topics.[27]

The setup of the blog is different from that of a forum. Only members (maximum of 32, now at 26) can post on the main page. These postings are usually longer pieces of criticism on a specific film or a TV series, and sometimes they are festival notes from around the world. On the comments pages, members and non-members can express their opinions about the post. This setup keeps the blog far more focused than the Forums have ever managed to be. In no time, a number of forumites began posting their writing at the blog. These included those who actually wrote film criticism in their offline lives. Membership is limited and by invitation only. The blog introduces its members as "a collective of writers who have come together because we are all opinionated, passionate lovers of film who wish to share with friends and strangers alike." So the essential aim of sharing filmic experiences remains central. Milk Plus takes its name from Stanley Kubrick's A Clockwork Orange (UK: 1971), and the yearly awards given out, in a manner similar to the Blanche Awards, are called The Droogies, after the same film. The site has quickly garnered attention, and was chosen by *Forbes* magazine as the second best movie blog, behind *rottentomatoes. com*, which is hardly a blog, since it collects the reviews of professional film critics and not amateurs. *Forbes* has said:

> The site confers posting privilege on literate and knowledgeable amateur movie critics and gives them space to post reviews, with an emphasis on non-Hollywood fare. The site succeeds in this goal to a considerable extent, allows for lively but serious discussion and provides links to leading professional critics and other film-related sites.[28]

In other words, Milk Plus has managed to step away from the "chatter" of the Forums, and it has been able to produce meaningful discussions on film. This chatter is not a problem specific to the *New York Times*, but is visible in most forum-type communities. It should not come as a surprise that two forumites who have noted that the Forums "have [their] fair share of 'Man, this film sucks,' one-line reviews, they're balanced by longer, more considered, analyses"[29] and that they wished "that the Forum would become more, it's not exactly the right word, but academic"[30] are among the regular contributors for Milk Plus.

Nearly two years after Milk Plus, another group separated from the *New York Times* Forums. This came as a response to the changes in the Forums, which included a tighter moderation in terms of off-topic postings, in addition to a new look and new moderators. For a close community with established rituals, these changes were unacceptable. After debates via private emails, 26 members set out to establish The Third Eye Film Community in May 2004. It is noteworthy that "community" became a part of the title. One of the members supplied the domain, and all have contributed to the cost of a programmer, who set up the site.[31] The Third Eye is closer in its setup to the Forums than it is to Milk Plus. Its members increased quickly, reaching 70 in three months, mostly from the Forums, some are also members of Milk Plus.

Like the *New York Times* Forums, The Third Eye has different topic headings, including Television and Music. Membership is fairly open, but the community is not largely advertised (unlike the *New York Times*), which ensures that membership remains small, and provides a more intimate and casual setting. As Nessim Watson discusses in his analysis of the phish.net fan community, intimacy plays a vital role in sustaining an online community.[32] Members can also send each other private messages if they want to continue their dialogue on a more personal level.

In "real life," there are restrictions in clubs, people are sometimes forced to leave or not admitted at all, and it is somewhat similar online. In the Forums, registration is a fairly simple procedure, open to all. But on occasion, there have been members who were banned. In Milk Plus, however, the "club" is more restrictive. According to the FAQs, "The decision to invite someone to join the blog is based upon merit and compatibility with the other blog members" and one needs the acceptance of at least two of the site administrators to be able to post on the main page. But because there is a tight admittance procedure, people are more open about their offline identities and there have been no problems in terms of having to ban a member.

The *New York Times* Forums continue, with some of the same people. Although former members have been disillusioned, there have been, and will continue to be, new members. And the Forums, although now more strictly moderated, do provide their members with a certain sense of belonging and community. For newer members joining in over the years, these Forums can be a stepping-stone to other online film communities, as they have been for the forumites discussed here.

Conclusion

Home viewing has indeed changed a lot in terms of film viewing practices. I do agree that no home theater can ever give the full experience of viewing a film in a movie theater. But one does not always (and everywhere) have the same access to films the way residents of large Western cities in the 1960s had, as it was glorified by Susan Sontag. So, one can now go and buy or rent videos or DVDs to watch at home. New cinephiles are well aware that home viewing may not offer the best conditions for film viewing, as suggested in this poem by *nilson2001*:

> I think that I shall never see
> A perfect unsmeared DVD
> As I relax at home in my BVDs
> I soak and scrub my DVDs;
> But scrub as I will, it's no matter,
> Still here a freezeframe, there a chatter;
> One night a stutter in PYRAMUS AND THISBE
> In rage I hurl it like a frisbee;
> Then a missing f-word in my CASINO,
> Sends me deep into a bottle of vino;
> And what's this frozen fish frame in JAWS?
> Some video lackey's unclean paws?
> And those missing seconds in SHICHIN NO BUSHI,
> A great pain in this cinephile's tushy![33]

Similarly, one is not always able to find people in his/her close circle of acquaintances to discuss films. With the internet, it has become possible to reach people with a love of cinema all over the world. The fact that the members of these communities cannot always meet each other face-to-face does not make them any less real, especially if the primary goal is to share ideas and opinions about films. And in fact, in this community, as in other online communities, members have managed to meet in person, or at least have contacted each other using other types of communication technologies. As members meet each other and the community becomes more intimate, the nature of the community changes from being "online" to "old-fashioned," and the difference is that now, the community consists of people who may know each other but happen to communicate via the internet. In any case, this cinephile community could not have come into existence and could not be sustained without information technology.

Kent Jones comments on how, in part because of home-viewing practices, we have become "our own islands": "[That is] why we scan the globe and are heartened to recognize something in others that we recognize in ourselves: real love."[34] For cinephiles around the world, the internet is the only place where one can find fellow film lovers. That's why it plays such a crucial role in the undying of cinephilia. As Bryant Frazer argues, "the Internet may well deliver a second century of cinephiles from video-bound solitude." I believe it already has.

Notes

1. *New York Times Film Forums. New York Times.* Edition November 2004. 11 November 2004. <http://forums.nytimes.com/top/opinion/readersopinions/forums/movies/homeviewing/index.html?offset=8780>.

2. In this article "Forum" with a capital letter refers to the *New York Times Forums* specifically, and "forum" refers to the type of online community in general.

3. Sontag, Susan. "The Decay of Cinema." *New York Times,* 25 February 1996: section 6, p. 60.

4. Panayides, Theo. "Permanent Ghosts: Cinephilia in the Age of the Internet and Video, Essay 2." *Senses of Cinema,* no. 4, March 2000. 17 Aug. 2004. <http://www.sensesofcinema.com/contents/00/4/cine2.html>.

5. Martin, Adrian. "Letters From (and To) Some Children of 1960." Rosenbaum, J. (ed.). *Film Quarterly,* fall 1998. 10 February 2002. <http://www.findarticles.com/p/articles/mi_m1070/is_1998_Fall/ai_53258011>.

6. Erickson, Steve. "Permanent Ghosts: Cinephilia in the Age of the Internet and Video, Essay 1." *Senses of Cinema,* no. 4, March 2000. 16 August 2004. <http://www.sensesofcinema.com/contents/00/4/cine1.html>.

7. *Video Search of Miami.* 18 August 2004. <http://www.vsom.com>.

8. Silverman, Jason. "Invasion of the Web Critics." *Wired*, 28 February 2004. 18 August 2004. <http://www.wired.com/news/digiwood/0%2C1412%2C62453%2C00.html>.

9. Frazer, Bryant. "Permanent Ghosts: Cinephilia in the Age of the Internet and Video, Essay 5." *Senses of Cinema*, no. 5. April 2000. 17 August 2004. <http://www.sensesof-cinema.com/contents/00/5/cine5.html>.

10. Jones, Steven G. "Information, Internet and Community: Notes Toward an Under-standing of Community in the Information Age." Jones, Steven (ed.). *Cybersociety 2.0*. Thousand Oaks, CA, London, and New Delhi: Sage Publications, 1998.

11. Rheingold, Howard. "The Virtual Community." Trend, David ed. *Reading Digital Culture*, Malden, MA and Oxford: Blackwell Publishers, 2001. 272-280. p. 272.

12. Schuler, Doug. *New Community Networks*. New York: ACM Press, 1996, p. 9.

13. Wellman, Barry and Milena Gulia. "Virtual Communities as Communities." Smith, Marc A. and Kollock, Peter (eds.). *Communities in Cyberspace*. London and New York: Routledge, 1999, 167-194. p. 187.

14. Hamman, Robin. "Introduction to Virtual Communities Research and Cybersociol-ogy Magazine Issue Two." *Cybersociology Magazine*, no. 2. 20 November 1997. 18 August 2004. <http://www.socio.demon.co.uk/magazine/2/is2intro.html>.

15. *New York Times Film Forums*. <http://forums.nytimes.com/top/opinion/readersopi-nions/forums/movies/indiesandworldcinema/index.html?offset=5280>

16. Osder, Elizabeth (editor of *NY Times* online at the time of the site launch). Email to the author. 23 January 2002.

17. Jones, Kent. "Letters From (and To) Some Children of 1960," J. Rosenbaum (ed.). *Film Quarterly*, Fall 1998. 10 February 2002. <http://www.findarticles.com/p/articles/mi_m1070/is_1998_Fall/ai_53258011>.

18. Doheny-Farina, Stephen. *The Wired Neighborhood*. New Haven: Yale University Press, 1996. p. 37.

19. Sontag, "The Decay of Cinema.".

20. *New York Times Film Forums*. Edition November 2004. 12 November 2004. <http://forums.nytimes.com/top/opinion/readersopinions/forums/movies/homeviewing/index.html?offset=17995>.

21. *pokerface11*. Email to the author. 31 January 2002.

22. *copywright*. Email to the author. 4 February 2002.

23. *shroom*. Email to the author. 12 February 2002.

24. *jeremybroad*. *New York Times Film Forums*. Edition November 2001. 8 November 2001. <http://forums.nytimes.com/webin/WebX?14@60.AUp5aJFFySW^1226029@.f06d782/43144>.

25. *Milk Plus: A Discussion of Film*. <http://milkplus.blogspot.com>.

26. *The Third Eye Film Community.* < http://www.thirdeyefilm.com/phpBB2/index.php >.

27. *Milk Plus Board Policies and FAQs*. 19 August 2004. <http://milkplus.blogspot.com/Board%20Policies%20and%20FAQs.htm>.

28. *Forbes.com*. 19 August 2004. <http://www.forbes.com/2003/09/30/cx_da_movieblogs-slide_2.html?thisSpeed=15000>.

29. *copywright*, idem.

30. *shroom*, idem.

31. Shapiro, Lorne. Email to the author. 6 September 2004.

32. Watson, Nessim. "Why We Argue About Virtual Community: A Case Study of the Phish.Net Fan Community." Jones, Steven G. (ed.) *Virtual Culture*. Thousand Oaks, CA / London / New Delhi: Sage Publications, 1997. pp. 109-110.

33. *New York Times Film Forums*. Edition November 2004. 11 November 2004. <http://forums.nytimes.com/top/opinion/readersopinions/forums/movies/homeviewing/index.html?offset=4355>.

34. Jones, K. "Letters From (and To) Some Children of 1960".

Re-disciplining the Audience

Godard's Rube-Carabinier

Wanda Strauven

In the late 1990s, I toured California in a roofless Jeep. After a long day of "tough" (windy) driving, I ended up, rather accidentally, in the "no-nonsense services town"[1] of Barstow. On the historic Route 66, I took a cheap room in a Best Motel. Fatigued and dazed by the trip, I nestled down on the queen-sized bed and switched on the color TV, one of the motel's amenities. There were probably over 100 channels. And, inevitably, I started zapping. I would prefer to see myself in this specific situation not as a couch potato, but as an active "homo zappens"[2] who is taking control of the multiplicity and the simultaneity of signs (or channels). This is, of course, self-deceit.

While "mindlessly surfing"[3] typical American television (soaps, sports, weather channels, CNN, lots of commercials…), I suddenly stumbled upon something different, something bizarre: it was a sequence of black and white images, in French, with English subtitles. In my zombie mood (or mode) I zapped forward; then, abruptly, I stopped and went back. I had to go back to those images. These were Nouvelle Vague images, there was no doubt about that. I was sure it wasn't Truffaut because it was too surreal. It had to be Godard. Once back in the Old World, I did some research and discovered that it was, indeed, LES CARABINIERS (France: 1963, THE RIFLEMEN).

"To Collect Photographs Is to Collect the World"

I was able to trace back LES CARABINIERS thanks to its picture postcard sequence, which is one of the most remarkable moments of the film. During this 12-minute sequence, the riflemen's wives (and the spectator) get a summary of their war conquests. Because: "To collect photographs is to collect the world," according to Susan Sontag who pays close attention to Godard's film from page one of her collection *On Photography*:

> In … LES CARABINIERS (1963), two sluggish lumpen-peasants are lured into joining the King's Army by the promise that they will be able to loot, rape, kill, or do whatever else they please to the enemy, and get rich. But the suitcase of booty that Michel-Ange and Ulysse triumphantly bring home, years later, to their wives turns out to contain

only picture postcards, hundreds of them, of Monuments, Department Stores, Mammals, Wonders of Nature, Methods of Transport, Works of Art, and other classified treasures from around the globe. Godard's gag vividly parodies the equivocal magic of the photographic image…. Photographs really are experience captured, and the camera is the ideal arm of consciousness in its acquisitive mood.[4]

With the exception of the photo of the sphinx, the riflemen did not take any of these photographs themselves; they just collected them, they did not shoot them. They only shot people. So, talking about the camera as an "ideal arm of consciousness" is, in my opinion, not really appropriate here.

More important is the intertextuality of the cinema that occurs between the different series (or "categories"[5]) of pictures. There is, as Jean-Louis Leutrat and Suzanne Liandrat-Guigues have quite properly observed, a transversal one, i.e., the "*série transversale cinéma.*"[6] For instance, among the mammals we see Felix the Cat (named after the cartoon hero), followed by the dog Rin Tin Tin. The Industry category contains a photo of the Technicolor Laboratories of Hollywood. And in the last category, which constitutes a "*catégorie à part*"[7] (namely women, naked or scantily dressed), there are images of Elizabeth Taylor, Brigitte Bardot, and Martine Carol (in her part as Lola Montès).

The pornographic aspect of this last series is interesting in how it sends us back to two previous moments in the film: first, the photographs of pin-up girls by which Michel-Ange and Ulysse are persuaded to become soldiers in the King's Army and, secondly, the very suggestive undressing and bathing of a lady that closes the sequence of Michel-Ange's first visit to a movie theater. It was this explicit meta-filmic instance, this scene-at-the-movies, that disciplined me in Barstow, but more specifically, it was Michel-Ange's attitude as a simpleton or "country rube"[8] that stopped me from zapping between the channels (pretty much as Hector Mann roused Professor Zimmer from his stupor in *The Book of Illusions*).

In this article, I explore the forces behind this scene-at-the-movies from the 1960s in order to understand why it attracted me in the first place, and why it prevented me from zapping any further. For that purpose, I will make a comparison with the disciplining of the early film audience through the genre of the rube films. Although my analysis focuses on a Nouvelle Vague film, which is an object of traditional (Parisian) cinephile practice, my interest is elsewhere: it's all about how late-night television in the postmodern/postclassical era can help engage us not only with old, forgotten masterpieces but also with the history of (early) cinema, and help us – maybe – to better understand that specific past.

Godard's Ambivalent Homage to Early Cinema

The scene-at-the-movies in Les carabiniers narrates Michel-Ange's first film experience. In other words, Michel-Ange is an immaculate film spectator, and his reaction to the moving image on the screen is comparable to that of the "historical" early cinemagoers; at least if we are to believe what the traditional film history has tried to make us believe.

Michel-Ange gets to see three attractions, which are remakes of respectively Lumière's l'arrivee d'un train (France: 1895, the arrival of a train), Lumière's repas de bebe (France: 1895, feeding the baby) and Méliès's apres le bal, le tub (France: 1897, after the ball, the bath). In terms of pastiche-imitation versus parody-transformation, the first attraction seems, at first glance, more "truthful" to the early cinema style than the other two. However, no passengers are waiting on the platform; in fact, the train does not stop, but passes right through (at high speed). And there is diegetic sound, accompanied with (extradiegetic) piano music. Our rube Michel-Ange tries to protect himself from this filmic danger by crossing his arms in front of his face.

The second attraction is a real subversion of the original: not only has the baby become a toddler, but it also comes with a spoken soundtrack (is this a deliberate metaphor for the cinema who has learned to walk and talk?); further, it contains anachronistic references to fascism (in the father's address to his son) and slapstick comedy (in the action of throwing whipped cream pies), which could lead us to read it as a pastiche in its literal sense (*pasticcio*): a mess. But we could also speculate on Godard's critical or satirical intentions in relation to the crisis of the modern family and consider it as a pre-postmodernist (or pre-postclassical) parody. Michel-Ange's reaction is excessive laughter.

The third and final attraction is, in contrast to the subversive rewriting of Lumière's family scene, a sublime rewriting of Méliès's first nude film, re-titled: le bain de la femme du monde (the society lady's bath). It is sublime not only in its display on the screen (within the screen), but also in its interaction with two kinds of spectators (outside and inside the film). Godard plays with the off-screen concept: to the amusement of the external spectator, Michel-Ange changes seats twice in order to see what is going on beyond the limits of the screen's frame. As in the first attraction, he acts like a typical rube in that he does not understand that the frame is the limit, that there is no beyond. But in a very subtle manner, Godard fools the external spectator because as the society lady starts taking off her gown, the framing is a medium-close-up; when she steps into the bath tub, the camera lifts slightly up; and when she goes down into the water, the camera tilts downward. Whose gaze is this? Who is imposing this gaze, this framing on us? Michel-Ange? Is he too intimidated, too prudish to look at her entire naked body? Very unlikely. I am tempted to think that his vision is less limited than ours, that to his eyes the lady's naked posterior is indeed visible (just as it is in Méliès's APRES LE BAL, LE TUB). Thus, Godard is re-framing the scene for the external spectator!

Only towards the end of LE BAIN DE LA FEMME DU MONDE do we see the actual size of the screen within the screen. Here, the framing is even less restricted than the full shot we have been contemplating from the beginning of the third attrac-tion. There is, of course, no proof that the framing has been fixed/immobile dur-ing the entire scene, but it should have been according to the early cinema tradi-tion (and along the lines of the first and second attractions). Another characteristic of the early ("primitive") cinema is the actress' "to-camera ad-dress,"[9] her direct look into the lens. Combined with the shot-reverse-shot tech-nique of narrative cinema – Godard is re-editing – her gaze becomes ambiva-lent: is she looking at us as external spectators? Or is she looking at the rube? And if so, is her gaze one of complicity, since she knows that he has seen more than we have? The fact is that Michel-Ange interprets her quick look as an in-vitation and climbs on stage to join her in/on the screen.

This entire scene-at-the-movies with its three attractions is a rather complex homage to early cinema. Instead of literally quoting, appropriating, early cine-ma "classics," Godard decides to rewrite them. While the Lumière "documen-tary" tradition is subverted (or even perverted), the Méliès "magical" tradition is displaced onto a level of meta-filmic tricks (who is fooled by whom?). Is Godard inviting us to look differently at early cinema? But why is he then re-establishing the myth of the credulous early cinemagoer that New Film History scholars have been trying to dismantle?[10] Michel-Ange's reaction to the first and the last attraction is clearly stereotypical in the defensive attitude towards the approaching train versus the offensive attitude he has when faced with the naked woman. Or are we being fooled again?

Rubes and Spectatorship(s)

The question is: Did early cinemagoers really duck in their seats for approach-ing trains? Did they really want to touch the actors on the screen? Dai Vaughan has observed that their "prodding of the screen [is] comparable with our own compulsion to reach out and "touch" a hologram."[11] One could add that the "shock moment" they experienced in front of THE ARRIVAL OF A TRAIN is similar to our viewing experience of 3D-movies, horror or special effects (I remember I ducked in my seat more than once watching Spielberg's JURASSIC PARK).

So, what is wrong with the myth of the first *cinématographe* screenings? Why did New Film History have to deconstruct this myth? A major concern was, no doubt, the revaluation (or updating) of the mentality of the early spectators, to point out that they were anything but stupid. André Gaudreault and Germain Lacasse have introduced the notion of the "neo-spectator" to indicate the so-called "virgin" film spectator at the end of the 19th century, in clear distinction with today's film spectator who carries along the cultural baggage of more than 100 years of cinema.[12] Because of this difference in visual memory, our reaction to the "primitive" films differs from the way neo-spectators would have reacted to it.

On the other hand, it is important to keep in mind that these neo-spectators were not entirely (or perfectly) virginal: they had already been initiated by a long series of optical toys – i.e., 19th-century visual memory – into the illusion of movement. I would like to emphasize the word illusion in that they knew (or must have known) that it was an illusion of movement, not actual movement. Tom Gunning goes a step further when he proposes interpreting people's screaming in front of THE ARRIVAL OF A TRAIN as an expression of their will to participate in modern life, to have an "encounter with modernity."[13] This would mean that the early cinemagoers pretended to be credulous, but were in fact incredulous, which characterized them as modern citizens.

This brings us to the difference between the city-dweller and the peasant, which was enhanced, or emblematized, by the genre of the early rube films that appeared around 1900. By displaying the ridiculous attitude of country men at the *cinématographe*, these films were – supposedly – meant to make the (urban) audience conscious of the "look, don't touch" rule. Actually, this specific genre of early cinema created the image of the credulous early cinemagoers! For instance, COUNTRY MAN AND THE CINEMATOGRAPH (UK: Robert W. Paul, 1901) and its remake UNCLE JOSH AT THE MOVING PICTURE SHOW (USA: Edwin S. Porter, 1902) both show the reactions of a country man in front of (the illusion of) an exotic dancer, an approaching train, and a courting couple. In front of the approaching train, the country man's reaction is – like Michel-Ange's – defensive he runs away from the filmic danger. And by the end of the last attraction – at least in Porter's version – the rube tears down the screen, as Michel-Ange does towards the end of LE BAIN DE LA FEMME DU MONDE.

Whereas several scholars have stressed their "didactic nature,"[14] Thomas Elsaesser has suggested reading these early rube films as a form of discipline. Through laughter the spectators were disciplined (rather than educated in cine-literacy), that is, they were prohibited from talking and creating other distractions; their attention was drawn to the screen portraying this stupid country man, and not to the legs of their attractive female neighbor.[15] In other words, these rube films inform us about the attitude of the early (urban) audience that, circa 1900, was very likely getting bored by the endless seriese of approaching trains.

If this is the case, we can only wonder what Godard's scene-at-the-movies in LES CARABINIERS is telling us about the 1960s spectator who, in the meantime, has also become a TV viewer. It seems as if Godard is trying to convince this (new) spectator to go back more often to the movies. With the help of the society lady and the complicity between her and the rube, Godard re-initiates the TV viewers into the experience of cinephilia, telling them that if you go to the movies, you will get to see what the rube sees. You get to see more than you see on TV! By the 1990s, this was no longer true: there was simply too much on TV. But that's probably why I got struck by the colorless, less-is-more images on my color TV in Barstow. Godard's carabinier kept me from zapping. I was disciplined not by laughter (as were the early cinemagoers around 1900) or old-fashioned cinephilia (as were the (French) TV-viewers in the 1960s), but through (film) historical curiosity. I wanted to understand to what degree Michel-Ange's attitude was similar to, or different from, Uncle Josh's. I wanted to understand how postclassical spectators can (still) be disciplined by rubes from the 1960s.

In this particular disciplining process, my historical curiosity was, without doubt, preceded or instigated by tenderness – I was touched by the rube-carabinier and specifically by his tender touching of the society lady on screen. After her inviting glimpse, Michel-Ange jumps on stage and starts caressing her arms very softly, delicately. Even the most obtuse rube should feel from the very first touch that the lady in the bathtub isn't real, that she is just a projected image. So, why does Michel-Ange continue touching her? And why does he try to enter the screen? Or is Godard maybe not telling us anything specific about the spectatorship of the 1960s after all? Maybe this scene-at-the-movie is merely creating the basis for the cinematic apparatus theory?

The Future(s) of Film: TV-Zapping

In 1924, Buster Keaton wonderfully prefigured the principles of the apparatus theory in one of the key scenes in SHERLOCK JUNIOR (USA: Buster Keaton & Roscoe Arbuckle, 1924). Keaton creates an image of the mechanism of film viewing, by means of a "modern" rube as we see projectionist Keaton entering the screen to participate in the drama on-screen. But it is not the body of the projectionist who literally enters the screen, it is his ghost (or double); his real body is asleep. It is merely his dream in which Keaton wants to save his girl from the malicious hands of his rival. Similarly, Michel-Ange might be considered as a double or as the embodiment of the film spectator's desires. It is striking that the other spectators – in the Le Mexico theater Michel-Ange enters, as well as in the theater where Keaton works as a projectionist – do not react. They don't even laugh at the rube, as if he is invisible.

Interesting enough, Keaton's SHERLOCK JUNIOR not only announces the apparatus theory, but the zapping mode as well. The projectionist's double remains within the same frame (TV screen), but the channel changes continuously. This could be interpreted as a new form of discipline (following the discipline through the thrills of the cinema of attractions and the discipline through the laughter in the rube films). Perhaps in the 1920s people were getting so used to the narrative tradition that they needed something like a purely meta-filmic moment, the non-narrative within the narrative. This would lead us to an explanation of the "birth" of experimental cinema as a necessity to entertain spectators who were getting bored by stories.

Whereas Keaton disciplines the 1920s spectators through the art of zapping, Godard's scene-at-the-movies had the exact opposite effect on me in the late 1990s: it *prevented* me from zapping. Like the spectators of the 1960s, I was re-initiated into cinephilia thanks to Michel-Ange's literal, bodily accentuated love for the screen. However, this 1990s cinephilia was not born in some *cinéclub*; it is instead fundamentally linked with my (American) TV experience. Thanks to TV zapping, I rediscovered LES CARABINIERS. It is revealing, then, what Godard actually has to say about television:

> Take away the text and you'll see what's left. In TV nothing is left. When I watch television I watch it on mute. Without the sound you see the gestures, you see the routines of the women journalists and hosts, you see a woman who doesn't show her legs, moves her lips, does the same thing, and occasionally is interrupted by so-called on-the-scene footage. She'll be the same the next day only the text will have changed. So there should only be the text; let's do radio. The more you want change, the more it's the same thing.[16]

Godard's only interest in television is its text. Paradoxically, this is the reason why he watches TV "on mute," as if it is silent cinema where he lets the gestures do the talking. But they don't have anything to say. In opposition to the "silent" images of early cinema, television images are meaningless. Without the sound, Godard says, "nothing is left." This might explain why my senses were struck by the images in LES CARABINIERS. As I was zapping through the immense TV text of meaningless images, I suddenly encountered images with a meaning of their own, images that did not need a text. Although these meaningful images also recur in the spoken scenes of LES CARABINIERS, they certainly reach their peak of "purity" in the two speechless (i.e., without text, not without sound) attractions of the scene-at-the-movies. The scene – let me repeat it once more – that disciplined me in Barstow.

Notes

1. According to the *Michelin Tour Guide*: "Once a 19C stop for miners, pioneers and farmers on the Old Spanish Trail, Barstow is now a no-nonsense service town about midway between Los Angeles and Las Vegas, 60 miles west of Mojave National Preserve. A mecca for outlet-mall shoppers, the former Southern Pacific railway hub still has 24-hr train switching. It also is remembered as a stop (in the 1940s and '50s) on Historic Route 66." *California*, Michelin Travel Publications, 1999, p. 82.

2. Jos de Mul introduced the term "homo zappens" to indicate the Futurist of the 21st century who – thanks to the electronic revolution and the advent of the internet – can simultaneously stay in "multiple virtual worlds" and fully experience Marinetti's concept of "imagination without strings" (or wireless imagination). See <http://www.eur.nl/fw/hyper/Artikelen/imag.htm>.

3. As Paul Auster's character David Zimmer does during six months after his wife and two sons died in an airplane crash, "anchored to [his] usual spot on the sofa, holding a glass of whiskey in one hand and the remote-control gadget in the other" (Auster, Paul. *The Book of Illusions*, London: Faber and Faber, 2003, p. 10). Zimmer remains numb, unfocused, till one night his senses get struck by a clip of Hector Mann who makes him laugh and changes his life (converting him from literature to (new) cinephilia!).

4. Sontag, Susan. *On Photography*, New York: Doubleday, 1977, p. 3.

5. According to Deleuze, Godard's cinema is characterized (or constituted) by "categories," which are always reflective, instead of conclusive. LES CARABINIERS, in its entirety, is a film of categories of war; "[ce] n'est pas un film de plus sur la guerre, pour la magnifier ou pour la dénoncer. Ce qui est très différent, il filme les catégories de la guerre. Or comme dit Godard, ce peut être des choses précises, armées de mer, de terre et d'air, ou bien des "idées précises", occupation, campagne, résistance, ou bien des "sentiments précis", violence, débandade, absence de passion, dérision, désordre, surprise, vide, ou bien des "phénomènes précis", bruit, silence." Deleuze, Gilles. *L'Image-temps*, Paris, Les Editions de Minuit, 1985, p. 243.

6. Leutrat and Liandrat-Guigues. "Le Sphinx." *L'Esprit Créateur*, 30/2 (Summer 1990), p. 87.

7. Ibid., p. 86.

8. See Hansen, Miriam. *Babel and Babylon*, Cambridge: Harvard University Press, 1991, p. 25: "The country rube was a stock character in vaudeville, comic strips, and other popular media, and early films seized upon the encounter of supposedly unsophisticated minds with city life, modern technology, and commercial entertainment as a comic theme and as a way of flaunting the marvels of that new urban world (compare RUBE AND MANDY AT CONEY ISLAND [Porter/Edison, 1903])."

9. With regard to Godard's use of "to-camera address" in general, David Bordwell observes: "This is not simple "reflexivity" (reminding us we're watching a film) but a self-conscious demonstration of the filmmaker's power over the profilmic event, a virtuosic display of the ability to govern what we see". According to Bordwell, Godard "refuses to identify the profilmic with the diegetic." Bordwell, David. *Narration in the Fiction Film*, London: Routledge, 1997, p. 326.

10. I am referring to the new wave of early film scholars that emerged after the 1978 FIAF conference held at Brighton. I am aware of the anachronism: in 1963 Godard is re-establishing a myth that has yet to be dismantled.

11. Vaughan, Dai. "Let There Be Lumière." Elsaesser, Thomas (ed.). *Early Cinema: Space Frame Narrative*, London: British Film Institute, 1990, p. 65.

12. Gaudreault, André, Germain Lacasse. "Premier regard: Les "néo-spectateurs" du Canada français." *Vertigo*, 10 (1993), p. 18.

13. Gunning, Tom. "An Aesthetic of Astonishment: Early Film and the (In)credulous Spectator." Braudy, Leo, Marshall Cohen (eds.). *Film Theory and Criticism*, New York and Oxford: Oxford University Press, 1999, p. 832.

14. Morissette, Isabelle. "Reflexivity in Spectatorship: The Didactic Nature of Early Silent Films." *Offscreen*, July 2002. <http://www.horschamp.qc.ca/new_offscreen/reflexivity.html>. On the "learning process," see also Hansen, op.cit., pp. 25-30.

15. Elsaesser, Thomas. *Filmgeschichte und frühes Kino. Archäologie eines Medienwandels*, München: edition text + kritik, 2002, pp. 71-74.

16. From the interview with Emmanuel Burdeau and Charles Tesson, May 2000. Godard, Jean-Luc. *The Future(s) of Film: Three Interviews 2000/01*, Bern: Verlag Gachnang & Springer, 2002, p. 20.

The Original Is Always Lost

Film History, Copyright Industries and the Problem of Reconstruction

Vinzenz Hediger

Over the last few decades, film archivists and copyright holders of films have become increasingly aware that the film heritage is under threat. Chemical decomposition and archival negligence, often due to lack of funds, eat away at the substance of what is left of the world's film heritage. Accordingly, conservation and reconstruction are the order of the day. In recent years, film archivists have developed the restoration of film into an archival discipline of its own, university programs are devoted to the preservation and presentation of films, entire festivals focus on the programming of restored works of film art, and increasingly such efforts receive funding from media companies who develop a renewed interest in their archival holdings. Supporting and structuring this cluster of activities of preservation and presentation are the twin notions of reconstruction and the original. Even though the notion of the original has recently come under discussion – and this essay will attempt to further contribute to that discussion – there is a general understanding among archivists and the alerted public that the key to the preservation of the film heritage is *the reconstruction the work of film art in its original form and shape*.[1] Few people question that there actually is a need to preserve the film heritage. It is a work of culture, as directors and cinephiles such as Martin Scorsese will tell us, and who would dare to disagree?[2]

However, from the outset, the reconstruction of films has been motivated as much by commercial interests as by cultural interests.[3] In the second half of the last century, and particularly in the last fifteen years, major media companies have embarked on a large-scale operation of exploiting their own archival holdings, an activity that the press, using a metaphor rich in historical references, aptly describes as the "mining of the archives for coin."[4] This process of "mining" the past, of turning the past into a resource, has become one of the major sources of revenue for the large media conglomerates that dominate the global media economy.[5] Clearly, film restoration represents not only a mission, but also a market for specialists in the field of preservation and presentation.

Routinely, however, mission and market clash. I personally learned as much during my research into the US distribution and reception history of Gustav Machaty's Czech *succès à scandale* EXSTASE (distributed in the US as ECSTASY) from 1932. On the occasion of Machaty's 100th birthday in 2001, the film was restored and edited on video by the Filmarchiv Austria in Vienna. We now have a version that can legitimately claim to be called the restored original version. However, if one looks at the production and distribution history of Machaty's film, of which a number of versions exist, one wonders just how useful the notion of the original is in a case like EXSTASE. The production and distribution history of the film in particular suggests that it is quite impossible to locate a single coherent text that could be characterized as the film's "original." But even though the notion of the original may lack a precise referent in this case, calling the restored version the original has its advantages for the film. Much like the notion of the auteur, the notion of the original focuses the attention of the public, the media and other institutions on a particular film or work to which it is attached. Whether it refers to an existing "original" or not, the notion of the original is one of the crucial structuring principles of any artistic heritage, separating what is important from what is not, what deserves to become part of the canon from what does not. Highlighting one film and one version at the expense of another, the notion of the original generates interest, creates visibility and shapes accessibility, even though the underlying choice of version may be questionable from a point of view of film historiography. In cases like this, then, the film historian has to negotiate her desire for philological accuracy with a desire to create visibility for a film. Unavoidably, the result will be a compromise.

Such conflicts are likely to become more frequent in the foreseeable future, particularly since assignments for work on critical DVD editions of films have now become a routine occupation for film historians – for the mining of the archives has turned film historiography into a knowledge industry *sui generis*. This might be as good a time as any, then, to raise a few questions with regard to more recent practices regarding the reconstruction of films, particularly of films that are then made available on DVDs.

In what follows, I will discuss the preservation of film heritage as a cultural practice that has its own history and relies on its own specific, and often tacit, assumptions. Addressing what I consider to be the key assumptions, I will turn my attention to the notions of reconstruction and the original, and in particular to the way that they inform current practices of preservation and presentation. What I propose in this contribution, then, are some thoughts towards a praxeology of preservation and presentation, an outline for an analysis of the current practices of the preservation of the film heritage based on a discussion of their guiding notions.[6] My own guiding notion is that there is no sustained, organized practice without theory, whether explicit or implicit. In cases where the theory of practice is merely implicit, it is the task of the praxeologist to reconstruct the theory, partly from what the practitioners do, and partly from what they say about what they do. In my discussion, I will not go into the technical details of reconstruction. I am neither an archivist nor a specialist in the technique of reconstruction. Instead, I will talk about reconstruction from the point of view of a film historian and a film scholar. In particular, I propose to discuss what you might call the *rhetoric of the original*, i.e., the discursive construction of the notion of the original and the ways in which this notion is used in various contexts: in film archives, in film studies, but also in the marketing of films, one of my areas of specialization. More specifically, I am interested in the notion of the original in so far as it structures and guides film historical research, the practices of reconstruction and the marketing of restored versions of classical films.

I would like to structure my contribution in three parts. First, I would like to briefly analyze what I call *the rhetoric of the original*, i.e., the discursive construction of the original. In particular, I would like to argue that the rhetoric of the original systematically suggests that the original is always already lost, the better to legitimize the need for reconstruction. Second, I would like to show how the rhetoric of the original, particularly in its more recent forms, is intricately linked to the film industry's shift from a cinema industry to a copyright industry. And third, I would like to use the case of Machaty's EXSTASE to discuss the problems and advantages that the notion of the original offers for film historical research.

I

Turner Classic Movies, a cable channel operating in the US and in Europe, advertises its program with a trailer made up of clips from classic movies from the MGM, Warner Bros. and RKO libraries. This trailer, which resembles Chuck Workman's film clip montages for the Academy Awards ceremonies,[7] lists great moments of films and invites the audience to a game of trivial pursuit: Guess that film, guess that star, etc. A somewhat breathless male voice-over reads a commentary that is basically a list of attributes: It's Spencer Tracy vs. Jimmy Stewart, It's the passion of the old south, etc. Closing off this list is the following sentence:

> Turner Classic Movies – It's what film was and can never be again.

First of all, the claim that this *is what film was and can never be again* refers to the films themselves. If you take advertising slogans seriously, you can argue that this slogan expresses a specific attitude towards film history. Generally speaking, this is the attitude of a generation of film historians such as the late William Everson, a generation that believed that all good films were made before 1960, and that most of what has come since has been decadence and decay. An intellectual and emotional twin of this attitude may be found in the hard-dying belief that film art reached its apogee in the silent feature era, and that the introduction of sound destroyed it all. Adding a more philosophical note to this inventory of scenarios of loss and death is Paolo Cherchi Usai's famous claim that cinema is essentially an ephemeral medium, and that every screening contributes to the destruction of the film, and thus to the death of cinema. In fact, so numerous are the companions in mourning of the TCM slogan about what film was and can never be again that one has to start thinking about just what it is in the film medium that prompts so much philosophizing in the "Alas! Too late!" mode.[8]

Apart from making a statement about the program content, the movies, the TCM slogan "it's what film was and can never be again" also makes a claim about the program itself, and about the television medium. The films themselves represent the lost grandeur of classic cinema. This lost grandeur has a present, and a future, however, thanks to cable TV and the programs that feature the films. TV, or rather the *"Medienverbund"* (media cluster) of television and film, the slogan suggests, is a device for the recreation and the reconstruction of the lost grandeur of cinema.

Before drawing a general conclusion from a cursory analysis of an innocent advertising slogan, it is useful to remember what we are dealing with: program advertising for a particular cable TV channel. TCM is of course just one of hundreds of cable channels. But then again, it's not just any channel. Created under the label of TNT, or Turner Network Television, in the 1980s, TCM serves as the outlet for the MGM, Warner Bros. and RKO film libraries. Until 1995, the station and programming were the property of Ted Turner, who acquired MGM/UA and the film libraries in 1986 and merged his company TBS (Turner Broadcasting System) with Time Warner in 1995. TCM and the film libraries now form one of the major assets of Time Warner, one of the seven major media conglomerates.[9] But I will go into that in more detail in the next section.

Given the combined value of TCM's assets, we can safely attribute a certain significance to the station motto. The slogan encapsulates the two key elements of what I propose to call the *rhetoric of the original*. The slogan presents the film as an object that is always already lost, as something that can never again be what it once was. Simultaneously, by a rhetoric sleight of hand, the slogan introduces a technique for the restitution of the lost object, a machine that brings back the irretrievably lost and lends it a new present and a new future. The original, the slogan claims, is always already lost, but we have the authentic copy, the accurate reconstruction, made available through the meeting of television and film.

Film historians working on DVD editions of classic films sometimes use a similar form of rhetoric of the original. A case in point is David Shepard, who has edited numerous American silent films on DVD. "The best silent films," Shepard claims, "possess as much intellectual, emotional and artistic validity as the best dramatic and visual works of any other sort." Talking specifically about his reconstruction of Flaherty's NANOOK OF THE NORTH (USA: 1922) Shepard says: "The first problem was to obtain an authentic text." In other words: First you make sure that the original is quite lost, then you create a search party for the lost original. Shepard goes on to state that the presentation of a silent film on DVD requires "acts of creative interpretation by the DVD production team."[10] To give a more specific idea of what these acts of creative interpretation are, Shepard quotes D.W. Griffith to draw an analogy between his work and that of the projectionist, or rather the film presenter, in the silent movie theatre.

"The projectionist," Griffith says, "is compelled in large measure to redirect the photoplay." As is generally known, films were presented rather than merely shown in silent era feature film theaters. Film were framed by stage numbers and prologues and accompanied with music, sound and light effects. To theater owners and impresarios like S.L. Rothapfel or Sid Grauman, the film text was essentially a pretext for a great shows, and their "redirections of the photoplay" made them quite as famous, if not more famous, than most film directors. It is not a reconstruction of these presentational modes that Shepard has in mind when he talks about "creative interpretation," however. He merely draws an analogy between himself and the likes of Grauman and Rothapfel in order to legitimate his "reinterpretation" of the "authentic text." In fact, Shepard defines himself as a kind of medium, bringing the old film in tune with contemporary audience tastes or, to use the language of the spiritualist tradition, to bring the dead body of the film alive for a contemporary audience, so that it may speak to them. "The transformation of a silent film to DVD is not a pouring of old wine into new bottles, but a transformation of the old film to accommodate a new medium with new audience expectations." This transformation of the old film concerns the version, but first and foremost it concerns the technical aspects of the film. Reconstruction in this sense means giving the film a steady projection speed, the cleaning up of scratches and artifacts, etc. In short, reconstruction means to digitally enhance the film so that it does not look, and feel, old in comparison to a new film.

Like every good medium, Shepard clearly knows his audience. In a recent essay, Barbara Klinger argues that to a large extent, the fan culture of DVD collectors is a fan culture focused on the technical aspects of the medium. The criteria according to which DVD collectors evaluate new editions in internet chat groups and magazines does not concern the films themselves as artistic products. Rather, they focus on features such as image quality, sound and the quantity and quality of bonus material.[11] Much in the same vein, the reconstruction Shepard proposes is not so much a reconstruction as it is an improvement: The true goal of a DVD edition of a silent film is "to transpose the original visual experience for modern eyes rather than to exactly replicate the original material or call attention to the technical processes of restoration."

The restoration, then, is not just a reconstruction but also an improvement. Much like the new theme casinos in Las Vegas that allow you to stroll along the canals of Venice under the summer sun without having to bear the stench of stale water, DVD editions of silent films allow you to watch the film without having to put up with all the interferences that come with an unreconstructed original.[12]

Shepard's argument runs largely along similar lines as that of the TCM slogan. First you confirm that the original is an important, albeit always already lost object. You claim that there exists, or that there used to exist, this important old thing of great "emotional force" and "artistic validity" that merits our attention and all our best efforts to bring it back to life. Unfortunately, the lost object is difficult to retrieve. In fact, it is quite impossible to locate in its original form (it is what film can never be again). Fortunately, however, new media technologies – TV or DVD coupled with film – allow us to bring the original back to life in a new, and improved, version for present and future generations. To sum up Shepard's theory of practice, the transformation of the authentic text into the new and improved original:

> It's what the film never was but can always be again.

Needless to say, the original, the Ur-referent or "authentic text" that the restoration transforms into the DVD's performance of the restored film, is, and remains, lost – for its loss is the enabling principle of the production of the new and improved original.

At this point, one might raise the objection that film historians like Shepard cater to the cable TV and DVD editions markets, and that their practices are a far cry from the serious work of less commercially minded film archivists and film scholars. I would like to address this objection in two ways: First, by briefly analyzing the industrial framework of what I propose to call the rhetoric of the original, and then by discussing a specific case that apparently seems to escape that institutional framework, but in fact does not escape it. As I would like to show, the rhetoric of the original reflected in Shepard's statements is far from marginal. If I suggested that film history is a growth industry of knowledge production at the beginning of this paper, I was also referring to the fact that the film industry increasingly utilizes the knowledge produced by film historians for its own ends and, in fact, depends on this knowledge to an important degree.

II

In the classical Hollywood era, the average commercial life span of a film was two years.[13] A film was first shown in urban first runs for a few days or weeks, was then withdrawn and released to second run houses down the same street a month later, only to continue its slide down the scales of the distribution ladder to end up in rural theaters about two years later. As a rule, there were never more than three hundred prints of one film circulating on the North American film market. To save storage space, the prints were destroyed once the film's run was over. In the silent feature era, and sometimes even later, the negative was destroyed along with the print. This helps to explain why no more than 25 percent of the entire silent film production survives in archives today. Studios destroyed the negatives because old films were of no value to them. Once the films had lost their novelty value, they only took up storage space. More valuable than the film itself was the screenplay, which could be remade under a different title after seven to ten years.

Of course, there were exceptions. In 1925, Pathé paid half a million dollars for the reissue rights to four Chaplin comedies from 1917 (A DOG'S LIFE, SHOULDER ARMS, A DAY'S PLEASURE and SUNNYSIDE). The films were bought for theatrical re-release, but in all probability also for circulation in the Pathé 9.5 mm home movie format, the earliest ancillary market for theatrical films.[14] According to the press release, the sum of $500,000 dollars was exactly the same that First National had originally paid for the films eight years earlier.[15] This transaction was of course an advertising stunt, at least partly. To pay less would have been to suggest that the films had actually lost some of their value. On the other hand, the procedure was rather unusual. Chaplin was one of a very small group of film artists whose work exceeded the two-year life span of the average Hollywood film; Walt Disney would be another important example. But as a statement, the half million that Pathé paid went further: The sum signaled that Chaplin films, in an industry whose products depreciated in value very rapidly, were still worth the same after eight years and would probably even increase in value over time, an unmistakable sign of Chaplin's truly exceptional status within the industry in the classical era.

Under the current conditions of film marketing, every film is a Chaplin film, at least potentially in terms of its commercial life span. If the commercial life span in the classical era was two years, it has been next to infinite for some time now. A film is first shown in theatres, with up to ten thousand prints worldwide rather than the few dozens of in the classic era. Next the film is shown on cable TV, then it is edited onto video and DVD, etc. Douglas Gomery points out that the current system of film distribution replicates the runs-and-zones system of classical film distribution, albeit under the inclusion of TV, cable, and other new media as outlets for theatrical films. Also, film prints are still routinely destroyed after the theatrical run of a film is over. What has changed is the value of the film negative. Once a film appears on the home video market, there are basically no time limits to its availability, nor are there apparently time limits to the audience's willingness to watch, and pay for, old films. The extension of the commercial life span of films began with the television broadcasts of old films in the 1950s and 1960s, but it took on a new dimension with the introduction of home video in the early 1980s. Theatre revenues now only account for about 25 percent of the total income that an average film generates; more than 50 percent comes from home video and DVD. The infinite extension of the commercial life span covers not only new films, however, but classic films as well. This is what gives film libraries their value. Film libraries, comprised of both classic and more recent films, generate a steady revenue stream for the major studios that not only significantly improves the overall performance of today's film-driven conglomerates, but also serves to offset many of the financial risks involved in the production of new films. As early as 1957, an MGM executive stated in an interview that "the real fat of this business is in film libraries"[16] and since then, industry analysts have repeatedly claimed that "in the volatile entertainment business, a film library is one of the few things a company can count on," assessing that "despite technological changes, what is going to be delivered in these systems is the movie… it will survive any technological upheaval."[17] In fact, in one recent statement an analyst claimed that "a film library is a one-of-a-kind asset. Most assets depreciate over time, but not film assets," citing Universal's extensive film library and the steady revenue the library guarantees under current business conditions as General Electric's primary motivation for buying Universal from Vivendi and entering the film business after decades of abstinence and hesitation.[18]

The extension of the commercial life span of films is a crucial element of a larger development that is best characterized as the film industry's shift from a theater or cinema industry to a copyright industry. In the classical era, the industry's main investment was in real estate. As Richard Maltby points out, of a total of 2 billion dollars in assets that the film industry controlled in 1940, 94 percent were invested in real estate and only 5 percent went into film production.[19] The economic well-being of the major film producers rested on their control of distribution and, most importantly, of the large theaters. In that sense, the film industry was a cinema industry. After the Paramount decree in the late 1940s and early 1950s, the studios shifted their focus from the control of the market through real estate to control of the market through the copyrights of the films they produced. As a result, the blockbuster film, a brand product that promises revenues in a whole string of subsidiary markets, emerged as the new paradigm of film production and distribution, and film marketing consolidated into an activity of intensive and long-term exploitation of the copyright for artistic products. Quite naturally, as part of this shift from a cinema to a copyright industry, the studios also increasingly focused on the revenue they could generate by marketing old films to which they owned the copyrights.

The shift from a cinema to a copyright industry matters to film historians in that the market for classic movies is also a market for the knowledge they produce. In the 1950s and 1960s, classic films were considered fillers in between television programs. Now they are marketed as valuable works of art and collectibles. This is particularly apparent with DVDs. When the DVD was first introduced, the studios tried to market films on DVD the way they had marketed them on VHS – a few trailers announcing coming releases, and then the film. This strategy ran into trouble not least because many of the early buyers of DVDs were collectors who had previously collected films on laser discs. Essentially a cinephile collector's format, the laser disc had emerged in the early 1990s as a site of careful editorial work, with laser disc editions often containing interviews with the filmmakers, photo galleries and other additional material of interest to the film buff. Used to the editorial standards of the laser disc, early DVD buyers began to warn each other against the poor DVD editions in internet chat groups and collector's magazines, thus forcing the distributors to adopt the editorial standards of the laser disc to the DVD. As a result no DVD edition is now complete without a certain philological apparatus.

With the introduction of the DVD, then, the consumer demands of an apparent minority of historically minded cinephiles became the standard for mainstream film editions. As an academic film scholar, you are frequently asked for which careers you train your students. The emergence of the DVD collector culture has made this question easier to answer. In a world where production anecdotes about Tim Burton's ED WOOD, a film produced in 1994, can appear as journalistic news content alongside current box office figures on CNN's entertainment website on the occasion of the film's DVD release in October 2004, film students clearly have a prospect of a career digging up nuggets of film historical knowledge for the audio commentaries, making-of films and press releases that now surround the DVD release of a film. There will always be more need for lawyers in the entertainment industry in the foreseeable future, and they will always be making more money than film historians, but the market for historians is definitely growing.

In this market of reconstruction and collector's editions, the notion of the original plays a decisive role in shaping the accessibility and driving the circulation of old films. The rhetoric of the original suggests that we are dealing with an important object, one that is all the more precious because it is always already lost and can only be retrieved in a new and improved original form through the use of new media technologies. Incidentally, the mere fact that these technologies are used to retrieve and reconstruct, or transform, the lost original confers an aura of importance on the film.

The rhetoric of the original thus contributes to the formation of canons and helps to differentiate the DVD product at the same time. The rhetoric of the original determines what is important, and what is important deserves to be bought.

As a marketing tool, the notion of the original is particularly efficient when it is coupled with the notion of the auteur. Far from signaling a director's position as an outsider at the margins of the system of film production, the notion of the auteur has been an operational concept of mainstream film production for some time now. Witness the current standard contract of the director's guild that stipulates that the director's name has to appear in a standardized "A XY [name of the director] film" formula in the credits. Even in Hollywood, the director is now officially the auteur of the film.

In film marketing, however, the old oppositional notion of the auteur as an artist whose authentic expression is obstructed by the crass commercialism of the system still prevails. Nowhere is this more evident than in the notion of the "director's cut." Turning the formerly oppositional notion of the auteur into a marketing device, the "director's cut" strikingly illustrates what some theorists see as capitalism's capacity to absorb its own contradictions in a productive way. An obvious case of *"Nachträglichkeit,"* of deferred action in the Freudian sense, the director's cut is the original that *truly* never was, the original that the director was never allowed to create due to pressures from the evil forces atop the studio hierarchy but that has now unexpectedly, but also somehow of necessity, come into being. Promising the revelation of the truth about a loved object heretofore not adequately known (and thus, not sufficiently loved), the label "director's cut" creates a strong incentive for the prospective buyer, but it also has its consequences for film historiography and the perception of film history. Film students now perceive the latest authenticated version as the true original, as in the case of Francis Ford Coppola and his Apocalypse Now Redux (USA: 1979/2001), for instance. Thus the deferred action of the director's cut rewrites, or overwrites, film history, turning previous originals into palimpsests.

But if the rhetoric of the original creates an interface between film marketing and film historiography, how does this affect the work of the film historian and the work of film reconstruction? This is what I would like to discuss in the last part of my contribution.

III

Let me clarify one point right way: I am not interested in unveiling and accusing the perpetrators of the supposed errors and fakes committed in the name of making historical films available and amenable "for modern eyes," to quote David Shepard once again. I will, in other words, not defend the true original against the rhetoric of the original, for, as I have argued, the truth of that rhetoric lies in its claim that the original is indeed always already lost. Rather, the question is what to do about the lost original, or about the loss of the original: Mend it, mourn it, or just forget about it? In order to answer this question, I would like to return to my discussion of Machaty's film EXSTASE.

On the occasion of the 100th birthday of Gustav Machaty, a series of events were organized in the director's honor in Vienna. Among those events was the presentation of a reconstruction of the original version of Machaty's EXSTASE. Events of this kind help to structure cultural memory. A birthday is an excellent opportunity to confer the status of auteur onto someone who should be in the canon but has not yet made it there, or to reconfirm the status of someone who already belongs to the canon. Journalists working for the culture pages have a name for this: they call it "calendar journalism": Anniversaries set the agenda, and the importance of the person in question can be measured fairly exactly by the number of lines alloted to the article in his or her honor.

For the restoration of the Machaty film, the Czech version was chosen as the one to be presented under the rubric of the "original version" on video. This makes good sense according to the criteria of the established film historiography, which tends to map film cultures according to the national origin of the films' directors. In fact, EXSTASE was shot in Prague by a Czech director, and there was a Czech language version.

My own contribution to the Machaty festivities was a brief study of the North American reception of EXSTASE.[20] EXSTASE was Hedy Kiesler's/Hedy Lamarr's third film and the one that made her famous. She played a young, unhappily married woman, who falls in love and runs away with a railway engineer. Unusual for the time, the star is seen naked in several scenes. Also, there is a close-up of her face at the moment of orgasm. Finally, the heroine escapes without punishment this sent tempers flaring in Europe and particularly in some ports of the US when Samuel Cummings, an independent distributor specializing in "art" (read: soft-core porn) films, tried to release the film in New York and other major cities. EXSTASE is a typical case of a multi-language version production from the early years of sound film.[21] The film was shot in German, Czech, and French language versions. The first American version, released in 1936, is based on the German and Czech versions. It contains a number of double exposures missing from the European versions that create redundancy and help to make the narrative more explicit. Also, the American soundtrack contains theme songs specifically composed for the American release. As could be expected, due to its explicit sexual content the film had a difficult distribution history in the US and elsewhere; "It would never get past the censor," *Variety* wrote in its original review of the French version in 1933.[22] From state to state, distribution copies varied in length and content. In New York, for instance, the film was not released to theaters until 1940, when it came out in a significantly altered form. The film was now told in a flashback structure that was added by distributor Cummings, who listed himself as the screenwriter in the film's credits. Even more interesting with regard to the problem of the original version is the fact that the film's director, Gustav Machaty, apparently authorized each and every version he was asked to authorize by distributors, up to and including Cummings' creative reinterpretation (or should we say: transformation) of his film from 1940. Another interesting feature is the ending of the 1936 version, which contains landscape shots that do not appear in the European versions, but were obviously shot by the same camera team.

In the case of Exstase, the proliferation of different versions can largely be attributed to the intervention of censorship. Nonetheless, the fact that there are so many different versions raises interesting questions with regard to the notion of the original. Various narratives offer themselves to implement the rhetoric of the original in this case. Probably the most obvious of those narratives runs as follows: Censorship is the enemy of the artist; by reconstructing the uncensored original version, the film historian helps the artist to recover his original artistic vision. This is the narrative underlying, and justifying, the anniversary edition of the film. The problem, however, is that Machaty the artist personally authorized a number of censored versions of the film. Reconstructing the uncensored original in this case means defending the artist against himself. In fact, choosing one version as the only true original means to deprive the auteur, in the name of a higher interest, be it the building of a canon or be they commercial interests, of his right to determine which is the original version. In the case of Exstase, then, the rhetoric of the original eliminates and excludes from the canon a number of versions that, according to the rhetoric's own criteria, qualify as the original version as well.

Another possible narrative for the history of the different versions of Ex-stase/Ecstasy is a more Foucauldian one. According to this narrative, censorship could be understood as a productive, not a prohibitive force. By implication, then, the corpus of the original should include all the versions produced by the various interventions of censorship. One argument in favor of such a reading is the fact that the first American version contains material that was obviously produced by the same crew as the rest of the film but is not in the European versions. How do we explain the existence of this material and its inclusion in the American version? Clearly, it would be naive to assume that the producers of a film that went completely against the standards of decency then current in film production were taken by surprise by the reaction of the censors in the various countries to which they sold the film. In all likelihood, they anticipated such a reaction. Accordingly, it seems plausible to assume that they planned the film rather as a set of components rather than as a single coherent, "authentic" text. Not only were different language versions produced. The producers probably also shot additional material to allow distributors to create versions that would pacify the censors and allow the film to pass. Accordingly, the interventions of the censorship authorities represent not so much infractions of the artistic liberty of the author/director. Rather, censorship constitutes the last step in post-production and delivers the matrices for the film's completion.

From such a perspective, there can be no single original *text*. Instead, it seems useful to think of the original as a *set of practices*, a set of practices employed in the production and circulation of films. According to such a perspective, the original still must be given as lost. Divided up into a set of practices, the original is even more thoroughly lost than even the rhetoric of the original would allow it, at least as long as one holds onto an ideal of totality and replaces the search for the single true original text with a search for the totality of all the practices that constitute the original as a set of practices. Historical research must always come to terms with the single fact that a complete set of facts does not exist. A film historiography that defines the original as a set of practices would have to take this limitation into account.

Now you will probably object, and claim that it is impossible to represent an original in this sense as a film: Indeed, a set of practices is not a single film, but may include a whole bundle of "original" versions. My answer to that would be that the DVD offers just the medium that we need for a historiography of the original understood as a set of practices. The new medium, which is so well suited to the needs of the rhetoric of the original, may also be used to accommodate the approach that I propose. A DVD has the storage capacity and the navigational tools you need to represent an original as a set of practices and to re-present even the most unstoppable proliferation of original versions, even that of Ecstasy.

It remains to be seen whether the DVD will be used in such a way. One has to keep in mind that archival mining is an industrial occupation, as the mining metaphor indicates. It is part of what Bernard Stiegler calls the ongoing "industrialization of memory," and industrial production has its own laws. However, the main resource that archival mining draws on, other than the films themselves, is the cinephilia of the audience. In an age of niche markets, we cannot totally exclude the emergence of a significant audience perverse enough to care for dispersed sets of practices rather than for new and improved originals. Be prepared, then, for a rhetoric of the open series of multiple versions to supplement, if not supplant, the rhetoric of the original in a perhaps not too distant future.

Notes

1. Clearly, no one in his right mind would think that the way to preserve the film heritage is to cut up all archival holdings and recombine the material in interesting new ways – even though such procedures have been applied before in the domain of art: significant parts of the religious architectural heritage of France were reused as building blocks in public and private buildings after the French Revolution (a case in point is the Cluny cathedral in Burgundy, once a church larger than St. Peter's in Rome, of which now only fragments survive).

2. In their standard work *Restoration of Motion Picture Film*, Oxford et al.: Butterworth Heinemann, Paul Read, and Mark-Paul Meyer discuss the question "Why film restoration?" on page 2 in their introduction. As an answer to that question, they state that "In general it is possible to say that in the past ten years there has been a growing awareness of the urgency to restore films before they are lost completely." What remains to be explained for the historian of film culture, however, is why there is such a growing awareness.

3. In fact, systematic preservation of films from major studio archives started in the mid-seventies when Twentieth Century Fox began to transfer its nitrate prints to newer supports. Cf. "Fox Converts Nitrate Film Library." *Daily Variety,* 14 November 1983.

4. One example may be found in an recent article on film libraries in the *Los Angeles Times*: "Studios in recent years have mined billions of dollars by releasing movies on digital videodiscs.... Home video divisions have become studio workhorses." Cf. "Vault Holds Vivendi Reel Value." *Los Angeles Times,* 26 August 2003.

5. Incidentally, Louis Chesler, a Canadian entrepreneur who bought the rights to Warner Bros. pre-1948 films for $21 million in 1956, thus initiating a series of similar sales by other major studios and establishing the film library as an important source of revenue for film companies, was a mining engineer by training, Cf. "Warners Film Library Sold." *Motion Picture Herald,* 202/10, 10 March 1956, p. 14.

6. I am taking my cue here from the history and sociology of science and the work of authors such as Ian Hacking and Bruno Latour, and from historians and ethnographers such as Jean-François Bayart. To test the viability of the praxeological approach would request a significantly more comprehensive analysis of actual archival practices and the accompanying theoretical debates it that I can undertake in the short space of this essay.

7. For a critical discussion of the Workman montages see Lisa Kernan: "Hollywood auf einem Stecknadelkopf. Oscar-Verleihungen und die Vermarktung von Filmgeschichte." Hediger, Vinzenz, Patrick Vonderau (eds.). *Demnächst in ihrem Kino.*

Grundlagen der Filmwerbung und Filmvermarktung, Marburg: Schüren, 2005, pp. 161-174.

8.   John Durham Peters argues that "all mediated communication is in a sense communication with the dead, insofar as media can store "phantasms of the living" for playback after bodily death." In that sense, cinephilia is always already tinged with a streak of necrophilia. Witness Bazin's illustration of his essay on the ontology of the film image with the imprint of Christ on the Turin funeral cloth. Cf. Peters, John Durham. *Speaking into the Air: A History of the Idea of Communication*, Chicago: Chicago University Press, 1999, p. 142.

9.   Murphy, A.D. "Warner Bros. Library Home after 40 Years in Wilderness." *Hollywood Reporter*, 25 September 1995.

10. Shepard, David. "Silent Film in the Digital Age." Loiperdinger, Martin (ed.). *Celluloid Goes Digital: Historical-Critical Editions of Films on DVD and the Internet*, Trier: Wissenschaftlicher Verlag, 2003, p. 23.

11. Klinger, Barbara. "The Contemporary Cinephile. Film Collecting in the Post-Video Era." Maltby, Richard, Melvin Stokes (eds.). *Hollywood Spectatorship: Changing Perceptions of Cinema Audiences*, London: BFI, 2001, pp. 132-151.

12. The practices of viewing "improved" old films should make for an interesting comparison with contemporary tourist practices. As David Nye points out in a discussion of tourists visiting the Grand Canyon, "[t]heir characteristic questions, recorded by park staff, assume that human beings either dug out the Canyon or that they ought to improve it, so that it might be viewed more quickly and easily....The contemporary tourist, viewing the landscape, thinks in terms of speed and immediacy: the strongest possible experience in a minimum of time." Nye, David S. *Narratives and Spaces: Technology and the Construction of American Culture*, New York: Columbia University Press, 1997, p. 22.

13. For the following analysis of distribution practices, see also my "'You Haven't Seen it Unless You Have Seen It At Least Twice': Film Spectatorship and the Discipline of Repeat Viewing.": *Cinema & Cie*, 5 (Fall 2004), pp. 24-42.

14. For a history of Pathé's home movie formats cf. Pinel, Vincent. "Le salon, la chambre d'enfant et la salle de village: les formats Pathé." *Pathé. Premier empire du cinéma*, Paris: Editions du Centre Pompidou, 1994, pp. 196-217.

15. "Chaplin Reissues Bought by Pathé for Half Million." *Exhibitors Herald*, 23/3, 10 October 1925, p. 30.

16. Prayor, Thomas. "Professional Estimate." *New York Times*, 13 January 1957.

17. "Analysts Bullish on Pic Libraries." *Daily Variety*, 15 August 1991.

18. Cf. Footnote 4.

19. Maltby, Richard. *Hollywood Cinema*, Oxford: Blackwell, 1995, p. 60.

20. Cf. my "'The Ecstasy of Physical Relations and Not Normal Marriage.' Gustav Machatys *Ecstasy* in den USA," Cargnelli, Christian (ed.). *Gustav Machaty*, Wien: Synema, 2005.

21. For the most up-to-date research on multiple-language versions, cf. *Cinema & Cie*, 4 (spring 2004), a special issue devoted to the topic edited by Nataša Ďurovičová.

22. "Review of Exstase" *Variety*, 110/4, 11 April, 1933, p. 20.

III

Techniques of Cinephilia

Bootlegging and Sampling

The Future of Anachronism

Todd Haynes and the Magnificent Andersons

Elena Gorfinkel

> Speaking nostalgically, it is our grandfathers and grandmothers in general
> that we regret, not just their aesthetic response and opportunities to enjoy a
> perished art of the theater, but also their clothes, their relative moral simpli-
> city, and above all the dignity, along with charming quaintness, which their
> traditional images can inspire in our feelings.
>
> Parker Tyler, "On the Cult of Displaced Laughter"[1]

Parker Tyler's early treatise on the retrospective pleasures of cinematic artifacts,
despite its having been written close to 46 years ago, reflects some of the "retro"
stylistic tendencies in the recent work of American independent filmmakers,
Todd Haynes' FAR FROM HEAVEN (USA: 2002), Paul Thomas Anderson's BOO-
GIE NIGHTS (USA: 1997) and Wes Anderson's THE ROYAL TENENBAUMS (USA:
2001). For these directors, the "anachronistic" become, subjected to different
aesthetic and narrative strategies, in which reference to "outdated" historical
periods and objects invites spectators to engage affectively, though not necessarily uncritically, with history. The work of these American art-house auteurs has
been spoken of both in terms of a "new sincerity" within vernacular criticism,
but also in terms of irony, parody, and pastiche. Jeffrey Sconce, discussing the
etiology of the "smart film" of the 1990s, suggests that these filmmakers,
through their static tableaus and deadpan presentation, "render the uncomfortable and unspeakable through acute blankness."[2] Although seemingly redolent
with such examples of blankness and ironic distance, it will be argued here that
the films and the way in which they position the viewer, are actually invested in
imagining an audience from the past, in a desire to reinstate a more earnest
mode of film reception. Employing a *film historical imaginary*, these directors'
aesthetics capitalize on the visibility of anachronism as a means of highlighting
the pathos of historical difference. The poignancy of the irrecoverable gap between past and present – between the 1950s, the 1970s and today, and between
childhood and adulthood – becomes the subject of these films.

Negotiating cinephile attachments through a re-working of Hollywood's
codes of representation, the films under discussion – FAR FROM HEAVEN, BOOGIE
NIGHTS, and THE ROYAL TENENBAUMS – point to a particular historical, historiographic, and "retro" sensibility that diverges from the concerns of historical

authenticity or veracity ascribed to the traditional "period film." Although the three filmmakers are unique in their own respective ways, their films are illustrative of tendencies within American independent cinema towards a flurry of recycles, remakes, and period films set in the recent history of the 1970s and 1980s – in films such as THE WEDDING SINGER (USA: Frank Coraci, 1998), 54 (USA: Mark Christopher, 1998), LAST DAYS OF DISCO (USA: Whit Stillman, 1998), 200 CIGARETTES (USA: Risa Bramon Garcia, 1998), ALMOST FAMOUS (USA: Cameron Crowe, 2000), SUMMER OF SAM (USA: Spike Lee, 1998), to name a few. Furthermore, the release of the films DOWN WITH LOVE (USA: Peyton Reed, 2003), NAPOLEON DYNAMITE (USA: Jared Hess, 2004), AUTO FOCUS (USA: Paul Schrader, 2002), THE MAN WHO WASN'T THERE (USA: Joel and Ethan Coen, 2001), O BROTHER WHERE ART THOU? (USA: Joel and Ethan Coen, 2000) and PLEASANTVILLE (USA: Gary Ross, 1998) attests to a renewed and re-mediated filmmaking practice that creatively uses the film historical past.

Anachronism After Allusionism

Yet the "filmmaker as practicing cinephile" is, in itself, not a new phenomenon, but one that spans back to the emergence of cineaste culture in the 1960s, in Europe and the United States. Noël Carroll, in his essay on the uses of allusion in films of the 1970s, analyzes the penchant for the citation and appropriation of styles, themes, devices and genres from film history in the work of New Hollywood directors such as Brian DePalma, Robert Altman, Francis Ford Coppola, and Steven Spielberg. Carroll suggests that by the early 1980s, allusion had become a full-blown aesthetic sensibility in the Hollywood cinema. This expressive predilection for quotation and memorialization was, for Carroll, a result of the particular mélange of historical forces which defined American cinema in the 1960s: the conditions of film industrial reorganization, the flowering of a vibrant and literate film culture which claimed motion pictures as an art form rather than mass entertainment, the emergence of the auteur theory as a hermeneutic tool in the United States, and the cineaste education of young filmmakers at film schools. Out of this context could emerge Lawrence Kasdan's BODY HEAT (USA: 1981), as Carroll remarks,

> It's an old story. Or, to be more exact, it's an old movie – shades of THE POSTMAN ALWAYS RINGS TWICE (USA: 1946) and DOUBLE INDEMNITY (USA: 1944). And yet of course it's a new movie…. Nor does BODY HEAT merely rework an old plot. It tries to evoke the old films, films of the forties that the plot was a part of. BODY HEAT's costumes are contemporary, but of a nostalgic variety that lets us – no, asks us – to see the film as a shifting figure, shifting between past and present…. We understand

BODY HEAT's plot complications because we know its sources – in fact, because through its heavy handed allusions, we've been told its sources. Without this knowledge, without these references, would BODY HEAT make much sense?[3]

It is particularly in the use of allusion to create a bridge between the past and the present through the act of reworking and restaging film history, that it becomes evident that Haynes, P.T. Anderson, and Wes Anderson are heirs to the appropriative tradition which Carroll diagrams in his essay, and that Fredric Jameson would one year later come to term, within a rather different exegetic context, the "nostalgia film."[4] And it is hardly surprising that the work of the 1970s "movie brats" has been incorporated and itself quoted by the new breed of young directors, in a feat of historical and generational assimilation. Altman, Scorsese, DePalma, Coppola and others appear as guiding presences in the work of these independent directors now operating on the edges of mainstream Hollywood.

But while there is indeed a use of allusion in the work of the younger 1990s group, it seems necessary to understand how the films of Haynes and the Andersons move beyond the recycling devices of 1970s New Hollywood. Rather than a seamless allusion which showcases professional virtuosity and technical skill, which Carroll claims was an industrial impetus for the 1970s directors,[5] Haynes and the Andersons utilize allusion, but also eclipse it, in their preference for a kind of overt aesthetic and temporal disjunction, creating an intended rift within the constitutive aspects of their filmic worlds. The viewer always inevitably becomes aware of his or her own position, caught between different periods, in a region of illegible temporality and mobile film historical space.

In all three cases, these films are *about* anachronism as much as they *use* anachronism as an aesthetic resource. Haynes and the Andersons employ overtly "outmoded" or obsolete elements within their mise-en-scène and narrative. In FAR FROM HEAVEN, it is a simulation of 1950s melodrama, with oversaturated jewel tones coordinated among décor, costume, props and lighting, hyperbolically blowing autumn leaves, windswept scarves, and the stock small talk of the petty middle class. BOOGIE NIGHTS showcases the delusionally cheery and naïve milieu of late 1970s Californian pornography. The film overlaps the leftover traces of the sexual revolution with the insurgent beats of disco, the texture of shag rugs, sparkling swimming pools, cocaine parties and rollerskates. In THE ROYAL TENENBAUMS, the Tenenbaums appear as a throwback storybook clan of the J.D. Salinger, John Irving, and Charles Addams variety in a mythically timeless New York. Their discordant family genealogy is mapped by each anomalous member, each an anachronism unto him- or herself: Richie the tennis champion, Chas the real estate and accounting whiz, Margot the award-winning teen playwright, Etheline the archaeologist, Raleigh the neurotic neurologist, Eli the drug-addicted cowboy novelist, and Royal the brashly acerbic, absentee patriarch and disbarred litigator. The film's references escape their origin, alluding to its cinematic influences – from Orson Welles to Woody Allen – yet simultaneously creating a resoundingly literary narrative universe. In their renegotiation of generic expectations – particularly melodrama - these filmmakers demand an affectionate return to historical objects or moments, through the artifacts, images and sounds of the 1950s, 1960s and 1970s.

Like allusionism, anachronism is prone to a measure of taxonomy, and here in order to make sense of the usefulness of the concept in thinking about Haynes, P.T Anderson, and Wes Anderson, we should pause to assess some historical approaches to the subject. Within a contemporary vernacular and in its commonplace meaning, to mark something, a cultural object or figure, as anachronistic is to suggest that it is out of place, misplaced from another time. It is often seen as a slight – anachronism is after all understood as a type of mistake in the practice of historical representation.[6] Varieties of anachronism and their classification in history and literature abound; they have been divided according to their level of historical veracity, iterative intention, and textual result.

Within literary history, scholar Thomas Greene organizes five types of anachronism according to both level of authorial intent in the making of the mistakes and their textual result. For Greene, a "naïve" anachronism claims no access to control of the history in question, an "abusive" anachronism involves a refusal to engage historically, a "serendipitous" anachronism entails well meaning mistakes but those which are nonetheless beneficial, a "creative" anachronism is transgressive, historically loyal and has cultural/political goals, and a "pathetic/tragic" anachronism is defined by an estrangement from history, which is mired in decline.[7]

Greene ascribes to the anachronism moral, behavioral and characterological descriptions. The anachronist takes on a relation to "proper" history, a relationship which must either be excused, justified or condemned. Considerations of anachronistic elements in cinema have become common in the past twenty five years of scholarship on history in, and of, cinema, as the disciplines of history and film studies have long debated the accuracy of historical representations in popular films. However, assessments of facticity and the burdens of filming history are less pertinent here than a concern with the ways in which anachronism as a concept and mode of aesthetic recognition becomes a direct means of dialoguing with popular cultural memories of the historical past. There is both a historicist and fabulist strain in the creative marshalling of anachronism in these works, one which hinges on sly misuses and creative revisions of historical and film historical referents.

Implausible and Impossible: Revising 1950s Melodrama

Todd Haynes' FAR FROM HEAVEN, perhaps the most "loyal" adaptation of a historical period as pictured and remembered within a film historical genre, continues the project of historiographic fiction pursued in his earlier film VELVET GOLDMINE (USA: 1998). The latter film, in its fictionalization of 1970s glam rock, attests to the director's interest in both past eras of popular cultural production, and the connotative associations these moments call up for spectators. But what makes FAR FROM HEAVEN anachronistic can be read on two registers, first in terms of its much discussed adaptation of and homage to Douglas Sirk's melodramas of the 1950s. On this level, the film appears as though it is a time machine, shuttling us backwards in time from the present into the social and aesthetic conditions of studio Hollywood in the 1950s. On the second register, FAR FROM HEAVEN engages cinephile knowledge, positioned as a contemporary allegory of race, sexuality, and the social regulation of the private sphere. The pleasure of the film rests in the retrospective knowledge that the viewer holds, and in an acknowledgment of the violation the anachronistic text enacts on its classical Hollywood forebears.

Haynes diverts his film from pure remake into "creative anachronism," infusing concerns of race, homosexuality and female agency into the saturated visual frame of 1950s melodrama. The film presents a narrative of marital decline, motored by the admission of homosexuality by a middle-class businessman (Frank Whitaker/Dennis Quaid), which spurs on a nascent romance between his shaken suburban wife (Cathy Whitaker/Julianne Moore) and her African-American gardener (Raymond Deagan/Dennis Haysbert). The repressive contexts of 1950s small town Americana are infused with an inductive melancholy, as the bittersweet denouements of Sirk's tragic narratives – in films like ALL THAT HEAVEN ALLOWS (USA: 1955), MAGNIFICENT OBSESSION (USA: 1954), and IMITATION OF LIFE (USA: 1959) – precede and frame the unraveling of Cathy and Raymond's romance.

Engaging the audience on the level of reception, and following in the footsteps set by Rainer Werner Fassbinder, whose Sirk-inspired film ANGST ESSEN SEELE AUF (Germany: 1973, ALI: FEAR EATS THE SOUL) serves as yet another intertext to FAR FROM HEAVEN, Haynes' cinephile devotion binds the viewer into a retrospective dialogue with the Sirkian audience. Acting, performance, sound, camera movement and mise-en-scène are exceedingly studied and self-consciously artificial, lending what some reviewers ascribe to Haynes as his "academic" mimesis of Sirk. Neither parody nor "blankly ironic," Haynes' total re-creation of the narrative and emotional universe of the 1950s family melodrama assembles the excessive signs of a lost Hollywood moment for a present-day historicist purpose. In his sense of responsibility to the film historical conventions which he mimics and transgresses, Haynes can be seen to be operating in the mode of anachronism Thomas Greene deems "creative," and his project is a labor of a political and historiographic nature. It points to the limitations and ellipses within past representations, precisely through the very mimesis of these now obsolete techniques of cinematic storytelling, in a format J. Hoberman wittily referred to as "filmed film criticism."[8]

One scene directly alludes to Douglas Sirk's racially charged melodrama IMITATION OF LIFE, in which Lora (Lana Turner) is surprised that her black housekeeper Annie (Juanita Moore) had any friends, and implicitly a life outside of her household obligations to Lora. Haynes restages a similar encounter between Cathy Whitaker and her black maid Sybil. Asking her maid whether she knows of any church groups or civic organizations to which she could donate old clothes, Sybil names two, saying "I always seem to be signing up for something." Cathy responds with some surprise, exclaiming, "I think that's marvelous, that you find the time, with all that you do for us." As Cathy rushes out the door, two NAACP organizers are standing on the steps and ask her to sign in support of the organization; Cathy, in a hurry, ironically makes Sybil sign her name for her.

While echoing Sirk, Haynes' film ups the ante in a kind of filmic superimposition, where the connotations of one film are overlaid with the new. Cathy Whitaker's stirrings of romantic feeling for Raymond complicate the alignment of her comments to Sybil with that of Lora's (Lana Turner) in IMITATION OF LIFE. The kind of film historical reflexivity at work in this scene, as the NAACP comes to the door, depends on the privileges afforded by hindsight. The directness with which the film deals with race and homosexuality distances the film from pure remake or homage status. The inclusion of such themes enacts the counterfactual "what if?" scenario so prevalent in the ancillary fantasy processes of spectatorship. The historical possibility of the NAACP – as well as the historical possibility of gay identity – is inserted into the film historical, Sirkian text. What if the NAACP came to the door in IMITATION OF LIFE? Or, what if a character came out of the closet in a 1950s family melodrama? This sort of presentation, as an opening into a film historical imaginary, *inserts the historically and socially possible into the film historically impossible.*

A similar tenor is struck when Cathy, under the pressure of prying eyes and vicious gossip in her fragile bourgeois world, must end her relationship with Raymond; Cathy's words have a double-edged meaning, as she tells Raymond that "it isn't plausible for me to be friends with you." The word *plausible* itself gains a bittersweet, poignant edge – as it can both refer to the conditions of possibility and visibility of interracial love in the film's narrative space, as well as referring outwards to the film historical context, in our knowledge of the under-representation of interracial relationships in the Hollywood movies of the 1950s. And it is hard to forget that "plausibility" is inevitably associated with a popular vernacular around realism, through which moviegoers talk of the "credible" and the "believable" in filmic representations.

Haynes' anachronistic and cinephile fiction locates the affective pull of his story in the deep conflict and ambivalence attributed to the paucity of social choices available to Cathy, Raymond and Frank. This ambivalence is enriched by the retrospective knowledge and shuttling of the audience between the imagined Sirkian reception paradigm, of an audience in the 1950s, and the contemporary context of film reception. What is "outdated," yet most deeply felt as the pain of the film, is the brutal force of repressive, racist and sexist social opinion, a place where history circumscribes limits on the possible and the nearly impossible. As film critic Steve Erickson suggests, "not only are the taboos of Sirk's times outdated, so is the appalled hush that accompanied them."[9] Such taboos in the Hollywood cinema were matched and enforced with a restrictive Production Code, which produced a certain set of cinematic conventions of the said and the unsaid. Haynes lovingly and meticulously adheres to both the social and the cinematic codes of the time. He states, "I've always had a hard time depicting the experience of radical revolt from culture, truly transgressive experience… In a way I'm more comfortable showing the limits that make that kind of response possible."[10]

Working with and through these self-imposed generic limits, while pushing the representations of social limits, in the present, Haynes is able to reconstruct and create a space of film historical identification that exists by virtue of our contemporary moment and our emotional relay from "now" to "then." Affect is channeled through the conjuring of a gap between contemporary and past social attitudes, and the manifestations of those attitudes through the inarticulateness of characters' speech and gestures in the cinema. The exacting price of racism and exclusion is most violently rendered through the exile of Raymond Deagan from Hartford to Baltimore and the foreclosure on his romance with Cathy. The bitter cruelty of the Sirkian oeuvre becomes mutually constitutive with the cruelty of an intransigent social order, of a time that remains rigid in its unwillingness to accept racial and sexual difference. Yet the syncretic temporal and historical experience of watching FAR FROM HEAVEN facilitates a kind of spectatorial imagining, as the audience is constantly oscillating between the film's diegesis and its extra-diegetic contexts. As one critic suggests of the bitter pleasures offered by the setting and execution of Haynes' period homage.

> Those pleasures are associated with a past as alluring as it is ultimately unreachable: the mythic 50s of precisely this kind of psychological melodrama, an era that… starts as a historical period… and turns into a region outside time, an operatic space where emotions, hemmed in, finally prove irrepressible.[11]

FAR FROM HEAVEN's willful anachronism, its condition as a film that appears out of place and out of time, makes its narrative impact somehow carry more of an affective charge. The intense artificiality of the mise-en-scène and the heightened constrictions on content in effect engine an earnestly emotional response, from an audience that recognizes the limits and myopias of the cultural past as seen through the fractured mirror of film history.

The Pathos of Obsolescence

The melancholia underlying the genre of the family melodrama also gets reinstated through a longing for a lost film historical moment in the work of Paul Thomas Anderson. The historiographic predilections of BOOGIE NIGHTS illustrate some of its affectionate appropriation of 1970s film culture. BOOGIE NIGHTS presents itself as a period film that unceremoniously unveils the misunderstood milieu of American pornographic filmmaking in 1970s California. Fictionalizing porn figures such as John Holmes – who Mark Wahlberg (former pop star Marky Mark) dramatizes as Dirk Diggler – Anderson recasts the impulses of the porn industry into a melodramatic narrative of belonging, class aspiration, stardom, and the much longed for "American Dream." The film emerges to resemble a reworked combination of GOODFELLAS (USA: Martin Scorsese, 1990) and NASHVILLE (USA: Robert Altman, 1975) for the vintage porn set. Serving to banalize the purveyors of the obscene, Anderson inverts the presumed sordidness of pornography into a sensibility of innocuous naiveté. Howard Hampton, writing in *Film Comment* suggests the extent to which the film operates as a throwback to the ideological currents of classical Hollywood.

> Instead of chaotic perversity lurking beneath society's respectable facades, Anderson gives us a sex industry where outward sleaze masks a secret lust for normality and convention. BOOGIE NIGHTS shares with its characters a yearning for the incestual-family trappings of post-Victorian hypocrisy…. Timid anti-Puritan pretensions aside, BOOGIE NIGHTS' satire turns out to be more old-fashioned than Hawks.[12]

The tenuousness of the film's narrative universe depends on the audience's knowledge of the fate of the porn industry and its rerouting from celluloid to video format. As a result, *Boogie Nights* possesses an overwhelming fixation with the "dated" status of 1970s porn; it is its very outmoded quality that imbues the film with bittersweet melancholia and wistful tragedy, as the obsolescence of porn on film becomes an allegory for various characters' mistakes, delusions and frailties. The characters are already relics in the late 1970s, as Anderson compresses the aspirations of early 1970s porno chic with the disco

depredations of the late 1970s. Jack Horner's (Burt Reynolds) elaborate longings, to make narrative films which compel the viewer to stay even after they've
jerked off to the sex scenes is itself an anachronism from the early 1970s. Circa
1972, in the era of DEEP THROAT (USA: Gerard Damiano, 1972), the dream of
making narrative features with explicit sex was still a potentiality, not yet closed
off by definitions of obscenity that deferred to states' rights, when legal clamp-
downs on traveling prints sent a chill through the industry and deferred its
more lofty hopes of cross-over cinematic appeal.

In BOOGIE NIGHTS, anachronism, obsolescence, and failure get thematized in
the emergence of video, and the extinction of porn on film. Both Jack Horner's
desire to make "legitimate" films and his refusal to change with the times also
marks him as a casualty of historical and industrial change, and it is a judgment
the audience recognizes in advance of the film's ending. Horner's character perhaps mirrors Thomas Greene's figure who emblematizes the "pathetic/tragic"
anachronism – as Horner is visibly alienated by the porn industry's insistence
on technological "progress."

On the narrative level, the film engenders a sense of pathos for the banal
everyday dreams of the members of Horner's porn commune – for example the
African-American porn actor Buck Swope's (Don Cheadle) insistent desire to
dress like a cowboy and open a hi-fi stereo store, in Julianne Moore's character's
wishful assignation of herself as a mother figure to the errant flock of porn children, and in Dirk Diggler's working-class aspirations for fame and greatness.
On the level of mise-en-scène, pathos is not too far from nostalgia, in the fetishization of historical objects and signs. Consider for example the tracking shot
through Dirk Diggler's new house once he has hit the big time as a porn star –
the indulgence in décor and 1970s fashion, the outré wall hangings, burnt ochre
and rust color schemes of his bachelor pad – seem to directly address the audience's and author's historical knowledge, their retro-kitsch sensibilities, their
cultural memories of the recent past, as well as their screen memories of New
Hollywood style. Anderson, in MAGNOLIA (USA: 1999) and BOOGIE NIGHTS, ap-
propriates and recycles certain narrative devices from his New Hollywood pre-
decessors. From Altman, Anderson borrows the ambling, disconnected story-
lines and the use of elaborate ensemble casts. And from Scorsese one can see
some cinematographic techniques – spatially mobile tracking and dolly shots,
long following shots, such as the homage to the Copacabana scene in GOODFEL-
LAS, echoed in the camera movements through Diggler's new house.

The use of sound in BOOGIE NIGHTS also plays into the larger anachronistic
strategy, in the sampling of pop songs of the 1970s and 1980s, and the express
associations they invoke in popular memory. As Kelly Ritter compellingly argues, BOOGIE NIGHTS is an instantiation of the musical genre, reconstructed for
the 1990s, in which popular music orchestrates the affective landscape of An-

derson's 1970s. In the film, Ritter claims, "there is no attempt to make a spectator feel visually part of the action; rather, one is a historical observer, watching
time and lives go by quite separately."[13] While the visual presentation of the
film connotes an element of historical distance, the use of popular songs of the
period, such as *Boogie Shoes* and *Jesse's Girl*, create a conflict with the manifest
and relatively detached images. Ritter argues that this tension refutes and de-
mythologizes the historical associations of the musical with a "utopian sensibility." The deployment of music in Anderson's film complicates the audience's
desire to seamlessly enter the diegesis, a spectatorial mode often encouraged by
the song-and-dance conventions of the traditional Hollywood musical.

In an anachronistic violation which both puzzled and outraged critics, P.T.
Anderson's follow-up film MAGNOLIA, in its nod to the classical musical, toys
with the possibility of reinstating this utopian mode. The SHORT CUTS-style narrative, that follows a group of disconnected characters through a night of their
lives in Los Angeles, offers a cathartic scene in which all of the disparate characters, in separate locations in the diegesis, begin to sing along in unison with
an extra-diegetic song, Aimee Mann's *Wise Up*. The scene's intentional rupture
of filmic space, in its commingling of extra-diegetic and diegetic worlds, becomes a very confrontational mode of address to its audience. This anomalous
moment in the film, precedes another pronounced instance of frame-breaking,
when a torrent of frogs falls on the dark town, in a hyperbolically biblical moment of magical realism. Anderson's willingness to privilege disjunction and
disruption over seamless flow of narrative has been branded pretentious and
self-congratulatory. However, one could argue that the sing-along effect invites
the audience towards a measure of self-reflexivity but also back into a mode of
affective absorption, almost as a function of their incredulity. Desiring an audi-
ence-text relation from the historical past by appropriating the means of the
musical genre, MAGNOLIA stages a performance of synchronicity between disconnected characters. This performed synchronicity between characters paradoxically threatens to disrupt narrative cohesion and continuity, as the over-
arching melodramatic realism of the film is made suddenly "implausible."
Through the orchestrated sing-along, the characters and the film acknowledge
and direct their attention outwards to the extra-diegetic – a space which is
usually the exclusive domain of the audience, and implicitly the filmmaker.
Thus, in both this example from MAGNOLIA and in BOOGIE NIGHTS as a whole,
Anderson utilizes anachronistic forms and themes in order to renegotiate a relationship to his audience – forcing the 1990s viewer to reconsider their own historical positioning in relation to film history and popular cultural memory.

Melancholy Objects, Out of Place

We can see a further dispersal of the function of anachronism into a sustained aesthetic approach which dominates the mise-en-scène in the work of Wes Anderson, whose earlier features included BOTTLE ROCKET (USA: 1996) and RUSHMORE (USA: 1998). Anderson's style appears the most disjunctive in its aesthetic strategies and in its use of cultural objects and historical referents, while extending and expanding some of the impulses of Paul Thomas Anderson's fetishization of historical signs. Wes Anderson's THE ROYAL TENENBAUMS produces a literalized storybook world in which a dysfunctional New York family, with three grown-up child geniuses (Gwyneth Paltrow, Ben Stiller, Luke Wilson) and an archaeologist mother (Anjelica Huston), attempts to reconcile with a ne'er-do-well patriarch (Gene Hackman). Again the thematics of failure, within a melodramatic mode, align with a larger anachronistic aesthetic strategy.

The mise-en-scène, constituted through static tableaus and the precisely peculiar arrangement of setting and props, privileges flatness and the accumulation of historical objects as signs of melancholia and lost promise. The film is most often lauded as a triumph of art direction and production design. The acknowledgement of Anderson's tactics of aesthetic and stylistic control is often paired with a criticism of his film's lack of character development and narrational depth. In the fashion of a diorama, a dollhouse or an antique store display window, Anderson arrays and fetishistically accumulates disparate historical objects and forces them into one plastic plane and narrative universe.

In a manner similar to FAR FROM HEAVEN and BOOGIE NIGHTS, the emotional investments and affective energies of the viewer are directed, shunted to the space of the mise-en-scène itself. Each filmic element – for example, Chas and his sons' red track suits, the use of titling in the style of 1960s sans serif Bauhaus style typeface, the eclectic furniture, wood tones and pink-walled décor of the Tenenbaum home, the multiple associations of 1960s and 1970s New York, the uses of counterculturally rich songs such as The Beatles' *Hey Jude*, Paul Simon's *Me & Julio Down by the Schoolyard*, and Nico's *These Days* and the literary allusions to the narrative worlds of J.D. Salinger, John Irving, and the *New Yorker Magazine* of the 1940s, as well as the various Hollywood stars employed – all of these referents are drawn attention to as singular and irreconcilable, at the same time that a hermetic and enclosed world is cobbled together from them, in their repetition and accumulation. Each individual object – for example Richie's dated 70s tennis headband – brings the viewer to recollect and discern the location of the object in its original place in the past, within a particular historical period or distinct text. There is a certain desire to relocate these objects back to their own historical or literary place – to place the trinket back on the shelf where it belongs – at the same time as the element is alienated in its current narrative context.

It is interesting that the narrative itself is shot through with nostalgia and mourning for the days of the Tenenbaum children's glorious childhoods. Ostensibly, the Tenenbaums children grew up in the 1970s, and now 22 years later, we are left with them in a presumably mutual present. However, the film's aesthetic format and mise-en-scène, attenuated by the children's refusal to grow up, produces a kind of visual arrested development. Margot perennially wears the same mink coat and heavy eyeliner she has had on since childhood, Richie persists in wearing his tennis clothes even after his tennis career is over, Chas and his sons are always in their red track suits. All return to live in their untouched childhood rooms. The uniformity of their demeanor across time lends the feeling of the "homey, familiar quality of the Sunday funnies,"[14] an abstract sense that aligns the film with the more graphic and flat space of children's drawings, comic strips, and pop-up storybooks. Yet it also creates a sensation of time suspended through the consistent organization of objects in space.

One such example comes in a crucial moment which breaks the film's mode of visual narration and pace of editing, as Margot Tenenbaum's past dalliances and secret identities are revealed, cued by the opening of her case file at a private detective's office. This fast paced montage sequence is scored to the 1970s Ramones' song *Judy Is a Punk*. One might ask: where is the anachronism located here? It seems that Gwyneth Paltrow is herself the anachronism, connecting through her erotic presence and match-on-action kisses, a series of utterly disconnected scenarios of culturally and socially diverse lovers. Her presence makes the space of the frame look "contemporary" while the relation between each of her partners is based on a principle of utter discontinuity – a Jamaican rasta, a mohawk-wielding punk rocker, a Papua New Guinea tribesman, her book publicity agent, a greaser, a ferry worker, a Parisian lesbian, and her childhood friend, the self-styled urban cowboy Eli Cash. Intruding into each of their discrete spaces in the mise-en-scène to form a narrative of an embrace, Margot's presence operates as both anachronistic disjunction and sequential continuity. The Ramones' song, its own singular object, at first seems to stabilize the historical time in the 1970s; the song is further inscribed with a punk gesture as it gets narrationally matched with Margot's first act of rebellion – covert smoking. Yet each subsequent scene further creates a conflict between the historicity of the song, the references supplied by the visual image and the tones of sexual transgression. The Rive Gauche lesbian scene seems to both reference 1960s New Wave cinema and Jacques Tati's PLAYTIME (France: 1967), in the reflection of the Eiffel Tower in the glass. Cultural and historical space begins to stand in for time in this hyperbolic narrativization of Margot's sexual history, with the sans serif type titles indicating Margot's age and her location at each cut. We finally return to the anchor of the present in the final segment with Eli on the train, and to the immediate present, as the file abruptly closes and we are back in the detective's office, where Raleigh St. Clair, Margot's estranged husband states merely, "She smokes."

We might claim that the anachronisms of Wes Anderson are ones of uniting periods and elements which should be separated. On the other hand, this juxtaposition and fetishistic almost collector-oriented accumulation of signs and objects creates a narrative world which becomes in some sense "timeless." New York is constructed as a mythical location, where landmarks are intentionally invisible, where the expanse of the city stretches all the way up to 375th Street and is overrun by innumerable gypsy cabs. The fantasy construction of the storybook reinforces this notion of "timelessness" at the same time that it poses a question to what Anderson's relationship to history might be. Thomas Greene's definitions might pose another question, is this an abusive – ahistorical – or naive – with no historical control – anachronism? Anachronistic detail, while still recognized as such, is repeated and collected visually to the point of a break with a position of historical specificity, as it becomes a fully fledged plastic space of fantasy, placed outside of time because it is irreconcilable with any one moment or period.

Wes Anderson's THE ROYAL TENENBAUMS points to one extreme in the deployment of these anachronisms, as manifesting a desire to rework the material remains of the past into a creative fiction, while still retaining the unique pastness of these objects and texts in their circulation, repeated viewings and affective accumulation. Wes Anderson's predilection for objects and settings, for the texture of mise-en-scène, resonates with Todd Haynes and P.T. Anderson as well, who are meticulous, and studies in their aesthetics of décor, lighting, acting, makeup, and costume. Vivian Sobchack, reflecting on the nature of historical representations in films returns to the affective weight of objects and visual details, as carriers of historical meaning. Sobchack concludes:

> They at least, through their material means and the concrete purchase they give us on an absent past, make us care... sometimes the representation of phenomenal "things" like dirt and hair are, *in medias res*, all we have to hold on to – are where our purchase on temporality and its phenomenological possibilities as "history" are solidly grasped and allow us a place, a general premise, a ground (however base) from which to transcend our present and imagine the past as once having "real" existential presence and value.[15]

Although none of the films discussed are traditional historical films, their utilization of material things, within the texture of the mise-en-scène, and of film historical referents, gives the audience a sense of the palpability of history, even if the means through which the directors present that history is rendered through a rather stylized artifice. With narratives built around flawed characters and tropes of failure and loss, the obsolete and the anachronistic become tools for recognizing the meaningful gaps between past and present. What perhaps this sensibility which favors anachronism offers is the cinematic instantiation of a "historiographical consciousness,"[16] not in the service of writing history, but with the aim of using historical signs as a means for creating affecting fictions which can question the past from a new location. The nostalgic or retrospective tone of Todd Haynes, P.T. Anderson, and Wes Anderson's works reflects both a current of sincerity specifically tempered by an ironic detachment. In THE ROYAL TENENBAUMS, Eli Cash, the western novelist and Tenenbaum's neighbor, appears on a talk show, in which he is asked whether his new novel *Old Custer* is not in fact written in an "obsolete vernacular." Eli is puzzled and stupefied, yet this scene in a sense names the preoccupations of the film and by extension those of BOOGIE NIGHTS and FAR FROM HEAVEN; it is a persistent interest in making that which is forgotten, lost or outmoded, speak to us from beyond the grave.

Notes

1.   Tyler, Parker "On the Cult of Displaced Laughter." *The Three Faces of the Film*, New York: A.S. Barnes & Co., 1960. p. 132.
2.   Sconce, Jeffrey. "Irony, Nihilism, and the New American Smart Film." *Screen* 43/4 (Winter 2002), p. 362.
3.   Carroll, Noel. "The Future of Allusion: Hollywood in the Seventies (and Beyond)." *October* 20 (Spring 1982), p. 51.
4.   Jameson, Fredric. "Postmodernism and Consumer Society." Foster, Hal (ed.). *The Anti-Aesthetic: Essays on Postmodern Culture*, Seattle: Bay Press, 1983, pp.111-125.
5.   Carroll, Future, p. 80, n. 16.
6.   Aravamudan, Srinivas. "The Return of Anachronism." *MLQ: Modern Language Quarterly*, 62/4 (2001), pp. 331-353. For 18th-century Italian philosopher, Giambattista Vico, four kinds of errors can be delineated within the spectrum of anachronism, especially as they emerge in the writing of history: the ascription of events to a truly uneventful period, the marking of an uneventful period that is full of events, the error of uniting periods which should in fact be set apart, and the division of periods which should be organized together. Vico, Giambattista. *New Science: Principles of the New Science Concerning the Common Nature of Nations*, trans. David Marsh, 3rd ed., London: Penguin, 1999, p. 333.
7.   Greene, Thomas. "History and Anachronism." *The Vulnerable Text: Essays on Renaissance Literature*, New York: Columbia University Press, 1986, pp. 221-222.
8.   Hoberman, J. "Signs of the Times." *Village Voice*, 6-12 November 2002, n. p. <http://www.villagevoice.com/issues/0245/hoberman.php> (Accessed 31 August 2004).

9. Erickson, Steve. "Heaven Knows." *Los Angeles Magazine*, 47/12 (December 2002), p. 121.

10. O'Brien, Geoffrey. "Past Perfect: Todd Haynes' FAR FROM HEAVEN." *Art Forum*, 41/3 (November 2002), p. 152-6, 202.

11. O'Brien, Past, p. 153.

12. Hampton, Howard. "Whatever You Desire: Notes on Movieland and Pornotopia." *Film Comment*, 37/4, (July-August 2001), p. 39.

13. Ritter, Kelly. "Spectacle at the Disco: BOOGIE NIGHTS, Soundtrack, and the New American Musical." *Journal of Popular Film and Television*, 28/4 (winter 2001), p. 170.

14. Hoberman, J. "Look Homeward, Angel." *Village Voice*, 12-18 December 2001. <http://www.villagevoice.com/issues/0150/hoberman.php> (Accessed 30 August 2004)

15. Sobchack, Vivian. "The Insistent Fringe: Moving Images and the Palimpsest of Historical Consciousness." *Screening the Past Online Film Journal*, 6 (1 July 1999), n. p. <http://www.latrobe.edu.au?screeningthepast/firstrelease/fr0499/vsfr6b.htm> (Accessed 26 August 2004).

16. Sobchack, Vivian. "What is Film History? Or the Riddle of the Sphinxes." Gledhill, Christine, Linda Williams. *Reinventing Film Studies*, London: Arnold, 2000, p. 303.

Conceptual Cinephilia

On Jon Routson's Bootlegs

Lucas Hilderbrand

From the releases of George Lucas's blockbuster disappointment STAR WARS, EPISODE I: THE PHANTOM MENACE (USA: 1999) to acting twin Mary-Kate and Ashley Olsen's feature film flop NEW YORK MINUTE (USA: Danny Gordon, 2004), Baltimore-based conceptual artist Jon Routson (1969) recorded cinema screenings with his digital video camera. Routson would merely turn on his camera when the feature began, often cutting off the opening credits and jostling the image as he settled into his seat. He would rest the camera low on his chest or stomach to be inconspicuous and record without looking through the viewfinder in order to preserve the camera's batteries and to avoid attracting the theater ushers' attention. The footage often wandered out of focus, cropped the films, and reduced the big screens' grandeur to murky colors, low-resolution details, and harsh flickers. Occasionally elliptical jump-cuts interrupted the middle of recordings and end credits went missing, though all "editing" was done in-camera during the screening. Routson then burned the footage to DVD-R without any post-production alteration or creating menus or chapter settings. He has stated that he often didn't even watch his recordings before sending them to his gallery for instant exhibition. As an automated creative practice, these documents entailed no craftsmanship and only minimal technical proficiency, yet their imperfections allow us to reconsider the way we see films. In essence, these are reproductions of film exhibitions that stress the space of the cinema, the noise of the audience, and the grain and flicker of the films – showing us what spectators are supposedly perceptually ignoring.

Critical analysis of Routson's work has focused primarily on its novel challenge to traditional notions of authorship and its tenuous legality.[1] Despite prominent press attention, however, Routson has never faced litigation or received cease-and-desist orders. This, even though piracy paranoia has made the work timely and relevant – former Motion Picture Association of America President Jack Valenti's infamous campaign against piracy and the failed Academy Award video screener ban hit a fever pitch in fall 2003, exactly between Routson's two spring shows at Team Gallery in New York. Unlike European copyright laws, which privilege authors' moral rights, the US copyright code was conceived to promote the public interest by providing only temporary control and economic benefit to creators as an incentive to create, after which works would enter the public domain. The US "fair use" provision, amended in 1976, permits non-commercial reproduction of excerpts from copyrighted works for news reporting, critical, or scholarly purposes. European creators have more control over others' uses of their works, but in the US (in theory, at least) the public has more freedom to use and build from others' creations. In the past several years, however, US copyright codes have been expanded in the rights owners' favor with the 1998 Copyright Term Extension Act (aka the Sonny Bono Act) and the Digital Millennium Copyright Act, which governs not only uses of content but also reproduction technology itself.

Reeling from the rise of online music file sharing and the threat of increased moving image downloading, the entertainment industry has pushed for even more restrictive laws; these shifts not only threaten commercial piracy but also previously "fair" uses by artists and private consumers. Additionally, laws rendering uses of recording devices inside cinemas illegal have prompted the artist to stop making this series of bootlegs. Pirate tapes and DVDs have become increasingly scarce on the streets of New York, particularly along the formerly reliable and infamous Canal Street, as a result of police crackdowns. Simultaneously, more and more pirated copies are being accessed directly from industry insiders who leak near-final cuts out of post-production houses, as opposed to the old fashioned method of taking a camcorder into a theater and taping the screen.[2] Through Routson's work, these shoddy sorts of documents have migrated from Chinatown to Chelsea, from the black market to the white-walled art space. And, like pirated copies, Routson's recordings are often produced and reproduced on each film's opening day.

Contemporary fanatical attempts to prevent mass copyright infringement does not single-handedly make Routson's work interesting as art and only incidentally makes it political. These digital recordings in no way function as viable substitutes for the films; rather, they remediate the cinema as a whole – the exhibition space and its viewers, as well as the films. Significantly, the two terms used by Routson and his gallery are "recordings" (the title for both exhibitions at Team) and "bootleg" (the official title of each work). With a more neutral connotation, the term "recording" suggests both historical documentation and the materiality of the reproduction format. Yet, as Clinton Heylin argues, "An essential element of creativity separates the bootleggers from their piratical cousins – those who copy material but make no attempt to pass their product off as the original..."[3]

In a study of the underground music recording culture, he defines bootlegs as productive documents recorded by the fan/user of a live performance, in contrast to piracy, which entails the illegal duplication and sale of copies that compete with legitimate commercial releases.[4] Routson's recordings are not available for sale or distribution, so they pose no market competition to theatrical or home video releases. Additionally, their low-fidelity aesthetics give them little commercial value as pirate copies. In effect, the recordings' conceptual status and gallery context make them "art" rather than their contents (though they still operate as texts).

Routson's work is conceptual in the sense that it emphasizes process over product, jackass stunt over aesthetic achievement. In its seminal period from 1968-77 (also the first decade of video art), conceptual art challenged the authority, mastery, and commercialism of the art world through self-reflexivity and dematerialization: a work could just as sufficiently be described as created or seen, and as ephemeral or visually unremarkable "works," there was often no art object to sell.[5] Although emerging in a time of political upheaval, conceptual art did not necessarily possess Dada's satirical edge or total embrace of nonsense. Perhaps post-post-modern, Routson's latter-day recordings are conceptual works without ideas or politics. He challenges conceptions of authorship and artistic integrity as he does not "create" any of his images but steals or purchases them.[6] Like so much early conceptual art, these spectacles of spectatorship are presented as ephemeral installations that cannot be bought or owned.

In cutting films up or slowing them down, video artists have picked up where "classical" conceptual artists left off – though much early video art was rooted in conceptualism – by repurposing preexisting images and sounds for formal and discursive examination of perception, media, cultural practices, and (personal) histories. Coincidentally, the American fair use copyright provision does not protect *artistic* appropriation but does protect critical or transformative reuse – thereby necessitating a political edge or formal reinvention. Experiments in "found footage" began through reworking early, industrial, and educational films, but as video has made more content and technology accessible, popular cinema and television have become increasingly frequent resources and these practices have become exponentially more common. Routson's work was distinguished by his process of reshooting the content with a camera rather than merely duplicating it from deck to deck. Recording videos of film projections (almost) in their entireties, Routson's feature bootlegs are apparently devoid of the meaning, ideology, or political critique that marks much of this prior appropriation video work.[7] Instead, Routson's videos have elicited comparisons to Marcel Duchamp's readymades, Andy Warhol's affectless reproductions, and Douglas Gordon's video installations, which likewise appropriate whole Hollywood films but render them impossible to see in full.[8]

By seeing and recording films nearly indiscriminately – seeming to disregard canons or personal taste – Routson could be seen as either the ultimate cinephile or as altogether indifferent to the films. His exhibitions turned the Team Gallery space into an ad-hoc multiplex where three screens presented daily programming changes, with new works arriving as he produced them. Occasionally the three films on view during simultaneous screenings were thematically linked, at other times not. The low resolution videos on view for his first *Recordings* exhibition (22 March-26 April 2003) defaced aesthetically pristine pictures in BOOTLEG (FAR FROM HEAVEN) and BOOTLEG (CREMASTER 3), action spectaculars in BOOTLEG (SPIDER-MAN) and BOOTLEG (FINAL DESTINATION II), and low-brow fair in BOOTLEG (PHONE BOOTH) and BOOTLEG (BOAT TRIP), which was recorded following the opening after-party at McDonald's. His second show (3 April-8 May 2004) featured a repertory screening in BOOTLEG (SUNRISE), as well as a range of recent releases in BOOTLEG (ELEPHANT), BOOTLEG (ELF), BOOTLEG (MONSTER), and BOOTLEG (MEAN GIRLS).

At the opening for *Recordings II*, the gallery screened BOOTLEG (THE FOG OF WAR), BOOTLEG (THE PASSION OF THE CHRIST [SECOND RECORDING]), and BOOTLEG (KILL BILL, VOLUME 1). Each screening space was painted black with large-scale video projection against a white wall and a different seating configuration: a bench in the front and largest room, a leather couch in the intimate middle screening room, and metal folding chairs in the back gallery. Spatially, these layouts maintained a distance between the audience and the image; typically, viewers entering the galleries would not cross in front of seated viewers, nor would they approach the screen unless they kept close to the side walls. Keeping with a current trend in video art, these digital video recordings of theatrical screenings presented the work through projection configurations rather than on monitors – neither fully replicating the cinema experience nor home video viewing on television. Among the gallery's openings, *Recordings II* seemed sparsely attended, and as audio-visual art, discouraged the chatter and social scene typical of strictly visual art events. Screened as loops without predetermined start times, the bootlegs were nearly impossible to see from the beginning, and devoting the feature-length running time to each viewing would border on loitering. This is a problem for much looped video work installed in galleries, but these bootlegs do not seem intended to be viewed in their entireties. As they deny most of the pleasures of an evening at the movies, the videos are frankly too tedious to watch all the way through in the gallery, anyway. Instead, the recordings make the spectatorial disparity between cinematic film screenings and video installations resoundingly apparent. In contrast to the cinema, the video gallery does not presume an interpolated viewer who follows a linear plot; though the high art milieu might seem to demand more refined attention to the work, it instead allows the viewer a more casual and transient relation to the moving image and soundtrack – a brief aesthetic or theoretical encounter compared to a feature-length commitment. Like so much digital or conceptual art, these recordings are appreciated as experiences or as meta-texts. Liberated from any necessity of narrative cognition, the video bootleg viewer can instead ponder the theater's off-screen space or intertextual connections between simultaneous screenings.

Contingency played a role in both the bootlegs' production and, to a lesser extent, their exhibition. According to the gallery owner Jose Friere, the opening's three videos were not chosen for thematic reasons but for the more pragmatic one that only these DVD-Rs played back without skipping. Even though curated by chance, each recording offered a different perspective on film viewing. Bootleg (The Fog of War), shot from a distance, in focus and unobstructed, seems most blatantly a statement of copyright infringement – and perhaps even of respect; it does not work to destroy Errol Morris's political documentary. By comparison, the other two works on view were more successful in challenging classical cinematic spectatorship. Screening in the cozy video room, Bootleg (The Passion of the Christ, [second recording]) was shot with obscure framing that clearly interfered with any comprehension of Mel Gibson's film, and Bootleg (Kill Bill, Volume 1) similarly abstracts Quentin Tarantino's auteurist homage to genre films. The pleasures of these recordings are found in their details – in the specific ways they attract our attention away from the cinema screen or undermine the films' auteurist or narrative intentions.

During its first half-hour, Routson's Bootleg (Kill Bill, Volume 1) was shot in extreme close-up, showing only a small portion of the screen and none of the auditorium architecture. Save occasional glimpses of Uma Thurman's face, this film comprised of referential pastiche has itself been rendered almost unrecognizable, and it's through sound cues that viewers would most likely be able to place the film. Despite being mesmerized by Kill Bill upon seeing it in the theater months earlier, when I saw the bootleg at the opening, I couldn't identify it until I recognized the cue of Elle Driver's (Daryl Hannah) whistling. This portion of the recording allows us to really look at the texture of the film image in a way that we could never see it ourselves. In Routson's recording the pronounced celluloid grain has been punctuated by the projector's flicker, which produces an eye-straining strobe effect. A visually gorgeous and arrestingly violent film becomes painful to watch, while the graphic violence is abstracted, as is the game of intertextual citation. The extreme close-up framing, however, is only a temporary reconfiguration. When the camera zooms out, at the beginning of the anime section portraying O-ren Ishii's (Lucy Liu) back story, Routson's position in the auditorium is revealed. He apparently sat in the front row of raised stadium seating; a balcony bar splits the screen horizontally for the remainder of the recording. The bar so perfectly slashes across the screen's torso that it at first seems that the frame lines are simply out of register on the projector. In this second portion of the recording, featuring the majority of the film, the audio also marks the artist's and the audiences' presence. Now less subsumed in the film text, we begin to notice sniffles, mutterings about Japanese girls, laughs at the bloody stunts, and even a yawn during the drawn-out battle at the House of Blue Leaves.

In a series of correspondences about contemporary world cinephilia, Kent Jones comments that Tarantino, whose film knowledge is largely founded upon home video viewing rather than cinematheque attendance, would qualify as the "wrong kind of cinephile" according to Susan Sontag. Raymond Bellour concurs with the video-bashing charge, saying that Tarantino doesn't understand "the real weight of an image, which explains [his work's] ethical irresponsibility."[9] If Tarantino's love for cinema is perverse, one can only imagine what sort of heathen he would label Routson. He may or may not understand the "ethics" or the "real weight" of images, but in stealing and disfiguring Tarantino's, he allows us to ponder our perceptions of them. Both the extreme close-up and the far balcony bar framings function to disrupt a "perfect" perspective, but the effect differs: the former makes us see the film as something new and different, whereas the latter functions as an obstruction that merely frustrates the spectatorial experience.

Mediating both the religious message and the violence of Gibson's blockbuster religious biopic, BOOTLEG (THE PASSION OF THE CHRIST, [SECOND RECORDING]) was shot from a low angle behind a seat that cuts into the image and obscures its subtitles. (The dialogue was performed entirely in the dead languages of Latin and Aramaic.) By dramatizing explicit images of whipping, grueling cross bearing, and painful impaling on the cross, the film makes Jesus' sacrifice – for a religious audience – seem more profound and viscerally immediate. Any missionary potential the film may possess, however, has been bled from Routson's second bootleg. (Routson recorded three versions of the film, creating a video trinity that filled each of the gallery's screening rooms on three dates.) It performs an act of blasphemy by rendering Jesus' story incomprehensible and effectively censors much of the visual and verbal information. When the Jews first bring Jesus (Jim Caviezel) to be tried by Pontius Pilate (Hristo Naumov Shopov) – one of the few dialogue-intensive scenes – Routson shifted slightly in his seat so that fragments of the subtitles become visible on the right edge of the screen. This repositioning only proves more distracting as the viewer may engage in unsolvable puzzles of mentally filling in the missing words. With little visual stimulation keeping our attention on the screen image, we begin to look elsewhere and contemplate the theater space Routson documents. The auditorium's black, tile-drop ceiling reflects the screen during the film's brighter moments, and a red emergency exit sign glows like a beacon. The sound recording remarkably captures a flattened yet sensitive approximation of cinema acoustics, so that the effect of surround sound are still audible, even if the video is screened in standard stereo.

In the U.S., THE PASSION became a religious phenomenon, making ungodly sums of money during its sustained theatrical run when it became part of audiences' Sunday rituals: church groups would attend en masse repeatedly, week after week as an extension of religious services. As Routson reshot the film, it officially lost its ritual function or visceral-spiritual aura, and the framing behind an empty chair also made the theater space seem vacant. Only through audio disruption and inappropriate responses do we know that anyone was watching the film. At one point a cell phone rang, and the camera shifted as if it was Routson's own, which he had to maneuver to silence. Later, when the first establishing shot of crosses on a hilltop appeared an hour and a half into the film, someone near the camera muttered, "It's about time," expressing boredom and excitement for the crucifixion. We hear a loud belch at the moment Jesus' cross has been erected and a sarcastic, celebratory "yeh!" quietly cheered when Christ arose from the dead. It's ambiguous if the praise was for the resurrection or for the film's end.

Routson's bootleg not only presents a travesty of Gibson's film, but it also documented a singular screening performance, complete with audience commentary. Projection defects and audience responses are ephemeral, live events, and these bootlegs become video archives of historical reception. These bootlegs may be categorized as conceptual art because they are acts of appropriation, but as meta-cinema,[10] Routson's work provides an opportunity to interrogate how we watch films. The digital video camera's latter-day kino eye perceives the cinema differently than human spectators would – with zooms, out of focus, in close-up, and from uncomfortable angles. But by essentially shifting our points of view and the objects of our attention, these recordings refocus our gaze upon those elements of the cinema we are not supposed to see: the chairs, the ceilings, the illuminated exit signs, the bodies of other viewers, the projector's flicker, and even the grain of the celluloid. In the auditorium, all these aspects are present before us, but we are conditioned to ignore them. Like the rattle of the projector or the dust in the projected beam of light (which do not register in Routson's recordings), we only consciously consider the off-screen space when it either interferes as a distraction or when the film ceases to engross the viewer – that is, at moments when the apparatus has failed.

And yet, essential to cinema as a physical and social institution, the off-screen space must also be part of our apperception. Though exterior to the film *text*, it is not exterior to the cinematic *experience*. Vision and hearing are active processes of filtering information, and in the cinema we are assumed to not see (or pretend not to see) the surrounding mise-en-scène of the auditorium. Watching a film entails actively not seeing, by directing our attention to the screen and by relying upon the innate perceptual slowness that allows for the persistence of vision. As art historian and visual theorist James Elkins observes, blindness is an essential part of seeing:

> Because we cannot see what we do not understand or use or identify with, we see very little of the world – only the small pieces that are useful and harmless. Each act of vision mingles seeing with not seeing, so that vision can become less a way of gathering information than avoiding it.... [H]uman sight is not merely partial blindness or selective seeing but a determinate trading of blindness and insights.[11]

As Elkins comments, we sometimes fail to notice mundane details that we encounter repeatedly simply because the information isn't essential for our understanding. Similarly, our brains will fill in details as we process sights, so that we perceive objects as whole even if we only see fragmentary images. Even if a spectator's head blocks part of our line of vision, we can usually mentally compensate for the missing part of the image without confusion. Though we may strain our necks to peer around the intrusion, it does not ultimately alter our comprehension of the film. (As BOOTLEG [THE PASSION...] demonstrates, with subtitles this can pose more of a problem.)

By directing our attention away from the screen to the space of spectatorship, perhaps Routson's recordings allow us to reconceive reception. Considerable scholarly attention has reviewed the developmental history and cultural-aesthetic impact of audio reproduction; such work suggests that recordings function as preserved texts and, more interestingly, argue that each new technology has required different manners of performance and studio manipulation while creating new perceptual and consumptive relationships between the listener and the format/text.[12] This body of work remains indebted to Walter Benjamin, who expressed ambivalence about the status of the art object; removed from its former ritual function in the modern era, its reproduction can circulate more widely but without the aura of the original's physical presence. In taking film as his exemplary new medium for examination, however, Benjamin acknowledged that film technology and aesthetics have changed the way spectators *see*. As is too often overlooked, he wrote of perception and experience – of *reception* rather than *recording* per se.[13]

The space of the cinema and other spectators are generally considered irrelevant to our perception of the film. Yet, the occasional audio commentary in Routson's recordings suggest the sensibility of a viewer experienced in the specific milieu of interactive midnight movies and texts such as MYSTERY SCIENCE THEATER 3000 and DVD bonus features. Certainly responsive audiences contribute to the excitement of action and horror films, the pleasure of otherwise tedious cult flicks, and even enhance festival screenings of art films, for which applause appreciatively caps off the experience. Conversely, a rude neighbor can also spoil an otherwise pleasurable screening. Different types of venues, geographic locations, and even screening times also attract different audiences and social dynamics, from reverential to rowdy. The cinema is a social phenomenon, though we have been trained not to see or hear our fellow filmgoers as anything but a nuisance. (Or, in special romantic instances, the real subject of our attention.) As cinema historians have documented, early film audiences were even more vocal prior to narrative integration and feature running times; perhaps, then, it is spectatorial silence that is antithetical to the cinema, rather than bawdy participation.

Routson's recordings suggest a cinephilia of distractions. Critics writing on cinephilia have suggested, particularly in the wake of cinema's centenary, that there is a nostalgic impulse behind it – a fear of the cinema's death and an attempt to reclaim or maintain celluloid and public film culture.[14] Working with the vilified video medium, Routson reclaims the social, public exhibition of film. Annette Michelson has pointed out that cinephilia takes on variant modes in different periods, so there is no single or "proper" form of cinephilia.[15] She describes a specific early 1970s movement to eliminate social distraction and isolate a direct cinematic experience in the (curiously named) Invisible Cinema at the Anthology Film Archives; in this experiment, blinders were installed between each seat so that the faces and sounds of neighboring viewers would be blocked out. Routson's work perhaps seems antithetical to "classical" cinephilia's ideals of the primacy of celluloid screened in a cultural vacuum. (Ironically, total spectatorial privacy would not be available for most audiences until the advent of home video.)

Inverting the desire for asocial cinema or technically innovative venues, Routson's work emphasizes human disruption and the shortcomings of more decrepit spaces–the materiality of film exhibition. BOOTLEG (NASHVILLE) is especially – and probably accidentally – illustrative of the way film may be seen and heard.[16] Like most of his other recordings, this one begins abruptly; the image shifts about while Routson gets comfortable in his seat with the camera on, and silhouettes of latecomers cross in front of the screen. The audio track betrays the tinny echo of a lo-fi sound system so common to independent art houses, in comparison to the surround sound of new corporate theater complexes. In addition, film splotches and scratches – presumably at reel changeovers – are evident during this screening from an old and abused print. And, most importantly, the projector bulb is obviously too weak to evenly illuminate the widescreen framing, so the image is blatantly oval-shaped with dim corners.

The interference and the spaces of the cinema, complete with its restless and noisy audience, are precisely the subjects in Routson's work. The most exciting moments occur when the camera distorts the image or when someone talks over the soundtrack or gets up to leave the theater, blocking the screen. Routson's videos may be the exemplary cinephilic art in a moment of heightened

public attention to exhibitions spaces (particularly with sound systems and stadium seating) and to the convergence of piracy and media. These bootlegs are
less than pure spectatorial or art experiences – the works are neither fully conceptual (at times the viewer can get pulled into the narrative) nor cinematic
(there is too much interference for these videos to replace authentic film screenings). If anything, the recordings point to the fact that there is no such thing as
uncorrupted spectatorship in the cinema. There will always be a level of ambi-
ent distraction, of waning attention, of human shortcoming in any feature-
length viewing act, as much as theorists and buffs may want to pretend otherwise. Rather than hijacked films or artistic pirates, these recordings are reproductions of reception that call our attention to all that we don't see when we
watch films – or, perhaps, all that we do.

Thanks to Jose Friere and Miriam Katzoff at Team Gallery for making Routson's
work available for study.

Notes

1.   See Young, Michael. "The Art of Stealing Movies." *V-Life* [*Variety* supplement], Nov.
     2003: p. 76; McCabe, Brent. "Scene Stealer." *The Baltimore City Paper*, 21 January
     2004. <http://www.citypaper.com/2004-01-21/pf/feature_pf.html>; Smith, Roberta.
     "When One Man's Video Art Is Another's Copyright Crime." *The New York Times*, 6
     May 2004: E1 and E5; Lieberman, Rhonda. "Sound and Vision. John Routson." *Film
     Comment* (July/Aug. 2004): p. 17. In addition, his shows have been reviewed in *The
     Village Voice, Time Out New York, The New Yorker*, and *Flash Art*.
2.   For an ode to pirate tapes of Hollywood films, see Crouse, Edward E. "Mageddo:
     Adventures in Lo-Fi: Sampling Bootleg Videos Bought on New York Streets." *Film
     Comment* (May/June 2001): pp. 58-61.
3.   Heylin, Clinton. *Bootleg: The Secret History of the Other Recording Industry*. New York:
     St. Martin's Press, 1994: p. 8.
4.   Idem: p. 6.
5.   See Alberro, Alexander and Blake Stimson (eds.). *Conceptual Art: A Critical Anthol-
     ogy*. Cambridge, Mass.: MIT Press, 1999.
6.   In his earliest publicly exhibited works (both 1992), Routson produced a random,
     untitled VHS mix-tape by recording moments from television broadcasts that
     caught his interest and, as a work titled *Free Kittens*, released five felines to run loose
     in a gallery. He also has a continuing, long-term project of collecting commercial
     photographs of Easter bunnies taken at malls; these come from seasonal set-ups
     where parents pay for kitsch images of their children on the laps of adults in fuzzy
     white costumes, but Routson purchases photos of the rabbits alone, looking alter-
     nately cheery and desperate.

7. Found footage films and appropriation video have extensive histories; Joseph Cornell, Bruce Conner, and Ken Jacobs were the seminal innovators of found-footage film, Dara Birnbaum of appropriation video. Recent examples are far too numerous to recount in detail, but prominent contemporary artists continuing in these modes include Douglas Gordon, Christian Marclay, Peter Tscherkassky, Caspar Straake, Mike Hoolboom, Leah Gilliam, Nikolas Provost, Craig Baldwin, and Abigail Child; working specifically with early or damaged orphan films, Peter Delpeut's LYRICAL NITRATE (Netherlands: 1991) and Bill Morrison's DECASIA (USA: 2002) appropriate the texture of the medium itself more than its content. In addition to his feature film bootlegs, Routson has produced a pair of works that involve critical intervention through extensive re-working. With CARRIE/PORKY'S: ORIGINALITY, NEATNESS AND HYGIENE (USA: 2000) he created a stroboscopic work of gaze theory that alternates frames from shower scenes in CARRIE (USA: Brian DePalma, 1976) and PORKY'S (Canada/USA: Bob Clark, 1982). He also re-edited a bootleg of Matthew Barney's CREMASTER 4 (USA: 1995) for television, complete with network tags and station identification (for Disney-owned ABC) and commercials (beginning with an Audi ad prominently featuring the Solomon R. Guggenheim Museum in New York, one of Barney's major sponsors and exhibitors).

8. Gordon's 24 HOUR PSYCHO (1993) slows down Hitchcock's film to approximately 24 hours, playing out in stuttering slowness that makes the thriller tedious. His installation FIVE YEAR DRIVE BY (1995) extends duration of THE SEARCHERS (USA: John Ford, 1956) to a five-year running time, replicating the narrative's temporal span. In the installation BETWEEN DARKNESS AND LIGHT (AFTER WILLIAM BLAKE) (1997), THE SONG OF BERNADETTE (USA: Henry King, 1943) and THE EXORCIST (USA: William Friedkin, 1973) are projected on opposite sides of a translucent screen simultaneously so that the films' images dissolve into each other.

9. Bellour, Raymond, Kent Jones, et al, "Movie Mutations. Letters from (and to) Some Children of 1960." Rosenbaum, Jonathan, Adrian Martin, eds. *Movie Mutations: The Changing Face of World Cinephilia*. London: BFI, 2003: p. 8, pp. 28-29. See also Sontag, Susan. "The Decay of Cinema." *The New York Times Magazine*, 25 February 1996: p. 60.

10. In relation to Ken Jacobs's TOM, TOM, THE PIPER'S SON (USA: 1969), in which the camera moves around to focus on details within the frame as it reproduces an early film, Annette Michelson suggests that "cinephilia will now assume the guise of meta-cinema," also an apt description of Routson's work. Michelson, Annette. "Gnosis and Iconoclasm: A Case Study of Cinephilia." *October*, no. 83 (Winter 1998): pp. 15-16.

11. Elkins, James. *The Object Stares Back: On the Nature of Seeing*. New York: Simon and Schuster, 1996: pp. 201-202.

12. Several books have been published on the subject, but the most comprehensive and useful are Sterne, Jonathan. *The Audible Past: Cultural Origins of Sound Reproduction*. Durham: Duke University Press, 2004; and Chanan, Michael. *Repeated Takes: A Short History of Recording and Its Effects on Music*. New York: Verso, 1995.

13. Benjamin, Walter. *Illuminations: Essays and Reflections*. Arendt, Hannah (ed.), Zohn, Harry (trans.). New York: Schocken Books, 1969: pp. 217-251.

14. Paul Willemen suggests connections between cinephilia and both nostalgia and necrophilia in "Through a Glass Darkly: Cinephilia Reconsidered." *Looks and Frictions:*

Essays in Cultural Studies and Film Theory. Bloomington and London: Indiana University Press and BFI, 1994: pp. 223-257. Editors' note: see also Thomas Elsaesser on cinephilia as essentially necrophilic/vampiristic: Elsaesser, "Ueber den Nutzen der Enttaeschung: Filmkritik zwischen Cinephilie und Nekrophilie." Schenk, Irmbert (ed.). *Filmkritik. Bestandsaufnahmen und Perspectiven*. Marburg: Schueren, 1998: pp. 91-114.

15. Michelson, Annette. "Gnosis and Iconoclasm": p. 3.
16. An early scene takes on new significance in Routson's bootleg, as Haven Hamilton (Henry Gibson) expresses anger at the presence of the BBC reporter (Geraldine Chaplin) with her recording equipment in the studio; he says that if she wants a copy, she can wait and buy the album.

Playing the Waves

The Name of the Game is Dogme95

Jan Simons

Dogme95: Movement or Mimicry?

In hindsight, Dogme95 has been a spectacular but short-lived experience. The Danish film movement was launched in March 1995 at the conference "Cinema in its second century" in the Odeon Theater in Paris where Lars von Trier presented the Dogme95 Manifesto.[1] The closure of the Dogme95 secretariat was officially announced in June 2002.[2] If one takes into account that the first official Dogme films FESTEN (Denmark: Thomas Vinterberg, 1998) and IDIOTERNE (Denmark: Lars von Trier, 1998) were premiered at the 1998 edition of the Cannes Film Festival, one could argue that Dogme95 lasted for only four years. Considering that each of the four founding *brethren*, Lars von Trier, Thomas Vinterberg, Søren Kragh-Jacobsen, and Kristian Levring, made only one official Dogme film,[3] the movement starts to resemble an ephemeral *hype*. Some critics indeed saw the Dogme95 movement as nothing but a publicity stunt with the aim "to advertise one and only one item: Von Trier himself as a directorial value on the cultural stock market."[4] If so, one can only say that this PR stunt has been astonishingly successful. It raised Lars von Trier to international celebrity status, and between 1999 and 2000 some 35 films submitted by mainly young filmmakers from all over the world were awarded an official Dogme certificate.[5]

Dogme95 also achieved considerable critical success, though more because of its manifesto than its films. One may even wonder if films like FESTEN and IDIOTERNE would have become international hits if they had not been preceded by the manifesto. After all, Von Trier's earlier films THE ELEMENT OF CRIME (Denmark: 1984) and EUROPA (Denmark/Sweden/France/Germany/Switzerland: 1991) were not very successful even in Denmark and abroad they drew mainly the attention of a few Parisian *cinephiles*, while MIFUNE'S SIDSTE SANG (Denmark/Sweden: Anders Thomas Jensen, Søren Kragh-Jacobsen, 1999) and THE KING IS ALIVE (Sweden/Denmark/USA: Kristian Levring, 2000) scarcely received any distribution at all outside the international festival circuit. Nevertheless, books were published that celebrated the Dogme95 Brotherhood as "the gang that took on Hollywood,"[6] and in which the Dogme movement was held up as an example of "a small nation's response to globalization."[7] Essays were written that attributed no less than "film purity," "a neo-Bazinian ideal" and "humanism" to Dogme95.[8] Lars von Trier's newly acquired international reputation was authorized by the publication of a monograph in the series "World Directors" of the British Film Institute.[9]

> Dogme95 was perceived as an alternative to mainstream cinema that was dominated by the star and special effects-driven blockbusters of Hollywood. And this was, indeed, how it had presented itself. The Dogme95 Manifesto rejects the "illusions" the contemporary cinema produces with "trickery" and by "using new technology" which enables "anyone at any time (to) wash the last grains of truth away in the deadly embrace of sensation."[10]

Dogme95 was either vehemently rejected as a mere publicity stunt, or enthusiastically embraced as a viable alternative to the commercial blockbuster. Those who endorsed the Dogme95 program welcomed it as a call to arms for a new realism in cinema. They perceived Dogme95 as a replay of the oppositional stance of the movements of post-war modern European cinema, like Italian neo-realism (championed by André Bazin), the French Nouvelle Vague and other "waves" that followed in its wake. Richard Kelly, author of the first book on Dogme95, not only called the rules of the Vow of Chastity "surely the most audacious and conspicuous attempt to reinvent the cinema since, well, Godard", but even went so far as to write that "[l]acing between every line was a red thread, linking these Rules to Godard's pronouncements and actions, across four decades."[11] From Bazinian (neo-)realism to Godard, Dogme95 looked to many a critic and practitioner like a reincarnation of the European modernist cinema.

This is not surprising since the Dogme95 Manifesto itself reiterated much of the rhetoric of modernist artistic and political manifestos. Its opening sentence, "Dogme 95 has the expressed goal of countering 'certain tendencies' in the cinema today" is an explicit reference to François Truffaut's article "Une certaine tendence du cinéma français" published in the Cahiers du Cinéma of January 1954, which came to be considered the "manifesto" of the Nouvelle Vague.[12] Phrases like "In 1960 enough was enough! The cinema was dead and called for resurrection!" echoed the rhetoric of the Futurist Manifesto,[13] whereas the phrase "Today a technological storm is raging" also brings to mind the first sentence of the Communist Manifesto, "A spectre is haunting Europe."[14] The very rejection of "illusionism" is itself a recurrent trope in the rhetoric of the movements of modernist European cinema, which raises the question whether the "anti-illusionism" of the Manifesto should not be seen on a par with the references to other modernist manifestos: as a postmodern pastiche?

Von Trier's presentation of the Manifesto, which he read aloud and then threw into his audience printed on red leaflets, was a performance that echoed the actions of the Internationale Situationiste. Von Trier's gesture not only echoed a Situationist performance formally, but also in spirit. By summoning and summarizing the history of political and artistic modernism, Von Trier also accomplished a Situationist *détournement* of this history, including the Situationist gesture itself. As Karl Marx once remarked, history only repeats itself as a farce and this seems to be exactly the point Von Trier was making when he launched the Dogme95 Manifesto. According to its authors themselves, the Manifesto and the Vow of Chastity, had been "actually written in only 25 minutes and under continuous bursts of merry laughter...".[15] If then, as Von Trier and Vinterberg themselves claim, the Dogme95 Manifesto is at the same time deeply ironic and "most serious meant [sic],"[16] it is not be taken seriously at the level of its literal content or the substance of its rules, but at the level of its form.

The form of the Manifesto and Von Trier's performance were a simulation, a playing out of a model of modernist avant-gardism which no longer existed. It turned modernism into a play of mimicry and the foundation of a film movement itself into "a kind of play, a game called 'rule-making'."[17] That is, if Dogme95 is to be taken seriously as an alternative to Hollywood, it should not be interpreted from the perspective of the modernist movements of half a century ago but from the point of view of mimicry and mocking. Dogme95, I will argue, turns filmmaking itself into a game. Isn't Hollywood after all increasingly becoming a part of the games industry?[18]

Realism or Rules

The rules laid down in the Vow of Chastity are a call for a rigorous "back to basics." As the Manifesto puts it, "DOGME 95 counters the film of illusion by the presentation of an indisputable set of rules known as THE VOW OF CHASTITY [sic]."[19] The rules forbid the filmmaker from bringing props onto the set, using "special lighting," recording sound separately from the images, staging a scene for the camera ("The film must not take place where the camera is standing; shooting must take place where the film takes place") or to film "superficial action" ("Murders, weapons, etc. must not occur"). On a more positive note, they prescribe the use of mobile, handheld cameras (that must follow actions of the actors) and that the film "must take place here and now." Since the rules forbid any embellishment or any transformation of a film set, any manipulation of images and sound in post-production ("Optical work and filters are forbidden"), any conventional plot ("Genre movies are not acceptable") or what is somewhat mysteriously called "temporal and geographical alienation," they have been largely interpreted as a recipe for an unadorned, raw realism.

Words like "real," "reality," or "realism," however, do not occur in the Manifesto and in the Vow of Chastity. The "chastity" the rules require from the filmmaker is an abstinence from "trickery," but the Manifesto and the Vow of Chastity are silent on matters of representation, subject matter, themes, and content. The rules are not concerned with the film as it will appear on the screen, but the manner in which the film will be produced: they are production rules. The rules are not concerned with the film spectator but with the filmmaker. The Dogme95 rules do not prescribe certain film aesthetics but a therapy for professionals who, through Dogme, could forget the heavy load of the modern film production machinery for a while and instead develop and exercise their creativity.[20]

Abiding by the rules of the Manifesto, the "professional" filmmaker forces himself to go "back to basics" and to re-invent the practice of filmmaking. However, the rules do not commit the filmmaker to realism. The rules, for instance, do not preclude special effects or supernatural events – there is, for instance, a ghost appearance in FESTEN – but they forbid the use of certain "tricks" to produce them, like postproduction manipulation. If the use of special effects is necessary or desirable, the Dogme95 filmmaker must find ways to produce them within the constraints of the rules (or else confess cheats).

This is a far cry from a neo-Bazinian approach to filmmaking. André Bazin did not object to special effects either, and was also more concerned with the way they were recorded than with their "unrealistic" appearance. In his essay "Montage interdit" Bazin discusses the short children's film LE BALLON ROUGE (France: Albert Lamorrisse, 1956) in which a red balloon follows a little boy around the streets of Paris "like a little dog!"[21] Bazin is well aware that the balloon is "truqué" – the film is not "a documentary of a miracle or of a fakir at work"[22] – but according to Bazin the trickery is convincing because Lamorisse refrains from editing:

> "Essential cinema, seen for once in its pure state, on the contrary, is to be found in the straightforward photographic respect for the unity of space."[23]

The aesthetics of Bazin is aimed at a perceptual realism which "obtains to the degree that perceiving a cinematic representation of some thing or event is like perceiving that thing or event in salient respects."[24] That is, however the effect is achieved, even an improbable or impossible thing or event must look on the screen as it would look when perceived in reality. The Dogme95 aesthetics, which might be called "productional realism" is the exact reverse of this: however whatever a thing or event looks like on the screen, its image must be produced by abiding by the rules of the Manifesto. Since productional realism is not concerned with perceptual realism (nor with "content realism"), the question "why does Dogma not have a rule requiring unobtrusive editing and very long takes...?"[25] is beside the point. The purpose of productional realism is not to provide the spectator with a convincing representation of filmic objects and events, but to stimulate the creativity and inventiveness of the filmmaker.

The final scene of the Dogme&3 film MIFUNES SIDSTE SANG is a nice example of how the rules stimulate the creativity of the filmmaker in order to find ways around the constraints imposed by the rules. The film ends with a party where Kresten (Anders Berthelsen) and Liva (Iben Hjelje) dance while embracing and kissing each other, witnessed by Liva's sun Bjarke (Emil Tarding) and Kresten's mentally retarded little brother Rud (Jesper Asholt). Rud, who is filming the scene with a digital video camera, is pulled away by Bjarke, who says, "Let's get out of here, before it becomes pornography." "Idiot" Rud, using a digital video camera to film a love scene that has every chance of turning into hardcore porn is, of course, an ironic allusion to Lars von Trier's IDIOTERNE. But the scene is also an ironic comment on the Dogme rules themselves. A camera movement reveals an orchestra playing in the middle of the room where Kresten and Livia are dancing. As rule 2 of the Vow of Chastity decrees, the music "occurs where the scene is being shot."

This scene clarifies a few things about the rules. First, they are not geared towards a realism of any sort. The presence of the orchestra – and of Rud's digital video camera – is completely unmotivated and given the preceding story even quite improbable. Nor is Rud's digital video camera there as a self-reflective device to remind the spectators that they are "just watching a movie." Second, the rules are not repressive because they forbid the filmmaker to resort to conventional film practices, but they are productive because they challenge the filmmaker to find new ways to achieve his or her goals: the rules force the filmmaker to invent and develop new film practices, and by doing so, to make new kinds of films. Third, the rules are not to be taken (too) seriously and strictly obeyed, but to be mocked and to be played with light-heartedly. Whereas the final scene of MIFUNE mocks Von Trier's IDIOTERNE, this "ultimate Dogma work" (Peter Schepelern) itself can be seen as a demonstration, a parody, and a ridiculing of the Dogme rules.[26] Fourth, and most importantly, the purpose of the rules is not to add to the burden of filmmaking, but to transform the "heavy load of modern film production" into a joyful, pleasurable, and cheerful game.

The Dogme95 rules have all the characteristics of game rules. By prescribing what the player is obliged, forbidden or allowed to do, they set limits to how the player may achieve her goal.[27] Rules of games often allow a player to reach a goal only by using the least efficient means available, just as Dogme95 forbids the filmmaker to use the usual apparatus, methods and procedures of his trade. But, as computer game theoretician Jesper Juul says, "rules specify limitations and affordances" since they also set up potential actions and allow the player to make moves and find ways to achieve his goal.[28]

Dogme95, then, turns filmmaking into a game, and, as game rules, the Dogme95 rules are not aimed at a serious, "extra-ludic" goal, like achieving a "pure" representation of a bare truth. The main, and perhaps only function of the rules of a game is to make the game possible: they exist only for the sake of the game. As Juul points out, the rules of a game only make sense within a game, but are meaningless outside it.[29] Because nothing serious apart from the game itself depends on them, the rules of games are arbitrary: changing the rules may change the game or create a new game altogether, but they will still define "just a game." Any game is in principle as good as any other and a preference for one game rather than another is eventually a matter of personal preference. For Dogme95, too, the rules of the Vow of Chastity are just one particular set of arbitrary rules out of a vast, even infinite set of different sets of rules that specify different but equally valid games of filmmaking. As Von Trier said:

> But I still think that Dogme might persist in the sense that a director would be able to say, "I would feel like making that kind of film." I think that would be amusing. I'm sure a lot of people could profit from that. At which point you might argue that they could just as easily profit from a different set of rules. Yes, of course. But then go ahead and formulate them. Ours are just a proposal.[30]

Dogme95 thus defines filmmaking at a higher level first and foremost as a "rule-making game."[31] The particular set of rules that specifies a particular game of filmmaking is secondary to the primary principle that filmmaking – including Hollywood, art cinema and Dogme95 itself – is a playful, rule-based practice. A good demonstration of filmmaking as a rule-based game is provided by the film THE FIVE OBSTRUCTIONS (Denmark/Sweden/Belgium/France: Jørgen Leth, 2003), in which Lars von Trier gives his former mentor, filmmaker Jørgen Leth, a number of arbitrary rules for each of the five remakes of his 1967 film THE PERFECT HUMAN (Denmark: Jørgen Leth, 1967). The rules are arbitrary, and "following" them means finding ways around the constraints Von Trier imposed on Leth, who is subjected to the sort of therapy Von Trier and Vinterberg said Dogme95 was intended to be for professional film makers.

This also means that nothing particular depends on the Dogme95 rules as such, and the Brethren have been the first to exchange these rules for others. Asked whether either of his next film projects after FESTEN, THE THIRD LIE (Canada: 2000) and ALL ABOUT LOVE (USA/Japan/Sweden/UK/Denmark/Germany/Netherlands: 2003) was going to be a Dogme film, Thomas Vinterberg answered: "Definitely not. I mean, that's the whole point."[32] And although many critics have described Von Trier's musical DANCER IN THE DARK (Denmark/Germany/Netherlands/USA/UK/France/Sweden/Finland/Norway/Iceland: 2000) as a break with Dogme95 aesthetics, in the documentary VON

TRIER'S 100 ØJNE – VON TRIER'S 100 EYES (Denmark: Katia Forbert, 2000), Von Trier himself explained the conception of this film as just another game:

> I always wanted to make a musical, but I didn't know how to do it. I still don't know. But I'm very good at inventing games. I'm not good at playing games, though. This game was called "Let's make a musical!"

For DANCER IN THE DARK Von Trier wrote a "Selma Manifesto" in which the "rules" of this film are laid down.[33] In fact, the Dogme95 Manifesto is just one of the many manifestos Von Trier has written. Each of his films before and after the launching of Dogme95 was accompanied by a Manifesto in which he laid down the principles and rules for each particular film.[34] From this perspective, IDIOTERNE was just one film game among others.

Simulation

Although the Dogme95 Manifesto is silent about classic topics of modern film manifestos like subject matter, themes, or the relationship between film image and reality, Dogme's approach to filmmaking as a rule-based game is more than a formal redefinition. The Manifesto offers a radically new answer to Bazin's famous question "What is film?" which has been largely overlooked because the Manifesto has mostly been interpreted from a Bazinian point of view. This is all the more astonishing because the Manifesto very explicitly marks its distance from the modernist film movements. In fact, the Manifesto denounces any notion of film as an aesthetic object and the director as artist:

> Furthermore, I swear as a director to refrain from personal taste! I am no longer an artist. I swear to refrain from creating a "work," as I regard the instant as more important than the whole. My supreme goal is to force the truth out of my characters and settings. I swear to do so by all the means available and at the cost of any good taste and any aesthetic considerations.
>
> Thus I make my VOW OF CHASTITY.[35]

These enigmatic but certainly "provocative" sentences are strangely enough the ones least commented upon. If, however, one reads these lines and the rules of the Vow of Chastity that precede them in the light of the game approach to filmmaking, one starts to see the contours of a completely new conception of film that owes more to new media and computer games than to the classical and modernist cinema.

It is, of course, possible to see the denouncement of the status of artist and of the "individual film" either as "pure provocation" on the part of Von Trier, who usually has his name written in extra large type in the credits of his rather idio-syncratic films, or on a more positive note as the ultimate consequence of a rea-listic aesthetics that wants to make "reality speak for itself." But although the Rules deny the director a mention in the credits, they don't dismiss the director from the set. Rather they assign a different status and role to the filmmaker from that of the "individual" artist who has to "recede to the background"[36] in favor of "the truth of characters and settings."

To see what the altered status of the filmmaker is, one should read these lines in the spirit of the Dogme95 Manifesto, which addresses production methods and not the effects of these methods on the screen. In practically every mode of feature filmmaking, the basic unit of a film story is the scene, which is thought of as a correct, a probable or in some way effective representation of a unique (series of) event(s). Since the events are already "known," the task of the film director is to plan, design, orchestrate, and choreograph the re-enactment of the events in such a way that their representation on the screen is correct, convin-cing, and in the case of the "individual" *auteur* film, also expresses a "view" on the event. Mise-en-scène and framing are generally seen as the hallmarks of the film *auteur*.

Scenes, moreover, normally consist of several shots, which have to be staged and framed with the preceding and next shots in mind. Individual instances of a film are thus conceived, staged, framed and filmed from the perspective of the film as a whole. From Eisenstein to Hitchcock, from Godard to the contempo-rary Hollywood blockbuster, almost all filmmakers have taken this *storyboard* approach to filmmaking. The motivation and legitimization for this storyboard approach is the above-mentioned idea that a film is a representation of unique events that make up a story that has taken place before its narration.

Dogme95 proposes a completely different approach, which is partially ex-pressed in the third rule which requires the camera to *follow* the action instead of the action being staged *for* the camera. Other filmmakers, like John Cassa-vetes, practiced this approach to filming a scene as well, while remaining firmly within the realm of representational filmmaking. Improvisation, which opens up the possibility of chance, the unexpected and spontaneous, has certainly be-come an important part of Von Trier's film practice after his Dogme95 experi-ence, but is not crucial to the difference the Dogme95 approach makes.[37] As in a game, the rules only make sense when taken together. And, like game rules, they also only make sense within the context of the particular game they specify. Improvisation and following the actors with a camera have been practiced be-fore, but in the context of a different game where these practices take on a dif-ferent meaning and value.

First of all, for Dogme95, a scene is not a representation of unique events that must be reconstructed on the film set and eventually on the screen. The prohibition on specially made or brought props and sets (rule 1), non-diegetic sound (rule 2), artificial lighting (rule 4) and the use of "optical work and filters" (rule 5) are an injunction to keep the set cleared of everything that might suggest that what happens in front of the camera is a representational reconstitution of a fictional or historical past event. The only tools the rules allow are the set where the filming takes place, the actors who will embody the event, the story which specifies the event, and of course the "handheld camera" with which the action is to be recorded. With these tools, the filmmaker and the actors must bring about an enactment of one or some of the many ways the story event might evolve. The setting and the actors are the materials with which the director builds a *model* of the situation specified by processes and relationships as described in the script.

The Dogme director, that is, is not to create a *representation* of an event, but a *simulation*: the enacted and filmed event is a state in which the *model* of a situation described by the script settles. In science or in engineering, a model is not necessarily a representational simile of the "system" it models. Newton's mathematical equations do not "look like" the orbits of the planets. Lorenz's famous "butterfly graph" does not "look like" the changes in the weather conditions he was studying. The Newton's equations and Lorenz's graph capture some quantified properties of the systems the behavior of which they wanted to model for explanatory and predictive purposes. Models are also often used to study the behavior of "systems" under circumstances that are very unlikely to occur in reality, or are too dangerous or too expensive to carry out in reality. Models that simulate systems are radically different from representations of events: first of all, they do not necessarily have any visual or analogical similarity to the source system they model, and secondly, they do not necessarily, and in fact hardly ever, reconstruct events that have actually occurred but simulate events as they could or might have happened.[38]

Computer-based models in general and video games in particular are interesting examples because computer-generated virtual realities are visualizations of mathematical models (they are defined in terms of numbers, relations between numbers, and changes in numbers over time[39]). For reasons of clarity, designers may decide to give the mathematical model a visualization that is similar or analogous to the appearance of its source system. Weather forecasts on television, for instance, visualize the weather with images of clouds moving over a map, and game designers often visualize the mathematical models in which the game is captured with images of familiar environments (landscapes, cities) or well-known historical events. But these visualizations are not required by the model and can readily be exchanged for another visualization, provided that this visualization renders the relevant properties and behaviors. Game designers call the particular design of a visualization the "coloring" of a game.[40]

Games also reveal a third difference between simulations and representations relevant for an understanding of the Dogme95 approach to filmmaking. The model of a system's behavior reacts to certain stimuli according to a set of conditions or rules included in the model. Game players feed the model of the game they are playing with data by pushing buttons, moving a joystick or manipulating some other input device; an engineer may test the behavior of an airplane by feeding the model with various parameters like temperature, pressure, speed, height, weather conditions, etc. Simulations, whether in games or in scientific experiments, are used to explore the kinds of states a model gets into under certain circumstances. Models are generally not used to reconstruct events that have actually occurred (although that might be one of the applications of a model) but to explore and experiment with states the modeled system has never been in or in which it has very little chance of getting into.

Simulations, then, generally do not retrospectively reconstruct past states, but generate prospectively and hypothetically virtual states. The past actual states of a system are from the point of view of a simulation only a contingent subset of the vast "state space" of the system which contains all possible, actual and virtual states. Other than with representations, the states the model of a simulation will evolve into, are more often than not unknown to its designer/builder and user. The states the model of the system falls into, are not the *creations* of the designer or the user, but follow from the algorithms or rules that govern the behavior of the model and the parameters or variable conditions that are fed into the model. Computer artists who write algorithms and then feed them into computers to allow the computer to execute the steps, generally do not know what results the computer will produce. Since they only write the algorithms, they call themselves "algorists." They are a good example of "creators" who do not claim to be artists, and who do not let matters like "personal taste and aesthetic considerations" get in the way of the processes that generate the image.[41]

Simulation is also the *modus operandi* of the Dogme director. As argued above, the Dogme Rules oblige the filmmaker to keep the set cleared of anything that might "color" the model and distract from the elementary units from which it is built, "the story and the acting talent."[42] Dogme&4 THE KING IS ALIVE gives a nice demonstration of the modeling the Dogme95 rules impose: a group of tourists who are stranded in the Namibian desert and decide to rehearse Shakespeare's *King Lear* can only use the props they find on the spot and the natural light of the blazing sun. As is not unusual in (modern) theater, they "model" the world of Shakespeare's play, just like Von Trier in his film DOGVILLE (Denmark/Sweden/France/Norway/Netherlands/Finland/Germany/Italy/Japan/USA/UK: 2003) "modeled" the town of Dogville on a stage in a film studio with chalk lines and a few props. In Dogme#3, Kersten enacts one of the warrior roles of the Japanese actor Mifune using kitchen utensils found on his father's farm. The *spassers* in Von Trier's IDIOTERNE do not use any special props for their simulations of idiots.

Second, unlike the storyboard-filmmaker, the Dogme95 filmmaker does not know in advance how a scene will be executed. Like an algorist, the Dogme director disposes of an "initial state," specified by the story, some algorithms which are in his case a sequence of events specified by the script, some "building blocks" of his model in the form of actors and settings, and some external parameters he can feed this model like "mood." Just as an algorist lets the computer run his program, the Dogme95 director lets the actors "run the program" specified by the script and some variable parameters ("cheerful," "sad," "angry," "tender," "aggressive," etc.[43]). And just as the algorist must wait and see what state(s) the algorithms will generate, the Dogme95 director just registers the actions of the actors and waits and sees into what "state" the model formed by his settings and actors will settle into. The "coloring" or the "visualization" of the model is, like in modern theater, left to the imagination of the spectator.

How effective this procedure is in a media- and image-saturated culture of "real virtuality"[44] is nicely demonstrated by the photo sequence that closes DOGVILLE, which is accompanied by David Bowie's song "Young Americans." These photos from (among others) the Danish photographer Jacob Holdt's multi-media presentation *American Pictures* appear on the screen, as if only to confirm the visualizations with which the spectator had "colored" the scarce model of Dogville offered by the film using the knowledge of America the (non-American) s/he has acquired through photographs, films and TV programs. This photo sequence, however, points to another dimension of the simulation approach of Dogme95: it is not primarily focused on actual reality, but rather on the virtual.

Virtual Realism

Maybe because the Dogme95 Manifesto makes no comments on editing, most critics seem to have overlooked Dogme95's, or rather, Von Trier's radically innovative use of editing. Contrary to the Bazinian injunction to respect the spatio-temporal unity of the pro-filmic event, the editing in FESTEN and to various degrees, all of Von Trier's Dogme and post-Dogme films, is the very opposite of continuity editing. Not only are these films filled with jump cuts and mismatched shots, but more importantly, scenes are *sampled* by editing takes from different executions of the same scene and placed next to each other. In the scene in IDIOTERNE that leads up to Stoffer's challenging the others to *spass*, characters change places from one shot to the next, one character that was not present in one shot suddenly appears in the next, Stoffer is sitting in a wheel-chair in one shot and standing in the back of the room in the next, etc. Similar breaks and discontinuities can be observed in DANCER IN THE DARK and DOG-VILLE.

This editing style is a flagrant violation of the rules of classical cinema (an altogether different game), but entirely consistent with Dogme95's simulation approach to cinema. From the perspective of this simulation approach, the initial situation and the algorithms that govern the transitions to subsequent states define a so-called *state space* that consists of all the possible configurations that can be arrived at from the initial state by applying the algorithms.[45] For the Dogme director every execution of a scene is just one state out of a vast state space of possible versions of the events specified by the script and modalized by the parameters defined by the director. From a simulation perspective, no state is more "true," "authentic," "better," or "closer to the facts" than any other. As Von Trier explained his attempt to "dismantle psychological continuity" in his television mini series RIGET-THE KINGDOM (Denmark/France/Germany/Sweden, 1994):

> Each scene is filmed with as many different expressions and atmospheres as possible, allowing the actors to approach the material afresh each and every time. Then we edit our way to a more rapid psychological development, switching from tears to smiles in the course of a few seconds, for example – a task that is beyond most actors. The remarkable thing about this cut-and-paste method is that the viewers can't see the joints. They see a totality, the whole scene.[46]

Again, Von Trier was not the first in film history to use a "cut-and-paste method." In DEUX OU TROIS CHOSES QUE JE SAIS D'ELLE (France: 1967) Godard also shows several different executions of the same scene, but in order to emphasize the different meanings, modes and modalities that correlate with different types and genres of film (documentary, TV-report, feature film, etc.). Von Trier's cut-and-paste style wants the spectator on the contrary to gloss over the breaks and discontinuities and to synthesize them into "a totality."

Paradoxically, the discontinuities in Von Trier's films and in Vinterberg's FESTEN therefore seem to be a manifestation of the anti-montage aesthetics Lev Manovich identifies in new media practices ("where old media relied on montage, new media substitutes the aesthetics of continuity"[47]). More important than this perhaps superficial convergence with the aesthetics of new media, is that the "totality" this editing style aims at does not coincide with any single execution of the scene, nor is it a lowest common denominator. The totality that emerges from the sampled shots is, like the "America" that emerges from the photo sequence in DOGVILLE, a purely virtual pattern that underlies the state space but that is never fully actualized in any of the individual states.[48] If

Dogme95, then, focuses on "reality," it is a virtual reality, or rather the real as an actualization of the virtual. This "virtual realism" of Dogme95 is closer to Deleuze than to Bazin.

Dogme and Hollywood

Dogme95's virtual realism can be seen as a response to the special effects-driven Hollywood blockbusters. Hollywood certainly has promoted virtual realities as one of its main themes: from the MATRIX trilogy to LORD OF THE RINGS, from STAR TREK to MINORITY REPORT, the virtual seems to be ubiquitous. However, Hollywood also carefully keeps "reality" and "the virtual" firmly apart by always presenting the virtual as a computer-generated, illusionary technological effect. Paraphrasing Jean Baudrillard, one might say that by presenting virtual reality as a technological product, Hollywood makes the spectator forget the "real virtuality" of the "postmodern condition." Dogme95 does not "claim the real" against the spectacle of the virtual in Hollywood, but, instead, by refraining from advanced computer technologies, "trickeries," or artificially produced special effects, Dogme95's simulation-approach to cinema and Von Trier's virtual realism open up the virtual dimension in the real. The real as an actualised virtual, the virtual as part of the real: *bye bye Bazin* and *Stay Out of the Matrix*....

Notes

1. Von Trier, Lars, Thomas Vinterberg. "The Dogme95 Manifesto." 13 March 1995. <http://www.dogme95.dk>. There are several versions of the Manifesto in circulation, some of which are more elaborate than others. The version referred to in this chapter is the one published on the official Dogme95 website.
2. The closure of the secretariat was officially announced on the Dogme95 website. <http://www.dogme95.dk>. See also Stevenson, Jack. *Dogme Uncut: Lars von Trier, Thomas Vinterberg, and the Gang That Took on Hollywood.* Santa Monica, Ca: Santa Monica Press, 2003: pp. 291-292.
3. The other two films made by the "Brotherhood" are MIFUNE'S SIDSTE SANG (Denmark: Søren Kragh-Jacobsen, 1999) and THE KING IS ALIVE (Denmark/Sweden/USA: Kristian Levring, 2000).
4. Willemen, Paul. "Note on DANCER IN THE DARK." *Framework: The journal of cinema and media.* no. 42 (summer 2000). <http://www.frameworkonline.com/42pw.htm>.
5. The list of films officially acknowledged as Dogme films can also be found on the official Dogme95 website. Lists of Dogme films are also published in, amongst others, Stevenson, Jack. *Dogme Uncut*: pp. 271-280, and Hjort, Mette and Scott

MacKenzie (eds.). *Purity and Provocation: Dogma 95*. London: BFI Publishing, 2003: pp. 210-224. It is unknown how many Dogme films have actually been produced, because on the 9th of March 2000 the Brotherhood decided that certificates would be issued "solely on the basis of a signed and sworn statement to the effect that the Vow of Chastity has been adhered to in full and without any review of the applicant films!" *Dogme Certification. Press Release*. 9 March 2000. <http://www.dogme95.dk>.

6. Stevenson, Jack. *Dogme Uncut: Lars von Trier, Thomas Vinterberg and the Gang That Took on Hollywood*.

7. Hjort, Mette. "A Small Nation's Response to Globalization." Hjort, Mette, Scott MacKenzie. *Purity and Provocation*: pp. 31-47.

8. Conrich, Ian, Estella Tincknell. "Film purity, the Neo-Bazinian Ideal, and Humanism in Dogma 95." *P.O.V. Filmtidskrif.: A Danish Journal of Filmstudies*. no. 10, and "Aspects of Dogma." December 2000. <http://imv.au.dk/publikationer/pov/ Issue_10/section_4/artc7A.html>.

9. Stevenson. Jack. *Lars von Trier*. London: BFI, 2002.

10. Von Trier, Lars, Thomas Vinterberg. "The Dogme95 Manifesto."

11. Kelly, Richard. *The Name of This Book is Dogme95*. London: Faber & Faber, 2000: p. 4, p. 10.

12. Truffaut, François. "Une certaine tendance du cinéma français." *Cahiers du Cinéma*. no. 31 (January 1954): pp. 15-28.

13. In the Futurist Manifesto one finds phrases like: "Museums; cemetries!" and "You have objections? Enough! Enough!" Marinetti, F.T. "Manifesto of Futurism." *Le Figaro*. no. 20 (February 1909).

14. Marx, Karl, Friedrich Engels. *Manifesto of the Communist Party*. Paris, 1848.

15. Von Trier, Lars, Thomas Vinterberg. "Frequently Asked Questions. In general to Dogme95." <http://www.dogme95.dk>.

16. Idem.

17. Idem. The full paragraph out of which these quotes come reads:
"There is an implicit duplicity in The Dogme95 Manifesto. On one hand it contains a deep irony and on the other it is most serious meant. Irony and seriousness is interlinked in inseparable. What we have concerned ourselves with is the making of a set of rule. In this sense it is a kind of play, a game called 'rule-making'. Seriousness and play goes hand in hand. A clear example of this is that the very strict and serious Dogme95 Manifesto was actually written in only 25 minutes and under continuous bursts of merry laughter... Still, we maintain that we are in earnest. Dogme is not for fun. It is, however, liberating, merry, and almost fun to work under such a strict set of rules. It is this duplicity which is the magic of 'dogme.'"

18. At the time of writing this paper it was reported that Sony had bought MGM. According to CNN, "The purchase of MGM is in keeping with Chief Executive Nobuyuki Idei's vision of creating synergies between Sony's consumer electronics products and music, movies and games."

19. Von Trier, Lars, Thomas Vinterberg. "The Dogme95 Manifesto."

20. Idem.

21. Bazin, André. "Montage interdit." *Qu'est-ce que le cinéma? Édition définitive*. Paris: Les Éditions du Cerf, 1975: p. 53. Original French: "*comme un petit chien!*"

22. Bazin, André. "The Virtues and Limitations of Montage." *What Is Cinema? Essays Selected and Translated by Hugh Gray*. Vol. 1. Berkeley/Los Angeles/London: University of California Press, 2005, p.46.

23. Idem.

24. Gaut, Berys. "Naked film. Dogma and its limits." Hort, Mette, Scott MacKenzie. *Purity and provocation*: p. 98. Bazin himself described the effect of his preferred stylistic devices, *profondeur du champ* and *plan séquence*, the use of which results in "photographic respect of the unity of space" as:
"That depth of focus brings the spectator into a relation with the image closer to that which he enjoys with reality. Therefore it is correct to say that, independently of the content of the image, its structure is more realistic." Bazin, André. "The Evolution of the Language of Cinema. " *What Is Cinema?*: p. 35.

25. Gaut, Berys. "Naked film:" p. 99.

26. See Schepelern, Peter. "'Kill your darlings.' Lars von Trier and the origin of Dogma 95." Hjort, Mette, Scott MacKenzie. *Purity and provocation*: p. 65.

27. Järvinen, Aki. "Making and breaking games. A typology of rules." Copier, Marinka, Joost Raessens, eds. *Level Up. Digital games research conference*. Utrecht: University of Utrecht/DIGRA, 2003: p. 70-71.

28. Juul, Jesper. *Half-real. Video games between real rules and fictional worlds*. Diss. IT University of Copenhagen, Copenhagen, 2003: p. 55.

29. Idem.

30. MacKenzie, Scott. "Manifest destinies. Dogma 95 and the future of the film manifesto." Hjort, Mette, Scott MacKenzie. *Purity and provocation*: p. 56.

31. Von Trier, Lars, Thomas Vinterberg. "FAQs."

32. Kelly, Richard. *The name of this book is Dogme95*: p. 113.

33. The "Selma Manifesto" can be found on the official website of Dancer in the Dark: <http://www.tvropa.com/channels/dancerd/>.

34. Schepelern, Peter. "'Kill your darlings.'" pp. 59-60.

35. Von Trier, Lars, Thomas Vinterberg. "The Dogme95 Manifesto."

36. Von Trier, Lars, Thomas Vinterberg. "FAQs."

37. In the "FAQs" Von Trier and Vinterberg explicitly state that "… Dogme films don't have to be improvised" but that it has been an inspiration for the Dogme director "because it fits so perfectly with the freedom of the handheld camera."

38. "Shearing away detail is the very essence of model building. Whatever else we require, a model *must* be simpler than the thing modeled." Holland, John. *Emergence: From chaos to order*. Cambridge, Ma.: Perseus Books, 1998: p. 24.

39. Holland, John. *Emergence*: p. 27.

40. Costikyan, Greg. "I have no words & I must design." *Interactive Phantasy&2*, 1994. Also available on: <http://www.costik.com/nowords.html&Color>. On computer games as simulations see also: Frasca, Gonzalo. "Simulation versus narrative. Introduction to ludology." Wolf, Mark, J.P., Bernard Perron. *The Video Game Theory Reader*. London: Routledge, 2003: pp. 221-235.

41. On algorithmic art see Stephen Wilson, *Information Arts: Intersections of Art, Science, and Technology*. Cambridge, Ma: MIT Press, 2002, pp. 312-339.

42. Thomas Vinterberg. Von Trier, Lars, Thomas Vinterberg. "FAQs."

43. For a description of this production method see Stevenson, Jack. *Lars von Trier*: p. 84 a.f.

44. Castells, Manuel. *The Information Age: Economy, Society and Culture, Vol 1. The Rise of the Network Society.* Oxford: Blackwell Publishers, 1996: p. 327 ff.
45. Holland, John. *Emergence*: p. 34.
46. Stevenson, Jack. *Lars von Trier*: p. 84.
47. Manovich, Lev. *The Language of New Media.* Cambridge, Mass: MIT Press, 2001: p. 143.
48. One might think of the virtual as described by Sanford Kwinter:
     "The so-called emergence and evolution of form will no longer follow the classical, eidetic pathway determined by the possible and the real. Rather, it will follow the dynamic and uncertain processes that characterize the schema that links a virtual component to an actual one. What is most important to understand here is that unlike the previous schema where the "possible" had no reality (before emerging), here the virtual, though it may yet have no actuality, is nonetheless fully real. It exists, one might say, as a free difference or singularity, not yet combined with other differences into a complex ensemble or salient form. What this means is that the virtual does not have to be realized, but only actualized (activated and integrated); its adventure involves a developmental passage from one state to another. The virtual is gathered, selected – let us say incarnated – it passes from one moment-event (or complex) in order to emerge – differently, uniquely – within another. Indeed the actual does not resemble the virtual, as something preformed or preexisting itself. The relation of the virtual to the actual is therefore not one of resemblance but rather of difference, innovation, creation (every complex, or moment-event, is unique and new)." Kwinter, Sanford. *Architectures of Time: Toward a Theory of the Event in Modernist Culture.* Cambridge, Mass: MIT Press, 2001: p. 8.

The Parenthesis and the Standard

On a Film by Morgan Fisher

Federico Windhausen

The Fact of Industry

In his 16mm film Standard Gauge (USA: 1984), the American filmmaker Morgan Fisher presents, in a close-up long take of a light table, a series of frames from his collection of 35mm filmstrips. Throughout the course of his presentation, Fisher's voice-over narration frequently describes what connects him to each piece of film, while also providing fragments of a broader cultural history, tied to "the complex of economic activity that gives rise to an Industrial standard" such as the preferred gauge format of 35mm.[1]

Near the end of the film, as he recounts his work as editor and actor on a low-budget feature called Messiah of Evil (USA: Willard Huyck, 1974), he mentions that the printing lab was Technicolor. After noting that he rescued some films that the lab had been destroying ("with meat cleavers"), he makes the following commentary, which I quote in full:

> At that time Technicolor was still doing imbibition printing. Imbibition, or IB, printing was the dye transfer process that was the foundation of the Technicolor system. By means of filters, Technicolor would make a separation matrix from the original color negative for each of three colors: yellow, cyan, and magenta. To make a print, each matrix was immersed in a bath of the corresponding dye, which it would soak up, that is to say, imbibe. Each of the matrices was applied in turn to the print stock, each in correct registration with the others. All the photographic materials used in IB printing were monochrome, and the dyes were stable and resistant to fading, so the matrices and prints had a high degree of permanence. This is the head or tail, I don't know which, of the imbibition matrix for the magenta record. This material is beautiful to handle. It's more substantial than ordinary film. It's still pliable and limber, but in a different way. When IB release prints were ordered in large quantities, they were cheaper than other processes, and Technicolor was able to make money on the volume. But in the early seventies Technicolor came to a critical moment. The manufacture of IB prints was labor-intensive, and labor costs were going up. At the some time, studios became less confident of the market for their product and so began to order prints in smaller quantities. The only way Technicolor could offer IB printing and stay

competitive with other processes was to automate, but they didn't have the resources to do so. A few years after we finished working on the film, the Hollywood plant stopped making IB prints. The People's Republic of China was interested in the IB process, but they didn't want the old machines. Technicolor built new machines for them, closed the Hollywood plant, and sold the old machines for scrap. A few months after the Hollywood plant closed, a display ad appeared in *The Hollywood Reporter* that took the form of a memorial announcement. It read: "In Loving Memory, IB. Born 1927 – Died 1975. Hollywood's own dye-transfer process whose life was unrivaled for beauty, longevity, and flexibility. We salute you." It was signed, "The Friends of IB."[2]

This extended quotation can serve as an introduction to the work of Morgan Fisher, whose most recent film, entitled ( ) (USA: 2003), is the subject of this essay.

Many cinephiles would likely regard Fisher's disquisition as a valuable example of the ongoing struggle between the practical exigencies of the business of Hollywood and the utopian promise of the industry's artistic and technical innovations. In some of the more melancholy manifestations of cinephilia, a sense of aesthetic loss or decline is accompanied by the desire to preserve the material artifacts of a dying art and to document a range of interrelated, perhaps obsolete processes (economic, artisanal, and technical). This dual desire seems to have served as a major motivation for Fisher during the conceptualization and production of STANDARD GAUGE.

In an analysis written in 1999, film scholar David James describes STANDARD GAUGE as Fisher's "requiem" for the mode of "reflexive minimalism" associated with P. Adams Sitney's category of "structural film."[3] In James' view, STANDARD GAUGE asserts the "dependence of the avant-garde on the industry" while also suggesting "the passing of the antagonism to the culture industries that, however unconsciously, subtended it."[4] Interpreting the film as a "farewell to the artisanal mode of production and to the avant-garde cinema," James points out that Fisher "has not made any films since then – but he has sold an option on a script for a commercial feature, and is currently writing another that he hopes to direct himself." James' account of an artist's repudiatory gestures and his subsequent redefinition holds considerable appeal, but as Fisher's recent return to experimental filmmaking demonstrates, he neither abandoned nor renounced avant-garde cinema.[5]

In addition, the issue of whether the avant-garde is dependent on the industry, in any *generalizable* way, is not addressed in STANDARD GAUGE. Fisher does make clear in an interview, however, that he seeks, through his films, "to acknowledge the unalterable fact of the Industry, which there is no getting around, and to maintain an openness toward what it is and what it has given us. I regard the Industry as a source of ideas and material, as a subject, and in some ways as a model, even though I also criticize it."[6] In STANDARD GAUGE and his latest film, the filmmaker's reliance on industrially produced footage is the most salient indicator of his interest in Hollywood, and, as his statement indicates, his response to the industry is multifaceted.

This essay argues that ( ), Fisher's first film since STANDARD GAUGE, has its origins in the filmmaker's cinephilic tendencies, on the one hand, and, on the other, a set of self-imposed checks, limitations, and constraints designed to off-set or counter a familiar set of aesthetic conventions, ideas, and methods. In a manner roughly similar to STANDARD GAUGE, which avoids celebrating a predo-minantly subjective form of cinephilia by providing fragments of an industry's economic history, ( ) does not merely spotlight the beauty of its apparent subject matter, the often-marginalized "insert" shot (which comprises the entirety of its imagery).[7] ( ) is also an attempt to construct an alternative to two dominant montage traditions: editing for economic expressiveness and dramatic effect (in narrative film), and editing for poetic or metaphoric effect (in counter-Holly-wood film).[8] Unlike the historical and biographical narratives of STANDARD GAUGE, however, through which the filmmaker explains himself quite clearly and directly to the viewer, ( ) does not provide a clear indication *within the film* of the full extent of Fisher's concerns. The filmmaker's decision to refrain from providing an internal explanation of the film's dual subject matter (inserts and montage) is provocative, resisting commonly held notions about spectatorial experience and the value of supplemental information. Thus, Fisher's project assumes the challenges of an alternative approach to filmic construction and a revised view of the tasks of the spectator.

The Insert Made Visible

According to one definition, the insert shot presents "part of a scene as filmed from a different angle and/or focal length from the master shot. Inserts cover action already covered in the master shot, but emphasize a different aspect of that action due to the different framing... the term 'insert' is often confined to views of objects – and body parts, other than the [actor's] head" (or face).[9] Nar-rative silent films, for example, are especially inclined toward shots of letters, notes, and newspaper headlines because the insert allows for information to be conveyed from within the diegetic world, without recourse to conspicuous in-ter-titles.[10] The standard established during the silent era, of an unobtrusive, seamless insert, has been upheld throughout the long history of narrative sound films structured according to classical Hollywood principles.

In every normative case, the insert shot should be entirely functional, and therefore devoid of decorative supplements. In a written statement, Fisher observes that, despite their deeply subordinate nature, "Sometimes inserts are remarkably beautiful, but this beauty is usually hard to see because the only thing that registers is the news, the expository information, not what it is."[11] When Fisher presents his own archive of insert shots in ( ), he is asking viewers to take pleasure in the minimal, the functional, and the "utterly marginal."

The viewer of ( ) will notice a range of commonalities among the shots, including the prevalence of hands manipulating machines and technological devices of various kinds. Formal tendencies also emerge, in areas such as framing and lighting, along with a general sense of the insert's economy. Themes seem to be threaded throughout the film – most prominently, death and time. Paul Arthur's description of the film captures some of this:

> Detached from their enslavement to ongoing fictional events, shots of money, dice, knives, letters, pictures, and so on, come alive in dialogue with their neighbors. There are mysterious unmoored messages: "Meet you in front of this house at two o'clock"; "Do not disturb." Motifs spring up across the body of brief declarative close-ups: texts ranging from telegrams to tombstones; objects of danger; stealthy hand movements; measuring devices such as maps, cockpit gauges, an hourglass. Moreover, the narrative or genre *affect* originally pumped into the inserts by what preceded and came after them retains a kind of spectral presence. That is, even lacking the dramatic contexts in which these visual exclamation points carried out their tasks, we can sense an imminent anger or sadness or elation, heated onslaughts of betrayal, murder, insanity lurking just outside the frame.[12]

As Arthur points out, the spectator's experience tends to be informed by his or her previous knowledge of the insert's place within narrative film. It is this familiarity, borne of our affective investments in the cinema, that heightens the psychological resonance of the inserts in ( ): a knife in the back of a coat, wrists bound with rope, an object removed from a bloody palm, a fuse being lit, a mysterious powder being slipped into a teacup, a headline announcing "POLICE SEARCH CITY FOR GIRL STOWAWAY," a telegram prescribing a police raid "after the storm," a leg in chains, a government-issue license plate, a hand touching names carved in wood, and so on.

Of particular interest to Fisher is a paradox that lies at the heart of his project. For Fisher, inserts "embody" instrumentality "to the most extreme degree," and yet the fact that they are afforded "the least latitude for the exercise of expressive intelligence" makes them no less beautiful or psychologically engaging than conventionally expressive cinematic images. (And indeed, the inserts chosen by the filmmaker are evidence of a discerning eye.)[13] Fisher's grouping is motivated by the impulse to *liberate* inserts ("to release them from their self-effacing performance of drudge-work, to free them from their servitude to story") and to make the spectator *see differently* ("a way of making them visible").[14] Thus, ( ) has its origins not only in the cinephile's experience of visual beauty, but also in a basic set of avant-garde beliefs.

Models for a Montage Method

Viewers searching for a context for ( ) within prevailing avant-garde practices might look to the tradition of "found footage." Defined by its appropriation of previously shot imagery, found footage filmmaking makes extensive use of what Arthur calls a "bottomless repository of suppressed materials... tacky archival footage, anonymous home movies, porn, and, perhaps most pointedly, a panoply of tools and movie-production processes usually erased or mystified in the name of seductive entertainment."[15] Key bodies of work in the found footage tradition, such as the films of Bruce Conner and Ken Jacobs, have long been characterized as cultural salvage operations, produced by artists devoted to the uncovering of "lost" and often unfamiliar cultural artifacts. In this context, the practice of putting together a found footage montage is said to take on political dimensions, even if a particular film does not deal with politics in any direct or topical sense.

Given that the discernment of motifs and themes seems to be a central feature of the experience of watching Fisher's film, it might seem as if the filmmaker has elected to employ montage in various metaphoric or symbolic ways. After all, found footage practice has explored the rhetorical and expressive possibilities of montage extensively.[16] In support of this view, one could cite a recent found footage video that bears some resemblance to ( ), namely THE PHOENIX TAPES (1999), produced by German filmmaker Matthias Müller and German video artist Christoph Girardet. More specifically, the second section of this six-part work, entitled "Burden of Proof," is dominated by insert shots, all selected from the films of Alfred Hitchcock.[17] Hitchcockian insert images in this section include a Social Security card, a nametag, pins for ties and lapels, a warning written on a matchbook ("They're on to you"), a finger with blood on it, a shower head, a brush passing through a woman's hair, a hand reaching for a doorknob, a drawer opened to reveal a knife, a key dropped near a shoe, and a knife plunged into a coat. In contrast to Fisher's film, Müller and Girardet's video contains a carefully constructed soundtrack, comprised of incidental noises (including many foley artist creations), environmental sounds, musical excerpts (often orchestral), and portions of dialogue. Following a montage of eyes, "Burden of Proof" ends with the close-up image of a light shining into the eye of a doctor's patient, accompanied by a single line of dialogue: "Still can't understand how I fell down those stairs."

Through its cumulative structure, "Burden of Proof" manages to convey more than a general sense of danger and lurking menace, suggesting that Hitchcock's films are full of tense, neurotic, often homicidal characters. The partially-seen actors' jerky gestures and behavioral tics, for example, can be interpreted as pathological symptoms, with the doctor-patient scenario that ends the section taking on the qualities of a culmination or thematic restatement.

Despite the apparent resemblances between ( ) and "Burden of Proof," however, Fisher's film is distinguished by a crucial difference, one that is grounded in his ideas about the construction of meaning through purposive juxtaposition. As Fisher puts it, he sought out an "impersonal" system that could produce a film that was not "cut" or "edited" in any traditional sense of those terms.[18] In developing a set of anti-expressive, quasi-arbitrary montage principles, he allowed himself the freedom to borrow and modify structuring devices from literary and artistic genres (thus revealing the extent of his interest in disciplines and practices not commonly associated with the cinema). Fisher's ideal, then, is not the artfully interwoven tapestry of patterns and motifs created by the cinephile-turned-filmmaker, but rather the catalogue or database of the collector who seeks to remove himself from the archiving system after having chosen its contents.

The rule allowed Fisher to work out the structure of his film on paper, rather than the editing table. Since he only "needed the rule to make the film," the filmmaker does not describe in detail the system he constructed or the rules he followed, telling the reader of his explanatory statement that "it is not necessary for you to know what it is."[19] Fisher does divulge that his rule dictated the following: "No two shots from the same film appear in succession. Every cut is to another film." Seeking to avoid "the usual conventions of cutting, whether those of montage or those of story films" and to "free the inserts from their stories" through discontinuity, he adhered to a structuring device that ignores the specific content of his shots.

Fisher acknowledges that his role as the composer of the rule locates him as the author of the work, but he adds that "at least the rule introduces an intermediate term that does what it can to assign responsibility for the composing to somewhere else." Indeed, he views rules as being fundamentally "inconsonant with expressivity, as that notion is conventionally understood." This conventional understanding of expressivity is shaped by the following assumptions: the artistic ego can communicate to the receiver directly by mastering his or her medium, and mediating processes can neither alter the author's fundamental message nor dislodge the creative ego from its position of authority and accountability.

Fisher acknowledges that his questioning of such ideas is part of a long tradition. The practitioners he cites as precedents and influences come from the visual arts and literature – conceptual artist Sol LeWitt, writer Raymond Roussel, and filmmaker Thom Andersen.

An artist who is known for modular structures and serial drawings and paintings, all executed according to the instructions he provides for his assistants, LeWitt insists that the artist can be a planner who selects "the basic form and rules that would govern the solution of the problem. After that the fewer decisions made in the course of completing the work, the better. This eliminates the arbitrary, the capricious, and the subjective as much as possible."[20] The "problem" is shared by Fisher: How to circumvent the *dominance* of subjectivity? How to come up with a plan that can "design the work," in LeWitt's words? As David Batchelor notes, LeWitt's objective is not to incorporate "deeply significant ideas" into art or to raise art "to a form of quasi-scientific inquiry."[21] Rather, like Fisher, LeWitt seeks to discover whether his alternative approach to standard methods of construction can yield engaging images. Since neither LeWitt nor Fisher privileges the preconceived idea over the visual artifact, neither can be accurately characterized as an iconoclastic conceptualist.

In Roussel's work, Fisher sees how an "arbitrary and mechanical method" can produce, within "radically anti-dramatic" compositional structures, an array of disturbing "scenes utterly beyond the power of the imagination to invent."[22] The author composes the rules that will select a standard component (a word, phrase, line) of a text and determine which aspect of that component will be used for connective purposes – a word's double meanings, or its homonyms, for example. Roussel's strategies demonstrate that the author can treat his or her constructive processes as a self-contained puzzle, one that is no less solvable for being so intricate and complex.

Fisher acknowledges that Andersen introduced him to Roussel's work, and it is Andersen who demonstrates to Fisher, through his 1967 film entitled — ————— (made with Malcolm Brodwick), that a film made up diverse shots can be constructed according to rigorous rules. Beginning in the 1970s, through the completion of STANDARD GAUGE, Fisher has avoided conventional "editing" by restricting himself to single-take films. In STANDARD GAUGE, for example, the sequence of filmstrips and frames that Fisher manipulates by hand could only be called a "montage" in a very loosely defined sense. Like Andersen and Brodwick, Fisher allows himself to decide the sequence of frames (or shots) and the length of time that each will remain onscreen, thereby making choices in the production of STANDARD GAUGE that resemble those of the professional editor. In contrast, Fisher's rules for ( ) prevent his determination of sequential order or shot length.

An 11-minute documentary about rock and roll and American culture (with a musical soundtrack and no narration), Andersen and Brodwick's film is based on two rules. The first is used to determine the relative length of its shots, and the second to assign a "dominant hue" for each shot and to order those hues.[23] Fisher is particularly fascinated by what the first rule produces, an emotional effect that he describes as a progressive "sense of a diffusion, a relaxation of tension." The montage sequence that elicits such a response stands in direct contrast to a specific aesthetic norm – the shortening of shots in narrative films during moments of escalating dramatic intensity. As in all of the above cases, Andersen and Brodwick's preconceived or rule-bound method is generative, producing innovation in artistic practice and expanding aesthetic experience through specially designed works.

Among the many possible precedents Fisher does not mention, one film in particular is worth reviewing. In the 1970s, Ken Jacobs discovered a 16mm print of a drama entitled THE DOCTOR, a black-and-white short made for American television roughly twenty years earlier. In the seemingly banal story of a country doctor trying to cure a sick girl, Jacobs noticed various subtexts, including a perverse link between the elderly doctor and his young patient. Rather than tease out the short's Freudian subtext through a few carefully chosen juxtapositions of shots or scenes, however, he devised a simple, systematic process of reordering, executed by his university students (with a few mistakes he decided to keep). After determining the total number of shots in the original film, Jacobs began his own film, THE DOCTOR'S DREAM (USA: 1978), in the numerical center of THE DOCTOR, with the shot that lies precisely in the middle of the original film. Jacobs explains, "It then proceeds to the shot that came before that middle shot, then skips over to the other side and shows the shot that followed the middle shot and then keeps skipping back and forth to the outer shots."[24] Jacobs' method was inspired by a performance of Nam June Paik's, in which the artist began by playing the center keys of a piano, continued to alternating lower and higher notes, and finally progressed past the piano to alternating points in space.[25] Borrowing from Paik's performance art, in the tradition of experimental filmmakers adopting structural conceits from other disciplines, Jacobs finds a seemingly impersonal way to reveal implicit meanings or themes and suggest novel or unexpected views of conventional subject matter. As in Fisher's ( ), a montage method becomes a tool of discovery.[26]

Responses and Effects

Writing of the experience of reading the novels of Roussel, Fisher maintains that "you respond to what the method produced, some of the most extraordinary writing in all of literature," but he also acknowledges that Roussel felt the need to reveal his methods to his readership in *How I Wrote Certain of My Books*.[27] In doing so, Roussel differentiated his practice from that of the Surrealists, many of whom admired the dispassionate, dedramatized presentation of singularly strange scenarios in his texts. Unaware of Roussel's carefully structured approach to writing, of the constructive innovations that defined his practice, the Surrealists declared his work "magnificently poetic," in the words of Robert Desnos, based on its effect on the reader.[28] Fisher locates in his own film a roughly analogous pairing of conceptual methods and Surrealist effects: "( ) offers the improbable but nonetheless true case of a film that in its disjunctions and incongruous juxtapositions seems Surrealist, while in fact underneath it is a structural film. That was odd enough, I thought, that Surrealism and Structuralism could be joined, irrationality and chance on the one hand and clarity and order and predictability and graspability as to overall shape on the other."[29]

The viewer of ( ) can only discover this "odd" pairing with the aid of information that is not provided within the text of the film itself. Thus, the filmmaker allows for the possibility that ( ) is allegorical, insofar as "we need to know more than what we see in the work."[30] The notion that a work of art may need to be linked to an explanatory supplement runs counter to commonly-held beliefs regarding the autonomy and universal communicability of a completed film, but Fisher's attitude, which is less provocative in an artworld context than in movie culture, is consistent with his longstanding interest in the transformative impact of discursive elements upon our experience of images. Whereas STANDARD GAUGE provides a framework through its narration, however, ( ) allows the viewer both more and less freedom. On the one hand, since the film's supplement (Fisher's statement of purpose) performs an important didactic function, one type of cinephilic ideal, that of the self-contained film, is challenged; on the other hand, some cinephiles will doubtless appreciate that the film itself remains entirely visual, a feature that facilitates the perpetual rediscovery both of the insert and of new approaches to composition.

It should be noted that STANDARD GAUGE does point ahead to ( ) in certain moments. Near the end of the film, Fisher's narration becomes more fragmented and silently contemplative, taking more time to pause over filmstrips after simple introductory statements such as, "Here is a piece of film that to me is full of interesting incidents, none of them related to one another." In those moments, STANDARD GAUGE becomes more open-ended, allowing for a wide range of spectatorial reactions to its archived imagery. Such responses might be characterized as nostalgic, but Fisher would likely take a less restrictive view. His deictic gestures in the end of STANDARD GAUGE are driven, in part, by the impulse to provoke a variety of reflective and affective responses, within which the cinephile's melancholy longing for an obsolete photochemical film aesthetic stands as merely one historically circumscribed possibility. Another response, more common to ( ), might be distinguished by a sense that the irrational can be located within a wide array of cinematic images ("full of interesting incidents, none of them related to one another"). In the cultural life of both STANDARD GAUGE and ( ), many other reactions remain to be described and catalogued by the viewers with whom Fisher seeks to engage.

Practices in Relation

( ) is a doubly reflexive film, directing our attention to cinematic imagery and cinematic methods. Were Fisher merely a sensualist, a cinephile devoted to the beauty of film form, an artful compilation would suffice. Instead, by contributing to our understanding of a shot type that even film studies tend to neglect, the filmmaker functions as a cultural historian, albeit less explicitly than the narrator of STANDARD GAUGE. He also provides a model for the multidisciplinary reassessment of montage practice, by looking for alternatives in a range of methods rarely considered by found footage filmmakers or video artists.

With a final quotation, a revealing recollection from Fisher, we can return to the topic of experimental film's relation to Hollywood cinema:

> I became interested in filmmaking in the middle sixties, when *Film Culture* presented articles about the New American Cinema and films made in Hollywood on an equal footing. In the same issue were stills from FLAMING CREATURES and the opening sequence of THE NAKED KISS, where Constance Towers beats up her pimp. That was a golden moment. The unifying idea was that of being an artist in film, no matter where. There was also the implication, which I think is correct, that what independent films and commercial films have in common is as important, or perhaps more important, than what divides them. Soon afterwards the critical politics of the magazine shifted, and except for some old films that were enshrined in history, commercial films were dismissed as unspeakable.[31]

If *Film Culture* – and, according to David James, structural film – eventually came to represent a turn away from the attitude of receptivity and sense of relatedness Fisher recalls, then much of the output of found footage practice, STANDARD GAUGE and ( ) included, constitutes a counter-history, one in which visual pleasure and cultural critique are not assumed to be incompatible. Thus, despite its self-imposed limitations and constraints, Fisher's ( ) is, ultimately, the product of pluralist impulses. As such, it reflects the present state of avant-garde practice. The conceptual rigor with which Fisher treats the act of inserting, however, is a mark of distinction within a mode of production still dominated by expressive editing.

I thank Morgan Fisher for engaging in extensive exchanges with me regarding a number of aesthetic issues. His intellectual generosity and receptiveness made the process of working on this essay thoroughly enjoyable.

Notes

1. MacDonald, Scott. "Morgan Fisher." *A Critical Cinema: Interviews with Independent Filmmakers*, Berkeley and Los Angeles: University of California Press, 1988, p. 359.
2. Fisher, Morgan. "Script of STANDARD GAUGE." MacDonald, Scott (ed.). *Screen Writings: Scripts and Texts by Independent Filmmakers*, Berkeley and Los Angeles: University of California Press, 1995, p. 187.
3. James, David E. "Hollywood Extras: One Tradition of 'Avant-Garde' Film in Los Angeles." *October*, 90 (fall 1999), pp. 13, 17. Sitney's structural film essay and the debates it engendered are reviewed in Peterson, James. *Dreams of Chaos, Visions of Order: Understanding the American Avant-Garde Cinema*, Detroit: Wayne State University Press, 1994, pp. 72-77.
4. James, "Hollywood Extras," op. cit., pp. 16, 17.
5. For a useful introduction to Fisher's work, see MacDonald, Scott. "Morgan Fisher: Film on Film." *Cinema Journal*, 28/2 (winter 1989), pp. 13-27.
6. MacDonald, Morgan Fisher, op. cit., p. 357.
7. Fisher writes, "By chance I learned that the root of 'parenthesis' is a Greek word that means the act of inserting. And so I was given the title of the film." Morgan Fisher, "( )" (statement first distributed during screenings in 2003), n. p. Available: <http://www.filmlinc.com/nyff/avantgarde2003mf.htm>.
8. The distinction employed here is schematic. Obviously, both traditions are closely interrelated, and each is locatable within industrial and independent modes of production.
9. Anonymous. "Inserts." *Wikipedia*. Available: <http://en.wikipedia.org/wiki/Inserts>.
10. For brief discussions of diegetic inserts, see Salt, Barry. *Film Style and Technology: History and Analysis*, second edition, London: Starword, 1992, pp. 51, 138-139; Bordwell, David, Janet Staiger, and Kristin Thompson, *The Classical Hollywood Cinema: Film Style & Mode of Production to 1960*, New York: Columbia University Press, 1985, pp. 188-189.
11. Fisher, "( )," n.p.
12. Arthur, Paul. "( )." *Film Comment*, 40/1 (January/February 2004), p. 75.

13. Fisher acknowledges that he selected shots (from nearly 100 films purchased on the auction website eBay) that were "clear," that made an "impact," that were "incongruous, striking, arresting, mysterious," and possessed of a "classical simplicity." But he also asserts that he did not seek out any one dominant feature. Morgan Fisher, interview with the author, 18 August 2004.

14. Fisher. "( )," n.p.

15. Arthur. "( )," p. 75.

16. This is particularly evident in the case of the found footage essay (in film or video), which advances an argument or perspective through narration and compiled footage. A recent example is Thom Andersen's Los Angeles Plays Itself (USA: 2003). In three parts, "The City As Background," "The City As a Character" and "The City As Subject," Andersen's film develops an extensive critique of the representation of Los Angeles in Hollywood cinema and presents the filmmaker's alternative view of the city.

17. For an analysis of The Phoenix Tapes, see my article "Hitchcock and the Found Footage Installation: Müller and Girardet's The Phoenix Tapes." *Hitchcock Annual*, 12 (2003-04), pp. 100-125.

18. Recalling his days as an editor in the industry, Fisher cites a few standard questions that convey the approach he sought to avoid: "How can we tighten things up? What is the heart of the shot? How can you get rid of the stuff you don't absolutely need?" Each question assumes that editing entails making each shot "fit" into a narrative structure as economically and effectively as possible. Morgan Fisher, interview with the author, August 18, 2004.

19. Fisher, "( )," n.p. All quotations in this paragraph and the one that follows are taken from this text.

20. LeWitt, Sol. "Paragraphs on Conceptual Art" (1967). Zevi, Afdachiara (ed.). *Sol LeWitt: Critical Texts*, Rome: Libri de AEIOU, 1995, p. 79.

21. Batchelor, David. "Within and Between." *Sol LeWitt: Critical Texts*, p. 443. Batchelor's essay is an excellent introduction to LeWitt's art.

22. Fisher, "( )." n. p. This text includes a longer discussion of Roussel's work. See also Ford, Mark. *Raymond Roussel and the Republic of Dreams*, Ithaca: Cornell University Press, 2000, pp. 1-6; 187-201.

23. A more detailed description of the rules can be found in Fisher, "( )," n.p.

24. *Ken Jacobs: Interview by Lindley Hanlon June 10, June 12, 1979*, St. Paul and Minneapolis: Film in the Cities and Walker Art Center, 1979, p. 6.

25. Ken Jacobs, public discussion held at the American Museum of the Moving Image, New York City, 10 Nov. 2001.

26. Again, Paul Arthur provides a useful description: "Even though the spectator may not grasp the precise ordering principle, it is clear that as *Dream* unfolds the gaps in narrative logic between adjacent shots become increasingly attenuated and bizarre. With time wrenched out of joint, conventional markers of cause and effect get waylaid, producing weirdly expressive conjunctions... In this Kuleshov experiment in reverse, poetic themes and unsavory character motives seem to leap from the restirred detritus...." Arthur, Paul. "Creating Spectacle from Dross: The Chimeric Cinema of Ken Jacobs." *Film Comment*, 33/2 (March/April 1997), p. 61. For a more detailed analysis of Jacobs' film, see Gunning, Tom. "Doctor Jacobs' Dream Work." *Millennium Film Journal* 10/11 (fall/winter 1981-82), pp. 210-218.

27. Fisher. "( )," n. p. See also Roussel, Raymond. *How I Wrote Certain of My Books and other writings*, Trevor Winkfield (ed.), Boston: Exact Change, 1995.
28. Quoted in Ford, *Roussel and the Republic of Dreams*, p. 168.
29. Fisher, email correspondence with the author, 3 September 2004.
30. Fisher, email correspondence with the author, 26 August 2004.
31. MacDonald, Morgan Fisher, *A Critical Cinema*, p. 357.

The Secret Passion of the Cinephile

Peter Greenaway's A Zed and Two Noughts Meets Adriaan Ditvoorst's De Witte Waan

Gerwin van der Pol

> "Besides, what film is truly definitive?"
> Peter Greenaway[1]

During the 1986 International Rotterdam Film Festival I attended the Dutch premiere of A Zed and two Noughts (UK/Netherlands: Peter Greenaway, 1985).[2] As history records it, the film left behind a bewildered and amazed audience.[3] The opening credit scene gives so much visual and auditory information that the spectator is unable to "enter" the film. That may explain why many spectators talk about the film in spatial metaphors: the film was "beyond" them, or they felt "left out." Often mentioned in reviews of the film – and something Peter Greenaway seems to be proud of – is that watching the film is like seeing three films at once.[4] But that is not the only peculiarity of the film I noticed upon seeing the work. What really struck me was that the film resembled the Dutch film De Witte Waan / The White Madness / The White Delusion (Netherlands: Adriaan Ditvoorst, 1984).[5] Noticing this resemblance kept my attention focused on the screen.

In this article I intend to describe this film experience as a key to understanding the secret passion of the cinephile. It is not my intention to prove that Peter Greenaway was really influenced by De Witte Waan. Actually I think it is, for reasons to be revealed later, even better that this remains ambiguous. The only "fact" this chapter takes as a starting point, is that the films share similarities, for everyone to notice. In both films an older woman is involved in a car accident, partly recovers, lives on but is fully committed to dying anyway. Without any apparent reason, both women almost seem to welcome death. The woman in De Witte Waan (played by Pim Lambeau) confuses her own life with that of the roles she played as an actress in Tsjechow's plays (*The Cherry Orchard* in particular). Alba Bewick (Andréa Ferréol) in A ZOO confuses her own life with that of a woman in a Vermeer painting, and is even persuaded to have her legs amputated, so she looks more like her.

There are striking resemblances with the other characters as well. In De Witte Waan, two brother actors, Jules and Hans Croiset, play the father, the friend, and the driver of the car that caused the accident. That they look alike (and even play a double role) is a reason for the main character to be confused about their identity. The two twin brothers Oswald and Oliver (Brian and Eric Deacon) in A ZOO cause similar confusion to the other characters. Visually, the films share the eye-catching use of color. Each scene is based on one dominant color, reminiscent of the early cinema use of tinting and toning. Also, both films feature actors acting in a strange, detached, matter-of-fact way. Although they do react emotionally to certain events, most events hardly seem to affect them. Furthermore, both films are obsessed with animals, and the main argument made about them is their connection to death. In DE WITTE WAAN animals are shown on television (a seal pup beaten to death), as non-diegetic inserts, in paintings, as stuffed animals; and despite the fact that in the zoo, animals naturally are alive, the film A ZOO, too, stresses their connection to death. To me as a spectator, noticing this resemblance created a special film experience. Upon first noticing some of these similarities with DE WITTE WAAN, I started looking for more, and was rewarded with even more findings. At that time, it gave me a special feeling. Although this feeling is difficult to define, I recognized it from earlier film experiences. In fact, it is the possibility of the recurrence of this feeling that is a major reason for me to go see a next film. The search for this feeling is what defines me as a cinephile. And although it is not important to elaborate on the nature of this feeling, it is necessary to examine more closely how this discovery of similarities affected the film experience. The most important effect was that it fully engaged me with a film some other spectators could not engage with at all. To begin understanding the cinephile film experience, I will start by theorizing it along with theories that explain the relationship between spectator and film.

The best-known theory is Samuel Taylor Coleridge's "temporary and willing suspension of disbelief." This means that the spectator tends to take the fiction temporarily for granted, voluntarily accepting that real life laws do not necessarily apply. Noël Carroll has many reasons for introducing an alternative theory: "entertaining the thought."[6] According to Carroll a spectator can never forget that the fiction is just fiction. What the spectator actually does, according to Carroll, is entertain the thought that the fiction could be real. Kendall L. Walton posits a similar theory. Walton proposes in his book *Mimesis as Make-Believe* that in fiction spectators play certain games of make-believe.[7] Within a game of make-believe all events are fictionally true. Without any disrespect to the other two theories, I find Walton's suggestion of engaging with fiction as if it is were games particularly helpful, because it brings with it the concept of "rules of the game." The spectator can play the game following the rules set out by the author of the game, but is also free to change or add rules to the game. And since Walton shows that playing games is central to human life, it is not a necessity that the game of make believe is played within the film. It can also be played with the film as a prop in a different game of make believe, for example the one of comparing it to other films. Thus, applying Walton's theory to A ZOO, the following games are the key ones:

- the game of being in the world of A ZOO, and understanding its logic and characters;
- the game of understanding the film as typically "Greenaway";
- the game of understanding the film as typically postmodern;
- the cinephile game of understanding the film as resembling DE WITTE WAAN.

All four games can be played at will, simultaneously or alternately. However it is important to notice that they are separate games, and must remain (at least theoretically) separate. At first sight, it may seem like the resemblance with DE WITTE WAAN either fits the Greenaway game of quoting, or the postmodern game of quoting (both assuming that he did see the film). But to understand the fourth game as a typical cinephile game, it is necessary to distinguish it from the others. This will become clear after first showing how, respectively, the "Greenaway game" and the "postmodern game" engage the spectator with A ZOO. Playing the cinephile game will then be positioned in relation to the other games and distinguished in particular from the postmodern game.

Playing the A ZOO Game

The spectator tries to understand the characters and the events that befall them. The car accident has a huge impact on the lives of the two brothers Oswald and Oliver and also on Alba. The film shows their incapability of dealing with death, and that explains the strange choices they make, finally resulting in their deaths. The animals and many other aspects of the mise-en-scène look like important props necessary to play this game of make believe, but to the spectator the exact functions of those props remain unclear. This does not need to be a problem for the spectator, because it is obvious that at least the characters know how to use them. For example, Oliver eating the shattered glass of the car is not what the spectator would have done, but since the characters do seem to understand that the eating of glass as inevitable, spectators can try to understand their reasons for doing it.

Playing the Peter Greenaway Game

All the aspects that are difficult to understand when playing the A ZOO game are well understood by playing the Greenaway game. From his familiarity with other Greenaway films, the spectator recognizes all of the props as being parts of catalogues. Catalogues of animals, of black-and-white objects (is the zebra a white horse with black stripes, or a black horse with white stripes?), and of the alphabet (A-Z). And of course the film shows Greenaway's fascination for symmetry, decay, and Vermeer paintings. Within this game, it is no surprise that all these Greenaway motifs somehow coalesce, and construct the logic of the story. The logic of the motifs in Greenaway's films is a far stronger logic than the characters' motivations. Within the Greenaway game it is crystal clear that there is a doctor called Van Meegeren, who wants people to pose as if in the Vermeer paintings. The female character Alba Bewick looks very similar to one of the women in a painting by Vermeer. Unfortunately, the woman in the painting is shown without legs, and that makes Van Meegeren convince Alba of the necessity of amputating her legs.

Within the A ZOO game, the spectator can take this for granted without really understanding Alba's motivation for having her legs amputated. But in the Greenaway game the spectator is absolutely sure this was the only possible outcome, because they know how to explain the narrative turn with Greenaway's fascination for symmetry. In a similar vein, the spectator understands the two brothers. Oswald and Oliver (Brian and Eric Deacon) both lose their wives during a car accident, and throughout the rest of the film they try to understand the meaning of this loss. As biologists in the zoo, they are just as interested in living creatures as they are in the decay of animals. They photograph the process of decay, which results in stop-motion films of rotting flesh, all shown within the film A ZOO. Then they finally come to the notion that the time of decay is just as long as the time of pregnancy. And to prove themselves right, they have to conduct the ultimate experiment. That is, at the end of the film they commit suicide, to be automatically photographed for a stop-motion film showing their own decay and decomposition. For the Greenaway connoisseur this unusual behavior alludes to the familiar theme of decay in Greenaway's oeuvre.

Playing the Postmodern Game

In Greenaway's films, every shot, every part of the mise-en-scène is full of signs, there is a bombardment of signs and of quotes. Even the style of the film is a "quote" of a painting; the camera is always frontal to the set, so there is hardly any perception of depth. Most of the actors are shown in a fixed position, and when they walk, the camera tracks sideways with them. One can understand Baudrillard's pessimistic view that with all these extra meanings, in the end, there remains no meaning at all. From the moment the spectator learns that the swan that causes the car accident is called Leda, extra meanings begin to proliferate. Within the film A ZOO, the characters find extra meanings in the events that befall them, because they have a resemblance to other events; it is the quest of the scientists Oswald and Oliver. Faced with the tragic death of their wives, they start looking for the meaning of *death*, which in fact, becomes the meaning of their *lives*. Finding meaning in death, stillness, and rigor mortis brings dead objects back to life. A ZOO substantiates this reading by showing the stop-motion films of decay.

The rotting of flesh filmed through stop-motion in a certain way brings the animals back to life, just like the twins want to bring their wives back to life by deconstructing the accident that killed them. But there is no end to their analysis: via Leda, and her pregnancy, they become fixated on the origins of life, which means watching David Attenborough's nature documentaries. But they find a no-less profound meaning in the shattered glass pieces, or they applaud the logic of putting flies in the same cage with spiders because they have the same color. Through its abundance of signs, A ZOO exemplifies that one sign leads to another, and yet another. Within the postmodern game it is significant that there is a character called Venus de Milo. It alludes to the statue of the Venus de Milo, whose best-known feature is that she has no arms. This makes the spectator better understand the motif of the amputation of legs.[8]

Positioning the Cinephile Game

Of course, noticing the resemblance with DE WITTE WAAN could be part of the postmodern game. If we define the cinephile as someone who especially likes recognizing similarities and quotes, this sensation is common and available to all spectators. But is a spectator who notices some aspect of a film to be quotes from, or allusions to, another film, always a cinephile? When a spectator of A ZOO looks at the character Venus de Milo, is there anyone not thinking about the statue with the same name? The only effect this recognition of the allusion to another art object will have on spectators is that it makes them smile; postmodern quotes tend to have an ironic or parodic effect. But that is not what defines the cinephile experience.

Although the resemblance to DE WITTE WAAN can fit the postmodern game, and can result in a new reading of A ZOO, there is a difference in the feeling it causes the spectator to experience. In the postmodern game any cultured viewer can notice some of the quotes, citations, and tributes. What is usually problematic in the postmodern game, however, is that spectators become aware of the fact that they also *miss* many quotes shown in the film. This sensation of not coping, not being *art* literate enough to get all the meanings, can give the spectator a feeling of frustration and defeat. The cinephile game is the exact antithesis of the postmodern game. The spectator finds a quote that was possibly not deliberately put there, cannot be observed by other spectators, and thus exemplifies the mastery of the cinephile as a film expert. The cinephile experience is thus best defined as pride. This is what the cinephile is looking for; the true pleasure is finding connections between films that are not known to anyone, connections that only exist by virtue of the film catalogue (a collection of moving image memories) in the cinephile's mind. So the "Holy Grail" of knowledge for the cinephile is finding a novel connection. The cinephile wants to be absolutely sure that his/her found connection was never noticed before. The cinephile wants his find to remain utterly private. The cinephile is extremely proud, proud of his findings. A good example of this attitude can be found in the documentary CINEMANIA (Germany/USA: Angela Christlieb and Steven Kijak, 2002). The film follows five film buffs living in New York. Their world revolves around movies and they may see up to five films per day and 2,000 per year. Some have given up their jobs to dedicate their full attention to the cinema. Although the people portrayed in the film seem to exemplify society's low opinion of cinephiles as shameful characters – who for example feel that moviegoing is a worthy substitute for an active sex life – they nevertheless consider themselves champions, and are full of pride.

This strange coexistence of pride and shame that characterizes the extremist film buff can be explained via social psychology. For example, Fischer and Tangney argue, that the antecedents of pride are desirable actions; pride results in "displaying, engaging and feeling worthwhile."[9] Nevertheless, they also note that when displaying too much pride, or making it too public, pride can become shameful. With this perspective, the New York *cinemaniacs* can be understood as victims of their overly developed and expressed passion rather than as social misfits at heart who find shelter in the dream world of the silver screen. This partly explains why more normal cinephiles are modest about their expertise – the other reason being that communication with non-cinephiles is notoriously difficult, because there is no common ground of understanding and no shared knowledge of film trivia. Instead of displaying their knowledge at random in public, cinephiles tend to carefully select and form social groups; they meet in theaters, internet communities, and at film festivals. Here the personal discoveries are shared and discussed in a public setting that contributes to the individual cinephile engagement. This negotiation between personal revelations and the public discourse has been central to the cinephile experience since the earliest issues of *Cahiers de Cinéma*. The *Cahiers* critics "discovered" the auteur, especially in studio system films, and transformed this personal discovery into a "politique des auteurs."

In this light, Paul Willemen's thoughts about the cinephile are particularly relevant.[10] He traces the origin of cinephilia, "the privileged, pleasure-giving, fascinating moment," to the 1920s French discourse on *photogénie*, and Roland Barthes' *obtuse meaning*. For Barthes, the obtuse meaning "has something to do with disguise."[11] The concept of obtuse meaning is carefully distinguished from the *obvious* meaning. Cinephilia revolves around obtuse meanings; something unknown, not obvious, is revealed to the spectator. The question is whether these revelations can maintain their value as privileged moments for the cinephile when they become the subject of public discourse. I want to argue that the *Cahiers* critics' discussion of their findings in public, and even transformation of these findings into a *"politique"* did not affect their cinephile experience, because every film they watched continued to be open to new, personal interpretations, such as authorial signatures. Cinephile interpretations are by definition personal and cannot spoil the cinephile's experience when put down in words since the experience already belongs to the past. At most, making cinephile experiences public could influence how future cinemagoers experience this "privileged moment." This notion of spoiling strongly influences discussions about films; sometimes it even surfaces in film reviews and advertisements, consider for example the warning not to reveal the gender surprise in Neil Jordan's THE CRYING GAME (UK/Japan, 1992).

Conditions for Playing the Cinephile Game

From the moment a spectator starts playing the cinephile game, a sub-game begins to simultaneously be played. For the cinephile game to be as enjoyable as possible, the spectator has to be absolutely sure that the found connection is fully private, and not a fact of which the filmmaker was aware. This sub-game never ends. Although the spectator can be temporarily soothed by the thought that his findings are totally private, every new spectacular resemblance to DE WITTE WAAN will raise new doubts in the mind of the spectator.

One of the first questions that comes to a spectator's mind is whether this resemblance is a fact. That is, does the resemblance merely exist in the spectator's mind, or is it because Peter Greenaway has seen DE WITTE WAAN? Certainly at the International Rotterdam Film Festival, a spectator may have been aware of the fact that Greenaway had been a special guest at the festival a few years earlier in 1983. In the sub-game, the spectator might reconstruct the following scenario: In 1984 DE WITTE WAAN premiered at the IFFR, where Peter Greenaway saw the film. He must have, because there were many rumors circulating around the premiere and the film received a lot of attention in the press. Moreover, the film A ZOO is proof of Greenaway's detailed knowledge of the Netherlands (such as the Rotterdam Zoo Blijdorp where the film is partially shot, or such details as the work of architect Van Ravensteijn, and the painters Vermeer and Van Meegeren) and with all these direct references to Dutch culture it is simply unlikely that the references to the Dutch feature DE WITTE WAAN are coincidental. Although I may not be able to definitively conclude that Greenaway saw the film, all the evidence does support my observation that the two films are too much alike to have been conceived of completely separately from one another. [12]

The same sub-game can be played with different arguments. One is the institutional game in which the spectator assumes that Greenaway did indeed see the film, but had to remain quiet about it. The argument would go something like this: Within the discourse of the problematic relationship between Hollywood and Europe, the similarity between the two films simply does not make sense. In (European) auteur films, imitating a recent film is not an accepted practice. What *is* accepted, however, is the use of other artforms and finding inspiration in old films. Indeed, Greenaway's oeuvre is often discussed in relation to its quotations of various other artforms, especially painting, and in light of Greenaway's acknowledgment of being influenced by certain films. He often mentions Alain Resnais; this admiration resulted in securing Resnais' cameraman Sacha Vierny as his own cameraman. Whereas these quotations are emphasized and used to position Greenaway as a typical European art cinema director, he had to remain quiet about the importance of DE WITTE WAAN to A ZOO, because it would diminish his creative mastery over his own film.

The denial that A ZOO is a copy of a recent film shows how strong the reigning concepts are: European auteur cinema can be understood as appropriating other arts, quoting earlier films and deconstructing American films, but it cannot be understood in terms of quoting other recent auteur films.[13] Counterexamples probably exist, and need to be stressed in order to test this "folk-theory"; but this concept continues to reign, certainly in the film spectator's own mind. Being secretive about the influence of DE WITTE WAAN would certainly help Greenaway maintain his reputation as an innovator, claiming that film is dead, and "now" is the time to make a difference. In keeping with this concept of an artist, Greenaway does not hesitate to inflict (light) damage on the reputations of others, like David Cronenberg. On the recent DVD release of A ZOO, he explains how Cronenberg told him that DEAD RINGERS (Canada/USA: David Cronenberg, 1988) was created as a copy of A ZOO. This is exactly the sort of information Greenaway (consciously or unconsciously) prevents from becoming known about his own films.

Playing the Cinephile Game

For the enthusiastic cinephile, the game of finding similarities between the two films resembles a series of rewarding riddles that only he/she – as an informed cinephile – can solve:

1. In DE WITTE WAAN, there is a subplot about a man who wants to perform an ultimate experiment with sound. He wants to produce a sound louder than the Big Bang, which will echo throughout the entire universe and make everything silent again. In the end, the experiment is started, but it fails because the rats have gnawed through the electric wires. And the researcher is unable to repeat the experiment, because he dies. This is, by the way, exactly the same experiment as the two brothers perform in A ZOO. Oswald and Oliver commit suicide, in order to have their decay filmed in stop motion, to prove that their decay will take nine months, the same duration as that of a human pregnancy. Their experiment fails because the garden is full of snails, which causes a short circuit to the camera.[14] The sound experiment of DE WITTE WAAN is performed in order to conquer death by reversing maximum sound to create silence.[15] The visual experiment of A ZOO wants to reverse pregnancy and decay to create moving images that show what normally is understood as immobility and death. Even though one film makes its statement in terms of sound, and the other in terms of visual images, the spectator begins to comprehend how the two films relate to one another. They are not copies; but they are two sides of the same coin. Or, to use one of the narratives from A ZOO, they are like the brothers Oswald and Oliver. First they deny each other's existence, then they admit they are brothers, then we learn that they are twins, then that they are actually separated conjoined twins, and in the end, the once-joined twins can hardly wait to be reunited. This is also what happens to the two films as well: First they are separate, then they begin to bear a vague resemblance, and finally both films are forever related to each other.

2. Both films insist that human endeavor ends with animals reigning again. The David Attenborough documentary emphasizes this: First there were animals, then came human beings, then there were only animals again. It is perfect moment when at the end, all the animals are liberated from the Zoo.

3. The strange character Van Meegeren also begins to make much more sense. He is the Vermeer forger – in the film and in history.[16] The resemblance of Andréa Ferréol to the woman in a particular Vermeer painting inspires Van Meegeren to portray her as a replica of a Vermeer subject, and to make this resemblance perfect, she has to have her legs amputated. That may seem like a sick joke for Peter Greenaway, but it is keeping with what the brothers tell us about their desire to be reunited: "it feels incomplete." In other words, having a twin makes one truly alive. Alba Bewick becomes the twin of the lady in Vermeer's painting. And Vermeer's paintings come to life because Van Meegeren copies them.

4. The other theme, that of black and white as opposites is also resolved: the black-and-white dog is run over in a *zebra* crosswalk, and thus finds its twin.

The inherent opposition in the dog (is it white with black spots, or black with white spots) is resolved in it being perfectly akin to the zebra crossing.

A ZOO was disliked by many viewers because of its allusions to other arts and non-arts, which ultimately gave it a very non-narrative quality. But, compared to DE WITTE WAAN, the film actually looks like a well-told narrative. However, in contrast, the narrative (but not well-told) film DE WITTE WAAN impresses the spectator, in retrospect, as being a beautiful non-narrative. In this case, it even ultimately helps us to understand the strange title – A ZED AND TWO NOUGHTS. Greenaway himself offered several interpretations: for example the first two letters are A and Z, so it encompasses the whole alphabet. And the two O's are for Oswald and Oliver. But why didn't he just call it A ZOO instead of A ZED AND TWO NOUGHTS? The strange explanation of the title stresses the notion that the two Os should perhaps be read as zeros. And if they are zeros, you don't need them (that is why the brothers die, also for the sake of symmetry). We are left with just the letter "Z". Z and DE WITTE WAAN produces De Witte Zwaan (the white swan). That same white swan, Leda, who caused the accident, emphasizes (on a metaphorical level) the fact that the two films can never be totally untangled. They are, like the conjoined twins, finally reunited.

Notes

1. Greenaway, Peter. *A Zed & Two Noughts*. London, Boston: Faber and Faber, 1986. p. 9, Author's note: "Besides, what film is truly definitive? By the time you see the film it may very well be sub-titled, re-edited, shortened, even censored, and every film is viewed at the discretion of the projectionist, the cinema manager, the architect of the cinema, the comfort of your seat and the attention of your neighbour." My argument will be about other ways in which the film will never reach its definitive state.
2. As a shortcut, I will from here on use the short, albeit incorrect, title A ZOO.
3. *Variety* vol. CCCXXI no. 6 (4 December 1985) "In the end, it remains the work of a highly talented British eccentric who hasn't yet managed to thresh out his private fantasies and obscurantist intellectual preoccupations to connect with major concerns or touch the emotions." p. 26
4. DVD *A Zed and Two Noughts*, BFI, 2004.
5. Adriaan Ditvoorst was a very talented Dutch director, daring and unconventional. His film DE WITTE WAAN had a similar reception as A ZOO in that the audience and the critics had high hopes for it, but ultimately found the film too experimental to be understood in a single viewing. The producer even ordered a re-edit: "Disappointingly, pic met with a mixed reception from press and public, due to its willfully baffling aspects which even wellwishers found hard to stomach." *Variety* vol. CCCXV no. 4 (23 May 1984): p. 32. Compare this quote with note three. Nevertheless, ever since Ditvoorst committed suicide in 1987, his films, and especially his last

film DE WITTE WAAN, are considered highlights of Dutch film history. His collected works became recently available on DVD.

6. Carroll, Noël. *The Philosophy of Horror: Or Paradoxes of the Heart.* New York: Routledge, 1990.

7. Walton, Kendall L. *Mimesis as Make-Believe. On the Foundations of Representational Arts.* Cambridge, Mass.: Harvard University Press, 1990.

8. For further postmodern readings, see Woods, Alan. *Being Naked Playing Dead: The Art of Peter Greenaway.* Manchester: Manchester University Press, 1996; Stalpaert, Cristel (ed.). *Peter Greenaway's Prospero's Books: Critical Essays.* Gent: Academia Press, 2000; Pascoe, David. *Peter Greenaway: Museums and Moving Images.* London: Reaktion Books, 1997; and Schuster, Michael. *Malerei im Film. Peter Greenaway.* Hildesheim, Georg Olms Verlag, 1998.

9. Fischer, Kurt W., Tangney, June Price. "Self-Conscious Emotions and the Affect Revolution: Framework and Overview." Tangney, June Price and Fischer, Kurt W. (ed.). *Self-Conscious Emotions: The Psychology of Shame, Guilt, Embarrassment, and Pride.* New York: The Guilford Press, 1995: p.10.

10. Willemen, Paul. *Looks and Frictions: Essays in Cultural Studies and Film Theory.* London: BFI, 1994: pp. 223-257.

11. Barthes, Roland. "The third meaning," reprinted in: Barthes, Roland (translation Stephen Heath). *Image, Music, Text.* London: Fontana Press, 1977: p. 58.

12. The facts do not prove it, but it remains a possibility. At the International Rotterdam Film Festival (IFFR) 1983, where a retrospective of his Greenaway's films was shown, he met producer Kees Kasander, who suggested the making of a new film. There is no doubt that in the course of 1984, Greenaway wrote the script for A ZED AND TWO NOUGHTS, *after* the premiere of DE WITTE WAAN. In 1985, Peter Greenaway appeared at the Rotterdam festival with his film 4 AMERICAN COMPOSERS (UK: Peter Greenaway, 1983). In spring 1985, he began filming A ZED AND TWO NOUGHTS in the Netherlands. The film premiered in November 1985 at the London Film Festival, and was shown as the opening film at the IFFR in 1986. Other circumstantial evidence is the fact that during the IFFR, when DE WITTE WAAN was shown, Peter Greenaway made the deal for A ZOO at the Cinemart. This Cinemart "was fitted out for the occasion by Ben van Os and Jan Roelfs, two rising art directors." (Heijs, Jan, Westra, Frans. *Que Le Tigre Danse. Huub Bals a Biography.* Amsterdam: Otto Cramwinckel, 1996: p. 159). They were to eventually become the art directors on A ZOO and they may have been influenced by DE WITTE WAAN.

13. Postclassical films, on the other hand, can be understood as quoting or mimicking other American films, even very recent ones, or as remaking European films like WINGS OF DESIRE (Germany/France: Wim Wenders, 1987) as CITY OF ANGELS (USA: Brad Silberling, 1998), but not as European remakes of Hollywood films.

14. These scenes share even more similarities: the body of the researcher in DE WITTE WAAN is covered with snails, just like the bodies in A ZOO. In addition there is the same blinking of lights.

15. The character says: "Creating a sound that will destroy the echo of the Big Bang with unnatural speed. The subsequent explosion will be incredibly big, and will reverberate against the walls of infinity, thus destroying everything in its path. Nothing will remain, nothing but silence. Finally, everything will be silent." (my translation).

16. The film also mentions this, and explains that this Van Meegeren is *like* the historical figure Van Meegeren, but not one and the same.

Biographies

Melis Behlil is a Ph.D. candidate at ASCA, University of Amsterdam and teaches Film Studies at Istanbul Bilgi University. She contributes to local radio and TV shows, as well as several publications. Her PhD research focuses on Hollywood's foreign directors in the last few decades. Her other areas of interest are film industries, musicals and online communities.

Marijke de Valck is a Ph.D. candidate at the Department of Media Studies, University of Amsterdam. She was co-organizer of the second graduate conference on cinephilia, *Cinephilia Take-Two: Re-mastering, Re-purposing, Re-framing*, held in Amsterdam in 2003. Her dissertation is a functional-historical analysis of the international film festival circuit that focuses on major European festivals. It includes case studies on Berlin, Cannes, Rotterdam and Venice.

Thomas Elsaesser is Professor in the Department of Media Studies and Director of Research Film and Television at the University of Amsterdam. Widely published and translated into some fifteen languages, his writings include essays on film history and historiography, Early Cinema, European Cinema and Hollywood, digital media, cultural memory and installation art. Among his books as author are: *Fassbinder's Germany: History, Identity, Subject* (1996), *Weimar Cinema and After* (2000), *Metropolis* (2000), *Studying Contemporary American Film* (2002, with Warren Buckland) and *Filmgeschichte und Frühes Kino* (2002). His most recent books as (co-) editor include *Cinema Futures: Cain, Abel or Cable?* (1998), *The BFI Companion to German Cinema* (1999), *The Last Great American Picture Show: Hollywood Films in the 1970s* (2004) and *Harun Farocki: Working on the Sightlines* (2004).

Elena Gorfinkel is a Ph.D. candidate in the Department of Cinema Studies at New York University. Her dissertation concerns American sexploitation films of the 1960s. Previous publications include articles in *Underground USA: Filmmaking Beyond the Hollywood Canon* (Wallflower, 2002), and in *Unruly Pleasures: The Cult Film and its Critics* (FAB, 2000.)

Malte Hagener teaches film in the Department of Media Studies at Friedrich-Schiller-Universität Jena. His interests include European avant-garde of the interwar period, popular cinema of the 1930s and German film history. (Co-)editor of *Als die Filme singen lernten: Innovation und Tradition im Musikfilm 1928-38* (edition text + kritik 1999), *Geschlecht in Fesseln. Sexualität zwischen Aufklärung und Ausbeutung im Weimarer Kino* (edition text + kritik 2000), *Film: An International Bibliography* (Metzler 2002), *Die Spur durch den Spiegel. Der Film in der Kultur der Moderne* (Bertz 2004).

Vinzenz Hediger is Professor of Film and Media Studies at the Ruhr University, Bochum, Germany. His publications include a book on movie trailers, *Verführung zum Film. Der amerikanische Kinotrailer seit 1912* (Marburg: Schüren 2001; forthcoming in English as *Nostalgia for the Coming Attraction. American Movie Trailers and the Culture of Film Consumption*).

Lucas Hilderbrand is a Ph.D. candidate in cinema studies at New York University. His dissertation focuses on videotape bootlegging, U.S. fair use copyright codes, and home video aesthetics. His writings have appeared in *Camera Obscura* and *Film Quarterly*, and he has been a programmer for MIX: The New York Lesbian & Gay Experimental Film/Video Festival.

Charles Leary is a Ph.D. candidate in Cinema Studies at New York University. His dissertation focuses on the work of John Cassavetes and he has written on Hong Kong cinema for various publications.

Jenna Pei-Suin Ng graduated in law from the National University of Singapore and spent two years in private practice. She is currently a first-year PhD candidate in Film Studies at University College London, researching digital cinema. Her MA thesis, "Virtual Cinematography and the Digital Real", won third place in the 2004 SCMS Student Writing Awards and will be published in a forthcoming anthology, *The State of the Real: Essays on Aesthetics* (Damian Sutton, Ray MacKenzie, Sue Brind (eds.), I.B. Tauris, 2005).

Drehli Robnik teaches film studies at the University of Vienna and Masarykova univerzita Brno (focus: blockbuster culture; mass-market cinema's relation to history and memory). Other part-time occupations: film critic, disk-jockey, edutainer. Recent publications: 'Allegories of Post-Fordism in 1970s New Hollywood' in: Th. Elsaesser, A. Horwath, N. King (eds.): *The Last Great American Picture Show. New Hollywood Cinema in the 1970s*. Amsterdam University Press 2004; "Leben als Loch im Medium: Die Vermittlung des Films durch Siegfried Kracauer", kolik.film 2, 2004; "Ausrinnen als Einuebung: Splatterfilm als Perspektive auf flexibilisierte medienkulturelle Subjektivitaet", www.nachdem-film.de; "Verschiebungen an der Ostfront: Bilder des Vernichtungskrieges der Wehrmacht in bundesdeutschen Spielfilmen", *Zeitgeschichte* 3, 31, 2004. Robnik lives in Vienna-Erdberg.

Jan Simons is Associate Professor in New Media at the Department of Media Studies at the University of Amsterdam. He was editor-in-chief of the Dutch film magazine *Skrien* and film critic for some of the country's leading news papers and weekly magazines. He is the author of *Playing the Waves: Lars von Trier's Games from Dogme to Dogville* (Amsterdam: Amsterdam University Press, forthcoming).

Sutanya Singkhra (Bow) graduated with a B.A. degree in English and Comparative Literature from Chulalongkorn University, in 2002. She worked as a freelance screenwriter for a few Thai films, a columnist for local movie magazines, and a subtitle translator for a local television cable network before joining the M.A. Film Studies Programme at the University of Amsterdam. After completing her thesis she wishes to pursue a career as a writer, in both fictional and academic worlds.

Wanda Strauven is Assistant Professor in Film Studies at the University of Amsterdam. She co-edited *Homo orthopedicus: le corps et ses prothèses à l'époque (post) moderniste* (Paris: L'Harmattan, 2001), and published on early and avant-garde cinema in various international editions and journals (*CiNéMAS, Cinéma & Cie* and *Narrativa*). Her monograph *Marinetti e il cinema: tra attrazione e sperimentazione* is forthcoming (Udine: Campanotto).

Gerwin van der Pol is a film lecturer at the Department of Media Studies at the University of Amsterdam. He specializes in film analysis, genre and sound, and is currently writing his dissertation on the 'auteur' film and spectators' emotions. His articles have appeared in the Dutch film magazine *Skrien*.

Federico Windhausen is completing a dissertation on the work of Hollis Frampton, Paul Sharits, and Ken Jacobs in the 1970s, at New York University's Department of Cinema Studies. He has published essays in *October, The Hitchcock Annual*, and *Cabinet*.

Index of Names

Index of Film Titles

Film Culture in Transition
General Editor: *Thomas Elsaesser*

Double Trouble: Chiem van Houweninge on Writing and Filming
Thomas Elsaesser, Robert Kievit and Jan Simons (eds.)

Writing for the Medium: Television in Transition
Thomas Elsaesser, Jan Simons and Lucette Bronk (eds.)

Between Stage and Screen: Ingmar Bergman Directs
Egil Törnqvist

The Film Spectator: From Sign to Mind
Warren Buckland (ed.)

Film and the First World War
Karel Dibbets and Bert Hogenkamp (eds.)

A Second Life: German Cinema's First Decades
Thomas Elsaesser (ed.)

Fassbinder's Germany: History Identity Subject
Thomas Elsaesser

Cinema Futures: Cain, Abel or Cable? The Screen Arts in the Digital Age
Thomas Elsaesser and Kay Hoffmann (eds.)

Audiovisions: Cinema and Television as Entr'Actes in History
Siegfried Zielinski

Joris Ivens and the Documentary Context
Kees Bakker (ed.)

Ibsen, Strindberg and the Intimate Theatre: Studies in TV Presentation
Egil Törnqvist

The Cinema Alone: Essays on the Work of Jean-Luc Godard 1985-2000
Michael Temple and James S. Williams (eds.)

Micropolitics of Media Culture: Reading the Rhizomes of Deleuze and Guattari
Patricia Pisters and Catherine M. Lord (eds.)

Malaysian Cinema, Asian Film: Border Crossings and National Cultures
William van der Heide

Film Front Weimar: Representations of the First World War in German Films of the Weimar Period (1919-1933)
Bernadette Kester

Camera Obscura, Camera Lucida: Essays in Honor of Annette Michelson
Richard Allen and Malcolm Turvey (eds.)

Jean Desmet and the Early Dutch Film Trade
Ivo Blom

City of Darkness, City of Light: Émigré Filmmakers in Paris 1929-1939
Alastair Phillips

The Last Great American Picture Show: New Hollywood Cinema in the 1970s
Thomas Elsaesser, Alexander Horwath and Noel King (eds.)

Harun Farocki: Working on the Sight-Lines
Thomas Elsaesser (ed.)

Herr Lubitsch Goes to Hollywood: German and American Film after World War I
Kristin Thompson